HISTORY
OF THE
PALLAVAS OF KANCHI

HISTORY OF THE PALLAVAS OF KANCHI

R. GOPALAN

Published by

FacsiMile Publisher
12 Pragati Market
Ashok Vihar, Ph-2
Delhi - 110052, India
Phone: 011-47034999
Email: www.facsimilepublishers.com
info@facsimilepublishers.com

Distribution Network
gyanbooks.com
India, USA, Canada, UK, Australia

ISBN: 978-93-3340-119-7 (PB)

First Published, 1928

2nd Impression 2025

Printed at: Gyan Press, Delhi.

HISTORY OF THE PALLAVAS OF KANCHI
Arthur R. GOPALAN

HISTORY
OF THE
PALLAVAS OF KANCHI

BY

R. GOPALAN, M.A.,
University Research Student, 1920-1924,
Sub-Librarian, Connemara Public Library, Madras

EDITED FOR THE UNIVERSITY
WITH INTRODUCTION AND NOTES

BY

S. KRISHNASWAMY AIYANGAR, M.A., HONY. Ph.D.,
Professor of Indian History and Archæology, Madras University,
Honorary Correspondent of the Archæological Survey of India

PUBLISHED BY THE UNIVERSITY OF MADRAS
1928

CONTENTS

APPENDICES

PAGE

ILLUSTRATIONS AND MAPS

WORKS CONSULTED

Aiyar (K. V. S.) : *Historical Sketches of Ancient Dekkan.*

Archæological Reports of Mysore.

Archæological Survey of India Annual Reports for 1906–7.

Beal : *Buddhist Records of the Western World.*

Bombay Gazetteer.

Carr (Capt.) : *Desc. and Historical Papers on the Seven Pagodas.*

Coomaraswami (A.K.) : *A History of India and Indonesian Art.*

Crole : *Chingleput Manual.*

Epigraphia Indica.

Epigraphia Carnataca.

Fergusson (J.) and Burgess (J.) : *Cave Temples in India.*

Fergusson : *History of Indian and Eastern Architecture.*

Fleet : *Dynasties of the Kanarese Districts.*

" : *Gupta Inscriptions.*

Indian Antiquary.

Indian Historical Quarterly.

Journal of Indian History.

Journal of the Mythic Society.

Jouveau-Dubreuil (G) : *Archaéologie du Sud de l' Inde* (1914).

" : *Ancient History of Deccan* (1921).

" : *Dravidian Architecture.*

" : *Pallava Antiquities.*

" : *Pallavas* (1917).

" : *Pallava Painting.*

Kanakasabhai (V.) : *The Tamils Eighteen hundred Years Ago.*

Krishna Sastri (H.) : *Two Statues of Pallava Kings and Five Pallava Inscriptions on a Rock-temple at Mahabalipuram.* '*Mem. Arch. Sur. of India*', *No. 26.*

Krishnaswami Aiyangar (S.): *Ancient India* (1911).
,, ,, : *The Beginnings of South Indian History* (1917).
,, ,, : *Early History of Vaishnavism in South India.*
,, ,, : *Some Contributions of South India to Indian Culture* (1924).
,, ,, : *Origin and Early History of the Pallavas of Kāñchī.*
,, ,, : *Manimekhalai in its Historical Setting.*

Longhurst (A. H.): *Pallava Architecture. Parts I & II. ' Mem. Arch. Sur. of India ', Nos. 17 & 33.*

South Indian Epigraphy—*Annual Reports.*

The Influences of Indian Art (1925). By Strzygowski (J.) and others.

The Madras Journal of Literature and Science.

The Mahavamsa.

Nalayira Prabandam.

Rea (A.): *Pallava Architecture.*

Rice (L.): *The Mysore Gazetteer.* 2 Vols.

,, : *Mysore and Coorg from Inscriptions.*

Sentamil.

Sewell : *List of Antiquities in the Madras Presidency.* 2 Vols.

South Indian Inscriptions, Vols. I–V.

Srinivasa Aiyangar (P. T.): *History of Pallavas.* (Tamil.)

Srinivasa Aiyangar (M.): *Tamil Studies.*

Taylor (The Rev. William): Oriental Historical MSS. 2 Vols.

Transactions of the Second and Third All-India Oriental Conference—1924.

Travancore Sanskrit Series LV. The *Mattavilasaprahasána* of Sri Mahendravikramavarman.

Vaidya (C. V.): *A History of Mediæval Hindu India.*

INTRODUCTION

THE following pages embody the work of Mr. R. Gopalan, M.A., a Research Student at the University, who took up for his subject the History of the Pallavas of Kanchi. He worked through his full term, and the thesis incorporates his work on the subject. The thesis of just a little over 160 pages constitutes a dessertation on the Pallavas, which takes us as far as we can proceed on the subject with the material at our disposal. Many of the difficulties in the subject have been brought nearer to solution by the work of a number of scholars, all of which is considered in the work. It does not pretend to have solved all questions connected with the history of the Pallavas finally, but it may be stated that Mr. Gopalan's work carries us as near to an up-to-date history of the Pallavas as, in the circumstances, is possible.

Our purpose in this introduction is to draw attention to the salient features of the thesis and indicate points where more light would be welcome. Such advance as was possible in the study of the subject within the last year or two is also incorporated with a view to completing the work of Mr. Gopalan and to invite examination and criticism by those interested in Indian Historical Research.

The name Pallavas has been a problem for scholars, and has received attention from time to time from several of them, offering explanations of various kinds; the doubt and the difficulty alike have arisen from the fact that a race of people called '*Pahlavas*' were known and are referred to as such along with the Sakas and others, both in the North-west of India and nearer in the North-western coast of the Dakhan. This, in literary texts sometimes takes the alternative form 'Pallava', and thus two forms, 'Pahlava' and 'Pallava' occurring side by side, give colour to the assumption that the two words are identical. They are indeed identical in form, but do not preclude the possibility of another word assuming this identical form. The word 'Pallava' as it applies to the rulers of Kanchi is undoubtedly and invariably a later form. We do not meet with the form '*Pahlava*' in connection with the Pallavas of Kanchi in any record of their time. The question therefore would naturally arise whether we need necessarily regard the name '*Pallavas*' as applied to the rulers of Kanchi as at all equivalent to the other '*Pallavas*' either as a word or in regard to what the word stands for. The word as applied to 'Pallavas' in the first instance seems to be a translation of the Tamil words 'Tonḍaiyar' and 'Tonḍamān', and this finds confirmation in some of the copper-plate charters, which do bring in tender twigs of some kind in connection with the eponymous name 'Pallava'. This undoubtedly is a later use of the term, but gives the indication that even at that comparatively late period, the traditional notion was that they were not foreigners, such as the *Pahlavas* would have been. In all the material that has been examined, there is nothing to indicate either the migration of a people or even of a family that migh have ultimately raised itself into a dynasty from the North-west, so that the assumption of a connection between the one set of people and the other rests upon the mere doubtful ground of a possibility, whereas the translation or adaptation of a Southern word into Sanskrit is very much more than a possibility, as indeed a word like 'Dravida' or 'Dramida' would clearly indicate. The distinction that Rājaśēkhara makes between the Southern *Pallava* and the North-western *Pahlava* seems in the circumstances to be a crucial indication that in the estimation of scholarly folk of the ninth and tenth centuries, the two were to be regarded as distinct from each other. The foreign origin of the Pallavas therefore seems to have no ground to support it.

The Pallavas seem nevertheless to have been foreign to the locality as far as our evidence takes us at present. The rulers of Kanchi had continued to be known as Tonḍamāns all through historical times. The people of the locality were similarly known as Tonḍaiyar, the region occupied by the people consequently Tonḍamaṇḍalam. These names are all traceable in South Indian literature in the period of prominence of the Pallavas and even before. The name Pallava however is used generally in the charters ever since the Pallavas issued charters, so that historically speaking we would be justified if we took Pallava and Toṇḍamān to be synonymous, and this receives support in the use of the compound expression in one of the poems of Tirumangai Āḻvār, 'the Pallava, who is the ruler of the Toṇḍaiyar' (*Pallavan Toṇḍaiyar Kōn*). Therefore it is not as if literature did not know the term; much rather literary use regarded the two as synonymous, so that the Pallavas, whoever they were, were Toṇḍamāns, rulers of Toṇḍamaṇḍalam undoubtedly.

So far as the Pallavas of the charters are concerned, whether the charters be issued in Prakrit or in Sanskrit, they are termed, the Pallavas of Kanchi, though several of the charters happened to be issued from localities comparatively far to the north of Kanchi. Several of the places in which their inscriptions and copper-plate charters have been found, or from which these were issued, are capable of location from the Bellary District eastwards up to the River Krishna in the north. Even so they seem to exclude the region which might geographically be described as the region of the Nalla Malais and the Pacha-Malais extending southwards along the mountainous tracts of the Eastern Ghats till we come past Tirupati into Chittoor, and the Bay of Bengal. From the Śangam literature so-called of Tamil, we are enabled to make the following distribution of peoples, if not exactly of rulers and dynasties. The Pāṇḍya country was in the extreme south extending from coast to coast. The Chēra extended northwards from it along the coast stretching into the interior indefinitely, the actual eastern boundary varying from time to time almost up to the frontiers of Karur. Therefrom went northwards up to the borders of the great forest the territory known to Tamil literature as Koṇkānam (Konkan), over which ruled a particular chieftain known as Nannan till he was overthrown by the Chēras. The east coast region, however, beginning with the River Veḷḷār flowing across the state of

Pudukottah now and emptying itself into the Bay of Bengal which marked the orthodox southern boundary of the Cholas, constituted the Cholamaṇḍalam which actually extended northwards therefrom to as far as the River South Pennar where began the division known as Aruvānāḍu, which extended northwards along the coast almost as far as the Northern Pennar. This last division fell into two parts, Aruvānāḍu or Aruvā South and Aruvā Vaḍatalai or Aruvā North. The region set over this in the interior including perhaps even a considerable part of what is marked off as Aruvānāḍu constituted the Toṇḍamaṇḍalam, a division occupied by the Toṇḍayar and belonging to them. It is this Toṇḍamaṇḍalam that was dominated by Kanchi and extended vaguely northwards as far as Tirupati, which seems to have marked off the northern boundary, which sometimes extended farther northwards quite up to the northern borders of the Pulicat Lake, the region round Kāḷahasti on one side of it at any rate, being borne in the old accounts even now as Toṇḍamān *Māgaṇi.* We have evidence of an old chieftain by name Tiraiyan ruling over the territory dominated by Vēngaḍam or Tirupati whose capital was in a place called Pavattiri (Reddipalem in the Gudur Taluk of the Nellore District). At one time this region was known as Kākandināḍu, 'submerged by the sea,' Kākandi being the name of the Chola capital, Puhār, because of the semi-historical ruler, Kakandan. It seems as though this territory was a new conquest to which was given the name from the capital of the conquering rulers. Whether the name was actually so given to it or no, it is evident that the region was ruled by a Tiraiyan chieftain who is referred to in the poems of the *Ahanānūṛu* as Tiraiyan merely without a qualifying adjunct. The Chola Karikāla is given credit in tradition which has come down to us for having cleared forests, constructed tanks and made other irrigation works, and thus introduced civilization in Toṇḍamaṇḍalam, which till then remained, from the point of view of the Chola country, uncivilized. Chola viceroys were thereafter appointed at Kanchi, and the territory ruled over by the Viceroy at Kanchi is generally referred to as Toṇḍamaṇḍalam. What is traditional in the story finds confirmation in the Śangam poem *Paṭṭinapālai* and in another poem by the same author *Perumbāṇāṛṛupaḍai*, which had for its hero the Toṇḍamān Iḷaṁ-Tiraiyan as he is known to literature. He is described in the poem as of Chola birth and as a powerful ruler of Kanchi and is ascribed a descent from the Cholas, nay in fact the family of Rama, as in fact in the later Pauranic genealogy of these Cholas some of the Ikshvāku rulers are made to figure. This traditional connection is on a footing with that between the Ikshvākus and the Gurjara Pritiharas of Kanauj. During this period and almost contemporaneously with the Toṇḍamān-Iḷaṁ-Tiraiyan, the territory of the elder Tiraiyan seems to have been held in power by a chieftain generally associated with Vēngaḍam and described ordinarily by the name Pulli, chief of the Kaḷvar or, as the correcter reading would warrant, Kaḷavar. The forest region therefore in the middle seems to have constituted a block inhabited by the people Kaḷavar who had their tribal ruler with headquarters at Vēngaḍam. That is the position that we derive from the Śangam literature of Tamil as such. Toṇḍamān-Iḷaṁ-Tiraiyan passed away and with him Śangam literature as well perhaps, and we are left in the dark altogether as to what had befallen Kanchi or the territory dependent thereon. That is the Tamil side of the evidence from the Śangam literature leaving aside the question of the age of the Śangam for the present.

On the other side of it, the region round Adoni is described in early inscriptions as Sātāhani Āhāra, sometimes as Sātavāhani Rāshṭra perhaps giving us the indication that it was a settlement of Sātavāhanas, which may be recent or early. It probably indicates that the Sātavāhanas were perhaps not exactly native to the locality, but acquired the territory and gave it their name to mark a new acquisition unless it be that other people called it by that name as the homeland of the Sātavāhanas. In either case, we find the Sātavāhana rulers on this border of the Tamil country, and one of the inscriptions of Pulumāvi mentions a great Sātavāhana general, Mahā

Sēnātipati Skandanāga, probably an earlier governor of a troublesome border country. The records of the Pallavas similarly have reference to this region, and are couched in a form like the Sātavāhana inscriptions in regard to language, the details of the definition of time, and even such details as do occur in regard to the very nature of the administration itself. The provenance of the ship-coins of lead or potin sometimes ascribed to the Pallavas, but more generally taken to be Sātavāhana coins, in the region extending from the Northern Pennar to the Southern gives an indication of an effort of the Sātavāhana to bring this region under their authority. The references to the successful struggle against the Āryans, which some of the Chola monarchs claim to themselves as well as the Malayamān ruler of Tirukovilūr perhaps is a reflex of this effort on the part of the Sātavāhanas. When the Pallavas therefore emerged from this region—and we are given the information in the earliest Pallava charter that the first great Pallava ruler of the locality referred to as Bappa Deva made a free distribution of a hundred thousand ox ploughs, etc., we seem to be introduced to an effort at civilizing the locality appearing very like an extension of the effort of Karikala to civilize Toṇḍamaṇḍalam itself. This will appear clearly from the sequel. The Pallava charters themselves seem to argue a connection with the Sātavāhanas of a more or less intimate character, political as well as institutional. This seems clear from the Prakrit charters much more pronouncedly than perhaps even the Sanskrit ones. The conclusion to which the epigraphists have arrived that the Pallavas of the Prakrit charters were earlier and ought so to be regarded seems well warranted by the circumstances of the case and the character of the documents as such. That these early rulers issued their charters in Sanskrit and Prakrit indifferently at the same time, and must be regarded as the same people is a conclusion which while it may cut the gordian knot seems to have little to justify it on the basis of the facts of the position. Superficial paleographical resemblances cannot be held to upset the more certain evidence of institutional continuity to which the Prakrit charters unmistakably point. Since the Pallavas issued their charters in Prakrit and of a style like that of the earlier Sātavāhana charters, does it not seem reasonable to argue that the early Pallavas of the Prakrit charters were officers of the Sātavāhanas, or at least officially connected with them and dependent upon their authority? It seems therefore reasonable to argue that the Sātavāhana governors of the south-eastern frontier gradually extended their territory, civilizing it as they conquered it, introducing the arts of agriculture and ultimately made themselves masters of the locality and extending southwards when the Tamil powers weakened to take into their territory Kanchi and Toṇḍamaṇḍalam. It was the conquest of this that gave them the standing to make themselves real rulers and whatever of title was wanting in it was made good ultimately by a marriage which brought along with it a further addition to the territory. This becomes clear both from the account that Mr. Gopalan has given of succeeding events as well as from the analysis of these inscriptions which he has provided in the appendix. The Pallavas of the Prakrit charters call themselves rulers of Kanchi. So do the Pallavas of the Sanskrit charters. But at the outset those Pallavas that issued these Sanskrit charters lay claim to having acquired their royal position by an influential marriage with a Nāga princess and by that means became 'possessed of a wife and a kingdom simultaneously'. This could only mean that the Nāga alliance brought in an accession of territory which put their claim to independent rule on a really more legitimate footing than that of mere conquest or occupation, which might have been regarded as a mere act of usurpation.

In the empire of the Sātavāhanas which began to break up early in the third century, the dismemberment seems to have been due somewhat earlier to the provincial governors setting themselves up in some kind of independence. The south-western block seems to have remained in its integrity the latest, while the aggressions of the Kshatrapas in the north and north-west to some extent, and the advance of the Vākāṭakas from the middle to a larger extent, deprived them of what was the headquarters block of the Sātavāhana empire. The eastern and south-eastern portion must similarly have separated themselves, and we find on the farther side of the Krishna river the Sālankāyana first and Vishnukundins later occupying the territory north of the Krishna. There was perhaps similar disintegration noticeable further south along the East coast, so that when (about a century after the passing away of Andhra rule completely), Samudragupta's invasion came south, there were many kingdoms in the region which submitted to his authority and accepted a feudatory position to his overlordship. A ruler of Kanchi by name Vishṇugopa figures in the list, and although he is not called a Pallava in the Samudragupta inscription—we have no right to expect this where every ruler is simply defined by references to his capital, not to his family or dynasty and Vishnugopa was ruler of Kanchi—leaves but little doubt, and the occurrence of a number of Vishṇugopas in the list of Pallava rulers of Kanchi leaves us in no uncertainty that this Vishṇugopa was as well a Pallava ruler. It is this disturbing influence of Samudragupta's invasion that introduced a change, which necessitated the succeeding ruler of Kanchi to make an effort at legitimizing his own particular position as ruler of Kanchi. This was done, in all probability, by a marriage alliance with the heiress of the south-western block of the Sātavāhana territory, the territory dependent upon the viceroyalty of Banavasi. The rulers were known generally as Chūṭu Nāgas, and, if a princess of that family had been married to a Pallava, it would be a Nāga alliance that would give at the same time a sort of a claim to the territory of which she was heiress to the Pallavas. Otherwise the overlordship claimed by the Pallavas and acknowledged readily by the Gangas, and none the less acknowledged though less readily by the Kadambas, would be inexplicable. Mayūraśarman almost shows himself rebel against Pallava authority. The Ganga rulers readily acknowledged it, two of their kings having been installed by their Pallava overlords Simhavarman and Skandavarman. This means that the Pallavas claimed authority over the whole of the territory of the

Sātavāhanas in the south, and that is what really accounts for the implacable enmity between the Great Pallavas and the early Chāḷukyas, who became rulers of the territory in the immediate neighbourhood of the kingdom of Banavasi of the Kadambas. It seems, thefore, clear that the Pallavas began as officers of the Sātavāhanas and ultimately rose to undisputed possession of the territory of Kanchi, the right to which they strengthened by an alliance with the heiress of the southern block of the Sātavāhana territory, thus in a way becoming titular descendants of the Sātavāhanas over the whole of the southern region of Sātavāhana territory including in it their own new conquest, the territory of Toṇḍamaṇḍalam dependent upon Kanchi.

From what is stated in the foregoing pages, it would have become clear that the Pallavas of the charters starting from the south-eastern marches of the Sātavāhana territory gradually occupied the region of Kurnool, Nellore and part of the Cuddapah Districts, and extended southwards till they gradually appropriated the town of Kanchi itself and the territory dependent thereon, in other words, what is known to the Tamils as Toṇḍamaṇḍalam. In this process of gradual conquest and appropriation of the territory intervening the south-eastern frontier of the Andhra kingdom and the northern viceroyalty of the Cholas, they must have dislodged the people who were in occupation of the territory under the elder Tiraiyan of Pavattiri, and latterly the chiefs of Vēngaḍam, of whom Pulli's name is familiar to the Śangam literature. It is this dislodgement of the tribe of people known hitherto as *Kaḷvar*, but more appropriately speaking, *Kaḷavar*, that brought about the disorder in the territory lying immediately to the south of the Nellore District extending southwards to the banks of the Kaveri. It is this region that gets involved in the Kaḷabhra[1] trouble and the process of expansion of the Kaḷabhras is reflected in the disorder and unsettlement which is noticeable

[1] For a detailed account of the Kaḷabhras see my paper 'The Kaḷabhra interregnum and what it means in South Indian History' presented to the International Congress of Orientalists held at Oxford, August 1928.

even in the kingdom of the Pallavas of the Sanskrit charters. The period beginning therefore with the middle of the third century and extending onwards is the period of these migrations of the Kaḷabhras from their original home in a general southward movement, which overturned the territory of Toṇḍamaṇḍalam, created confusion and disorder and brought about even the ultimate extinction of the well-established monarchies of the Tamil land. It is a movement like what is actually under reference in the details that we get of a Kaḷabhra interregnum, as the epigraphists call it, from the Vēḷvikuḍi plates of the Pandyas of the latter half of the eighth century A.D.

Any reasonable investigation of this particular question requires a general idea of the whole position. Without assuming too much, we may take it that these are known facts in regard to the Pallavas. The first, according to generally accepted opinion, is that the earliest of them issued charters in Prakrit much in the style of the Sātavāhana charters; of which we have knowledge of the localities concerned. Three or four generations of these Pallavas happen to be known. The Allahabad Prasasti of Samudragupta makes mention of a Vishṇugopa of Kanchi. Without pausing to enquire whether this Vishṇugopa was a Pallava or no—there is nothing in the context of the inscription to indicate that he was not a Pallava as no ruler is mentioned by his dynastic name, but all of them are associated with their capitals—Vishṇugopa must have been a ruler of Kanchi contemporary with Samudragupta. This may be taken to be the second established fact. Then it is that we come upon a confused dark period where more light would certainly be welcome. But soon after, for a couple of hundred years, we find a dynasty of rulers, the order of whose succession, we cannot as yet fix very definitely. These rulers for some reason or other issued their charters always in Sanskrit, and called themselves invariably rulers of Kanchi, although some of their charters were issued from various 'victorious camps' of which there are as many as three or four capable of location in the Nellore District, that is, the region north of Toṇḍamaṇḍalam proper. With these few main facts, which may be taken as established, we have to build up the history of the period from such glimpses as we get of details by setting them in a reasonable order on the basis of what is generally known. One general fact of Pallava history of this period—the period of the Sanskrit charters—is that it was a period of some amount of confusion, in which the succession to the throne itself could not have been in any very regular established order. There had been wars to the north, and wars to the south, and confusion in the interior of the territory of the Pallavas themselves. That seems to have been a period in which the Kadambas rose to power and the Gangas came into historical view on the one side. The Cholas almost passed into oblivion and the Tamil country suffered some kind of a confusion, as to the nature of which we have been in the dark till the Vēḷvikuḍi plates threw some light upon it by stating categorically that a certain set of rulers, at the head of the people Kaḷabhras, overthrew the Tamil rulers of the south, the famous three crowned kings of Śangam literature. What is the cause of all this confusion and what is it that could satisfactorily explain all the facts mentioned above categorically? We have a specific lead in the Vēḷvikuḍi plates for this, namely, that the Kaḷabhras came into the Tamil country as far south as the territory of the Pandyas, and upset the settled order to the extent of destroying a *Brahmadēya* gift (a free gift of land to Brahmans) which in orthodox parlance implies the destruction of a settled order of rule by the creation of a very considerable amount of confusion in the administration. If we could know something of these Kaḷabhras, we may possibly throw some light upon the causes of all the confusion in the history of the Pallavas during the period. For this again, there is a certain amount of light that we can derive from the Vēḷvikuḍi plates themselves. The plates were issued by an individual sovereign, who restored the grant to the living representative of its original donee on satisfactory proof that the village was originally granted in the manner claimed. His father, generally known to epigraphists by the titles

Tĕrmăran Rājasimha, we know, beyond doubt, was a contemporary of Nandivarman Pallavamalla (*cir.* A.D. 717 to *cir.* A.D. 782). Alloting him to somewhere about the middle of the long reign of Nandivarman, we may roughly place him in about A.D. 750 or A.D. 740. We want six generations to come to the period when the Pandya country emerged from out of the Kaḷabhra rule and got back into Pandya rule, and a certain ruler by name Kaḍuṁkon is stated in the grant to have done this. Even allowing the moderate span of twenty-five years' rule to each of these six generations, Kaḍuṁkon's rule would come to somewhere about A.D. 600 more or less, bringing him roughly into contemporaneity with the first great Pallava ruler, Simhavishṇu. The period of the Kaḷabhra interregnum, according to the Vēḷvikuḍi plates thus coincides with the period of Pallava history under the rule of the Pallavas of the Sanskrit charters. If the Kaḷabhras created confusion in the Tamil country, they must have come from elsewhere into it. Wherefrom did they come? It is obvious that they did not come from the south. The Pandya country seems the southern limit of their reach. During the period, Chola rule seems to have gone into eclipse of a more or less thorough character. The natural inference therefore would be that they probably advanced southwards. If they were in the Chola country before coming to the Pandya, could we not reasonably infer that they had been in the Pallava country before coming into the Chola, or at least had something to do with the Pallava? If so, who could these Kaḷabhras be, why were they so-called, and what would be the cause of their southward migration?

We have stated above on the authority of the Prakrit charters that the so-called Pallavas were viceroys of the south-eastern marches of the Andhra country, and they gradually extended their territory so as to occupy the region dominated by the hill Vēngaḍam, and ruled over by tribal chieftains, the earlier one known to literature being Tiraiyan of Pavattiri and the later one Pulli of Vēngaḍam. The latter chief is generally spoken of as the chief of the Kaḷvar in the so-called Śangam literature. But the learned editor of these works has since discovered that the correcter reading, on manuscript authority, would be *Kaḷavar* and not *Kaḷvar*. In the region which they occupied in the period of the later Sātavāhanas, and therefore the period immediately preceding that of the Pallavas, they had been a set of frontier people, at least somewhat predatory in point of character, accustomed to lifting cattle from the northern frontier and thereby flourishing upon it as a profession, and that is how Pulli is described in the Śangam literature. The tightening of the hold of the Pallavas even as viceroys of the Andhras by a pressure applied both from the north and west, must have dislodged these people from the locality of their denizenship, and set forward their migration which ultimately overturned the Toṇḍamaṇḍalam first, Cholamaṇḍalam next, and a considerable part of the Pāṇḍyamaṇḍalam after that. Perhaps it is this disturbance, and possibly the confusion caused by the invasion of Samudragupta through some of these regions, that must have ultimately brought about the subversion of the settled order and the introduction of the confusion, from out of which emerged the Pallavas of Kanchi of the Sanskrit charters. That period, it will be found, is the period in which something of a radical change had been taking place in the south-western viceroyalty—the palatine viceroyalty of the Andhras—of Banavasi. We see in that region, a set of rulers who called themselves Chūṭu Nāgas, claim relationship with the ruling family of the Sātavāhanas and achieving political distinction by wars against the Śakas and the Kshatrapas, the enemies of the great Sātavāhana, Gautamīputra Sātakarṇi. In the best days of their power, their territory seems to have extended as far north as the Godavari, but it began to shrink on the northern side, so that they became a purely southern power. The illuminating detail that the Vēlūrpāḷayam plates give us of Virakūrcha becoming, heir to a kingdom by a marriage with a wife, by which, as is stated in the quaint language of the charter, 'he simultaneously obtained a wife and a kingdom.' This seems to be no more than his marrying the heiress of the Chūṭu Nāgas and, by securing a wife of that distinction, he became also the heir to that territory either in his own person, or, possibly better, in that of his son. It is this alone that can account for the very important historical fact that we know of in the history of the Pallavas later,—the acknowledgment of allegiance to the Pallavas by the Gangas, two successive rulers of the Gangas having been installed on their hereditary throne by the contemporary Pallavas. That seems to be the position also in regard to the Kadambas, who became heir to the territory of the Chūṭu Nāgas clearly by conquest, as the story of Mayūraśarman indicates.

The Kaḷabhras then were the *Kaḷavar* of the region immediately north of Toṇḍamaṇḍalam, who being dislodged by the pressure of the Andhras, penetrated the Toṇḍamaṇḍalam itself, and as the Andhra power itself advanced, moved southwards, occupying the territory gradually till in the course of generations, they subverted the Chola rule and spread themselves farther south, to the occupation of the territory of the Pandyas so as to produce the interregnum referred to in the Vēḷvikuḍi plates in the Pandya country. This interregnum followed when the grant of the village Vēḷvikuḍi was made to the Brahman and had been enjoyed for a considerable length of time by him and his successors. The interregnum itself must have lasted for some considerable time, and to justify the lapse of the grant being forgotten for five or six generations after the restoration of Pandya rule. The Pallavas of the Sanskrit charters therefore had to advance into the country dependent upon Kanchi, dislodge the Kaḷabhras or Kaḷavars that were in occupation as a normal continuation of the struggle which must have begun between them and the Kaḷabhras somewhat earlier, till they could master possession of the region. It is probably in this process of conquest that the invasion of Samudragupta introduced another element of confusion, to provide against which an alliance with the more powerful neighbour, the Chūṭu Nāgas of the west, must have been felt to be necessary by the Pallavas of Kanchi. Whether the Vishṇugopa of Kanchi referred to in the Harisena inscription of Sumudragupta is Kāṇagopa identified with

Kumāravishṇu I is more than we can assert at present. It is possible that the Kāṇagopa of the later charters had a name Kumāravishṇu or Vishṇugopa. But in the absence of any lead, such a statement would be nothing but a guess, and it may be safer to leave Vishṇugopa the contemporary of Samudragupta unidentified with any of the names in the genealogy of the Pallavas of the Sanskrit charters for the present. When the Pallavas of the Sanskrit charters established themselves in the region of Toṇḍamaṇḍalam, their struggles with Kaḷabhras of the south must have begun, as a continuation of the struggle that dislodged them from the territory of Toṇḍamaṇḍalam. It is this that is reflected in the statement that Kumāravishṇu retook the capital from some enemy undescribed, and that Buddhavarman, one of the rulers of this dynasty, won victories against the 'ocean-like army' of the Cholas, which at the time could only mean the Kaḷabhras established in the Chola territory, as about that time we do hear of a Kaḷamba ruler by name Acchyutavikrānta holding rule at the Chola capital, Puhār over the Chola Rāshṭra, according to Buddhadatta, a contemporary of Buddhagosha. The establishment of the Kaḷabhras in the Chola country therefore seems to have been a settled fact by the middle of the sixth century. They were found there by Simhavishṇu at the end of the sixth; by Narasimhavarman I in the middle of the seventh, and by the Chaḷukyas about the end of the seventh and almost the middle of the eighth centuries. It seems to be these Kaḷabhras that come into view later on near Tanjore and Koḍumbāḷūr as Muttaraīyan chiefs bearing names and titles very much like that of Acchyutavikrānta. We come to the spectacle in the eighth century of the Tanjore chiefs being feudatories of the Pallavas and the Koḍumbāḷūr chiefs those of the Pandyas, and fighting against each other in consequence. The Kaḷabhra migration, the movement of the *Kaḷavar* southwards from their orignal home, seems thus to provide the explanation for the disappearance of the settled order in the Tamil country as portrayed in the Śangam literature and offers the explanation of the interval of obscurity and oblivion in Chola rule till the rising of the later Cholas to power in the latter half of the ninth century.

The narration of events above, it would have been noted, assumes the existence of a period of prosperity reflected in the Śangam literature anterior to the coming of the Pallavas of Kanchi into the region of Toṇḍamaṇḍalam. The assumption is based on evidence which an effort has been made to upset by another assumption without any valid evidence, we should say, of a Chola interregnum in the rule of the Pallavas of Kanchi on the basis of the statement that Kumāravishṇu II had to retake his capital from his enemies. The difficulties against accepting this assumption are many and fundamental; anything like a capture of Kanchi by the Cholas and even its retention in the hands of the Cholas for some little time till recapture by Kumāravishṇu, would hardly satisfy the conditions of the Chola Karikāla's capture of Kanchi, because the Chola Karikāla is associated, in the Śangam literature so called, with a succession of rulers extending over three or four generations, during which since his conquest Kanchi remained a Chola viceroyalty. The provision of an interval of that length before Kumāravishṇu II retook Kanchi would be on the face of it impossible. Karikāla is supposed to have introduced the arts of agriculture and civilization into the bulk of the region constituting Toṇḍamaṇḍalam, and the viceroyality was held with distinction by Chola princes immediately following him and subsequently by an illegitimate scion of the Chola family, Toṇḍamān-Iḷaṁ-Tiraiyan, before it passed into the possession of the Pallavas of the inscriptions. There is not the slightest hint of all this in the various charters, of which we have information, and Bappa Dēva's civilizing effort in the region farther north seems almost to indicate an extension of the effort of Karikāla. Looked at from any point of view therefore, it seems impossible to postulate a Chola interregnum in the middle of the succession of Pallava rulers of the Sanskrit charters and the effort seems to us futile. We have almost fifteen generations of rulers subsequent to the Samudragupta invasion. Although we cannot be very definite about the order of succession or of the detailed history of the period, the general trend seems clear enough to rule out the possibility of this interregnum. There is the evidence of the Śangam literature by itself and the evidence of the later Pandya charters leading thereto, and they seem alike to negative this possibility. Whether the Śangam actually existed or no, the existence of something like a Śangam and of a body of literature known as Śangam literature came to be an accepted article of faith among the Tamils at the commencement of the seventh century A.D. among the Tevāram hymners like Appar and Sambandar. For a tradition like that to grow and for a body of literature to get thus distinctly classified, we do require a certain efflux of time, and that could not be less than half a dozen generations or more, and thus the indication seems to be that the period of the Śangam literature will have to be referred to a time anterior to the advent of the Pallavas of the Sanskrit charters into the region of Kanchi. A Chola interregnum associated with the name of Karikāla in the generations immediately preceding Kumāravishṇu II seems impossible of justification. The period of the Pallavas of the Sanskrit charters marks the advent of a new dynasty, their long, but fairly successful, struggle against hostile occupation of the territory of Toṇḍamaṇḍalam, probably by the Kaḷabhras, their assertion of their overlordship over the Gangas, and a similar recognition of their overlordship at any rate, by the Kadambas after a struggle ending in the final establishment of the Pallava authority there till Simhavarman, the father of Simhavishṇu the first Great Pallava, founded a dynasty of powerful rulers for the next two centuries and a half, all require the couple of centuries that are left between the invasion of Samudragupta and the accession of Simhavarman, the father of Simhavishṇu. The accession of these powerful rulers to authority in this region is almost coeval with the rise of the Chāḷukyas into view in the region north of their territory.

The origin of the Chāḷukyas and their accession to power in the period with which their name is associated is somewhat obscure. Their habitual hostility to the Pallavas and the constant warfare between the two that this hostility brought about are facts recognized all round, although the reason for this constant hostility has been far from clear. The one is perhaps to some extent associated with the other, and an explanation of the hostility does not seem altogether beyond recovery. In the traditional stories connected with their origin, the historians of the dynasty or the heraldic custodians of their traditional origin gave them credit for association with the Ikshvākus of Ayodhya. Whatever the reason the association with Ikshvākus seems to have been fashionable even in this distant south at this particular time. The Chāḷukyas connect themselves with the Ikshvākus and some well-known Ikshvāku rulers figure in Chola genealogies when they began to appear. Even before the days of genealogies, the Toṇḍaman ruler of Kanchi is associated with some of the Ikshvākus in one of the Śangam classics. So the Chāḷukya's claim to an association with the Ikshvākus, while historically possible because of the existence of Ikshvāku rulers in their neighbourhood in the Andhra country, still remains unproved in the face of the fact that they have to invent a kind of explanation, at the very best unsatisfactory, for the name Chāḷukya. This defect seems to make them an indigenous dynasty of feudatory rulers, who raised themselves to power gradually, and set themselves up independently. The fact of their obscure origin coupled with the boar ensign on the one hand, and the impossible derivation of the word from Sanskrit on the other, seem alike to indicate a southern origin for them on a reasonable basis. Feudatory dynasties placed in rule over the less hospitable regions of the Tamil country went by the name generally *Vēḷpula Araśar* or *Śaḷukki Vēndar*. They were given the flag of the boar indicative of the nature of the territory over which they ruled and of the character of that rule. It is a family of chieftains like this probably that ultimately raised themselves to a position of higher dignity that became the Chāḷukyas of a later period. That this is so is reflected in the term sometimes being used in the form Salki, used as a term of contempt with reference to Salki Bhima, who is spoken of as a disloyal person. These petty chieftains seem to have risen first to power in the northern region of the Vākāṭaka territory, perhaps in succession to the Naḷas, or, at any rate, as one of the tributaries along with them. They then gradually spread southwards, extending their territory, and under the sons of Pulikesan I, they conquered the Kadambas and the Gangas and so extended their operations gradually as to come into contact with the territory of the Pallavas with the set object of recovering the southern block of the territory under the Andhras included in the viceroyalty of Banavasi. It was stated already that the Pallavas probably laid claim to this very territory on the basis of a marriage, and naturally, therefore, the two powers had a reason for perpetual hostility on an important, and at the same time, a vulnerable frontier for both of them. Therefore it is that since the Chāḷukyas established their power by the conquest of the Naḷas, the Mauryas and the Kadambas, they are seen in the full tide of their hostility to the Pallavas and this hostility continued, now the one, now the other getting the better, till one of the dynasties, the Chāḷukyas vanished from Dakhan politics. That accounts for the Chāḷukya invasion in the reign of Mahēndravarman, who from his headquarters beat them back, and left it to his son to carry the war into the enemy's country, destroy their capital and bring about an interregnum, which lasted for thirteen years. This happened at the end of the reign of Pulikesan II, and his son Vikramāditya was able to turn the tables upon the Pallavas and carry the war into their territory by a flank movement, so as to fight on the banks of the Kaveri near Trichinopoly against the Pallavas supported by all the Tamil powers this time. One of his successors was able to carry the war into Kanchi itself, occupied the town in his turn, and, instead of destroying it, as the Pallava Narasimhavarman had done at Vatāpi, their capital, not merely restored, but even made a fresh donation to the temple, showing thus distinctly that he was more humane in warfare than perhaps the Southern power. It is in revenge for this insult that Nandivarman Pallavamalla took the tide on the turn when, on the occasion of a marriage alliance brought about diplomatically between the Ganga princess, the daughter of Śrī Purusha Muttarasa, and the Pandyan prince, Neḍum-Śaḍaiyan Parāntaka, the donor of the Veḷvikuḍi plates, the Pallavas led the combination of the southern powers, in which the Pandyan minister got distinction, and inflicted a crushing defeat upon the Chāḷukyas at the battle of Veṇbai. Kīrtivarman II was so thoroughly defeated that the Chāḷukya power found it impossible to recover from the defeat. It is this again that was taken advantage of by the feudatory Rāshṭrakūṭa Dantidurga, himself, the son of a Chāḷukya princess to subvert the Chāḷukya power. He was able to do this by fortifying himself by an alliance with the great Pallava ruler Nandi to whom perhaps he gave his daughter in marriage and thus brought about his own elevation and the subversion of the dynasty of the early Chāḷukyas. The battle of Veṇbai is graphically described in detailing the achievements of the *āgnapati*, Māran-Kāri of Karavandapuram at whose instance the grant was made. Tirumangai Āḻvār's reference to Rāshṭrakūṭa Dantidurga, under his title Vairamēgha, and the deferential treatment which Nandivarman Pallavamalla is said to have accorded to him finds justification in this and the question how the early Chāḷukyas were ultimately overthrown and the Rāsṭrakūṭas established themselves in their stead is now put on a clear footing.

The accession of Nandivarman Pallavamalla to the Pallava throne and how it actually happened have alike remained a problem in Pallava history till recently. The publication of some of the Vaikunṭha Perumāḷ temple epigraphs[1] clears the doubt completely, though it does not altogether dispel the darkness that surrounded the actual character of his accession to power. From theepigraphs, it is clear that, when Paramēśvaravarman died, for some reason or other, the great citizens of the land had to be on the look out for a suitable successor, The position of the Pallavas at the time was far from easy. After some futile efforts they ultimately made up their minds

[1] *S.I.I.*, vol. iv, pp. 10–12.

to offer it to Hiraṇyavarma the collateral cousin through the younger brother of Simhavishṇu; but Hiraṇya shrank from the responsibility as an old man and offered the chance to each one of his four sons in turn. The three elder ones refused the responsibility and the youngest of them all, Pallavamalla by name, or Paramēśvaravarman Pallavamalla, agreed to accept the responsibility with an alacrity which was disconcerting to the father's paternal instincts. He was however allowed to succeed, and, when he reached Kanchi, he was duly installed under the title Nandivarman. Hence his full style Nandivarman Pallavamalla or Paramēśvaran Pallavamalla *alias* Nandivarman. This gives colour to some of the hymns of Tirumangai Āḷvar which celebrate the temple as Paramēśvara-Viṇṇagaram. It cannot now be taken that the Vishṇu temple was founded by Paramēśvaravarman II, nor even by Paramēśvaravarman I. It now becomes quite clear that the founder of this temple is the Pallava prince to whom the Āḷvār makes so many direct references. All of them refer to Nandivarman Pallavamalla in his family name Paramēśvaravarman. That apart, the accession, according to these records is a peaceful one by the choice of the people and therefore come to legitimately. But there are other charters which broadly state, as is recounted in the following pages, that he came to the throne as a result of fighting and by an act of usurpation. The two statements it is possible to reconcile, and it is hardly necessary to take them as irreconcilable alternatives. The facts seem to have been these. A Chāḷukya invasion seems to have been imminent, and the constant hostility of this power on the northern frontier together with the rising activity of the Pāṇḍyas in the south made the position of the Pallavas in the middle one of extreme anxiety. The maintenance of the Pallava power intact meant a Janus-faced fight, south against the Pāṇḍyas and north against the Chāḷukyas. When Paramēśvaravarman II died, if the responsible people of the kingdom felt that the ruler that succeeded him should be a man of ability and resource, and not a child succeeding a comparatively inefficient rule of a father, their offer of the throne to Hiraṇyavarman, possibly a veteran administrator at the time, would have valid justification on the basis of the fitness of the person. The legitimate successor, Chitramāya, or, whoever he was, may have been comparatively young and weak; and even later, the fight that could be put up in his favour does not appear to have been strong enough to make this assumption unwarranted. It was a useful change though the actual successor happened to be a young boy of twelve, supported as he must have been with all the resources of his father and brothers, and other officers of the kingdom. Those whose sympathies were on the legitimist side would naturally call such a succession an act of usurpation, while to those of the opposite faction Nandivarman's acceptance of the office was an honourable act of public beneficence for the well-being of the State. The thirteen or fourteen epigraphs that have been published throw very important light upon this position, and from these, what has hitherto been known regarding this succession receives fresh illumination. Nandivarman probably came to the throne and accepted the responsibility that it involved, by the invitation of those responsible for the welfare of the state; necessarily setting aside the legitimate claims of another prince of the family. The war which was a consequence necessarily, went against the legitimate prince, but the actual achievements of the general in behalf of Nandivarman seem fully to justify the anxiety of those who went out of their way to set aside the legitimate successor in favour of another. It need not therefore be the fault of Nandivarman Pallavamalla that he ascended the throne, not an act of his own, and merely for the sake of the position or the power that it carried with it. Though his earlier years were clouded by these wars, he managed to tide over these troubles both by successful war and by equally successful diplomacy, subverting the natural enemy, the Chāḷukyas in the north, and entering into a more or less permanent alliance with their successors, the Rāshṭrakūṭas; on the south, he got into perhaps a treaty of alliance with the Pāṇḍyas, after a good deal of fight with them on behalf of the rulers of Kongu, whose independence all his efforts could not sustain. When he died, his kingdom could pass down to his son without any difficulty and Pallava rule continued for another three or four generations, for almost a century, without distress.

There has been considerable discussion in regard to the successors of Nandivarman Pallavamalla and a controversy has raged over the fancied displacement of the dynasty and by the succession of a new dynasty called till recently by the epigraphists (Ganga-Pallavas.) Inscriptions published since this hypothesis was put forward seem entirely to negative the position taken and with the information at our disposal now, there is hardly any need to maintain the hypothesis, whatever justification it might have had in its origin. Nandivarman was succeeded by Dantivarman his son, Dantivarman by another Nandivarman, and then followed Nṛpatunga in a regular line of succession, all of them tracing their descent through Nandivarman Pallavamalla. Why a certain number of these should be distinctly marked off and given the name Ganga-Pallavas is far from clear. That there was some kind of a family connection between the Gangas and the Pallavas may be readily admitted. That is a connection which the Pallavas had with other royal families as well, namely, those of the Rāshṭrakūṭas and the Kadambas, taking the dynasty of Nandivarman Pallavamalla alone. A marriage alliance of this sort need not give a new direction unless we can specifically prove that a scion of the Ganga family through a daughter even, or through a Pallava princess set up rule in the territory of the Pallavas. For this, we have absolutely no lead. Comparatively minor changes in the titles of rulers at a certain stage of their history, or of the existence of a number of rulers simultaneously in the same territory, are not reasons that would justify a hypothesis as grave as this. What seems actually to have taken place is this. The Pallava-Pandya struggle in the time of the great Pallavamalla seems to have been more or less for the overlordship of Kongu to begin with. At some period of his reign that overlordship, if it was at any time exercised by the Pallavamalla at all, passed over to the Pandyas. To fortify this position, they entered into a marriage alliance with the Gangas across the Kongu frontier and this brought down upon them a great Chāḷukya invasion, as the Gangas were perhaps regarded as Chāḷukya feudatories at the time. Feudatory or no, the Gangas in alliance with the Pandyas would be a real danger on the flank of the Chāḷukya, having regard to the fact that they regarded the Pallavas as their standing enemies. That brought on the battle of Veṇbai which had for its ultimate result the subversion of the dynasty of the Chāḷukyas and the establishment, in their stead, of the rule of the Rāshṭrakūṭas who apparently fortified their position by an alliance with the Pallavas. This for the time settled the question of the political relationship between the Gangas, the Rāshṭrakūṭas and the Pallavas. Later on the wars continued between the Pandyas and the Pallavas on the one side, and hostility gradually developed between the Pallavas and the Rāshṭrakūṭas on the other. The Gangas in the middle now played the one part, now the other, till at last they were ultimately reduced to a position of subordination by the Rāshṭrakūṭas. This certainly was one element of weakness in the Pallavas. The Pandyas in consequence were slowly gaining the upper hand, and tightened their hold on the Pallavas, so that the Pallava territory which had at one time been so very extensive, was gradually shrinking to one of comparatively narrow dimensions. The final victory achieved by Varaguna II at Śripurambyam near Kumbakonam gave a crushing blow, if not the death blow, to the Pallava power, in which one section of the Gangas, the Gangas who held authority in the Bāṇa country, assisted the Pallavas. But the Pallavas still continued in a comparatively precarious position. This precarious condition of the Pallava power, as in the case of all other Indian imperial powers, brought about a dismemberment, which began usually with an independence of the provinces constituting the empire more or less definite, and this dismemberment is what is in evidence in our having a certain number of rulers in the Pallava territory, each issuing inscriptions, almost on his own authority simultaneously, when the power of the Cholas, newly come into existence under Vijayālaya, advanced northwards under his successor Āditya, and put an end to the crumbling empire of the Pallavas and annexed the whole of their territory to their own dominions, thus introducing a new overlordship, which was symbolized by the name Jayaṁkoṇḍacholamaṇḍalam given to the Pallava terrritory which till then was known Toṇḍamaṇḍalam. The existence therefore of several Pallava princes marks nothing more than a mere stage in the dismemberment of the kingdom or empire, and need not be regarded as the establishment of a separate dynasty of rulers distinct from the one who held rule from Kanchi. That seems the general trend of Pallava History, which Mr. Gopalan's work indicates. The purpose of this introduction is merely to supply a few gaps in the narrative, and thus to provide the few links required for the continuous story of the rise, growth, decay and the dissolution of the power of the Pallavas of Kanchi.

Mr. Gopalan has done the work with care and discrimination and has succeeded in providing a readable account of this interesting and extensive period of South Indian History, which, it is hoped, would be found useful by those interested in the subject.

S. KRISHNASWAMI AIYANGAR,
Professor of Indian History and Archæology,
University of Madras.

'MARINE VILLA',
October 15, 1928.

THE HISTORY OF THE PALLAVAS OF SOUTH INDIA

A.D. 200 to 900

CHAPTER I

INTRODUCTORY, HISTORY OF PREVIOUS RESEARCH AND SOURCES OF HISTORY FOR THE PALLAVAS

THE materials for writing a history of the Pallava kings of South India were until almost recent times exceedingly scanty and otherwise inadequate. They are moreover distorted by erroneous traditions and misleading accounts of mythical ancestry. A hundred years ago hardly any of their inscriptions on stone or on copper-plates, of which we have such large numbers now, were known. This becomes evident on a perusal of the Mackenzie Collection of MSS. relating to South Indian history which, mentioning dozens of members of the Chōḷa, Pāṇḍya and other dynasties of early South India, do not mention a single name of any of the members of the Pallava dynasty which had remained the dominant South Indian power for about seven centuries. This is remarkable seeing that the Pallavas wielded sovereign authority for several centuries in the Tamil land. Literary tradition embodied in the hymns of the Āḻvārs, and in the works *Nandik-kalambakam*, the *Periyapurāṇam*, *Chintāmaṇi*, *Avantisundari-kathāsāra*, etc., are far too scanty for historical purposes though they give a glowing idea of the culture of the Pallava period.

History of Research on the Pallavas.—The late Sir Walter Elliot did remarkable service for the cause of South Indian historical research by the publication of some early South Indian inscriptions in the *Journal of the Royal Asiatic*

Society [1] and in the *Madras Journal of Literature and Science* [2] as early as 1837. An important starting-point was made in his announcement in 1858 that in the sixth century, *the Pallava kings were dominant in South India.* Even earlier than this, in 1844, he had discovered that the monoliths in the Seven Pagodas were excavated by Pallava kings. At the same time Dr. Burnell succeeded in deciphering some of the inscriptions at this place belonging to Pallava kings. These inscriptions are included in Capt. Carr's well-known collection of papers on the Seven Pagodas. Another important contribution to Pallava history is the work of James Fergusson, *History of Indian and Eastern Architecture*, in which after a minute examination of the monuments at the Seven Pagodas he has attributed them to the sixth and seventh centuries A.D. But it was the second half of the last century that saw the discovery of numerous and important copper-plate charters and stone inscriptions belonging to this dynasty, which for the first time opened the eyes of scholars to the historical importance of this celebrated dynasty of kings, ruling in a part of the Tamil and Telugu country. This discovery has practically revolutionized the prevalent notions concerning Pallava history. The earliest of these records was edited by the late Dr. Fleet in the *Indian Antiquary* in its earlier numbers, with notes and translations. Towards the close of the last century stone inscriptions of this dynasty began to be discovered in various parts of the Tamil land along with a large number of Pallava monuments other than those found at Mahābalipuram. These records coupled with the inscriptions on the copper-plate charters form the most valuable raw material for the reconstruction of Pallava history. Many of the records have been edited, with great ability and learning, by Hultzsch, Venkayya, Fleet, Kielhorn, Krishna Sastri and others in the pages of the *Indian Antiquary*, *South Indian Inscriptions* and the *Epigraphia Indica.* The stone inscriptions and copper-plate records discovered year after

[1] vol. iv, pp. 1-41.

[2] vol. vii, pp. 193-232.

year are noticed in the *Annual Reports on South Indian Epigraphy* with notes and comments.

The first connected account of the Pallava kings was attempted more than forty years ago by the late Dr. Fleet in his *Dynasties of the Kanarese Districts*, which forms a part of the *Bombay Gazetteer*, where he has exploited for the first time all the records, inscriptions on stone and copper-plates, relating to the Pallavas which were accessible to him. The outline account of Dr. Fleet, though written so long ago, still remains in its main aspects authoritative and represents more or less the first attempt to write a scientific history of these kings. The next notable attempt to sketch the origin and history of the Pallavas was made by the late Mr. V. Venkayya in the *Archæological Annual Survey Report for 1906–7.*[1] This is a scholarly piece of research work on the subject, and embodies the author's life-long labours in the field of epigraphy and literature. This work written in 1906 takes into consideration the inscriptions and copper-plates discovered since the days when Dr. Fleet wrote, and the author's researches in the field of Tamil literature are also fully utilized. In many respects this account still remains an authority on the subject.

The next important work on the Pallavas is that of Prof. G. Jouveau-Dubreuil published in 1917. In this work the author has embodied the results of his independent research, and has propounded several original and ingenious theories regarding the origin, chronology, genealogy, art and architecture of the Pallavas. The author has succeeded, to a large extent, in establishing a connection between the Pallava kings of the Prakrit charters and the members of the Sanskrit records, and has attacked the intricate problem of their chronology and genealogy with critical ability. Many of the conclusions are based on the author's personal investigation which have resulted in the discovery of several new inscriptions and monuments hitherto unknown. The other

[1] pp. 217–43.

papers and monographs of the same author, such as those on 'the Pallava Antiquities', 'Pallava-painting', form important contributions to the subject and offer several new interpretations of parts of the subject. His latest work entitled the *Ancient History of the Deccan* embodies the author's latest views on the Pallavas, their origin and chronology.

Among other writers on the subject Dr. S. Krishnaswami Aiyangar has published a valuable account of 'The Origin and Early History of the Pallavas' in the *Journal of Indian History*, [1] then published in Allahabad. This contribution represents the author's latest investigations on this subject, and, having been published in 1923 is the most recent work on the subject of an authoritative character. A large number of papers on the inscriptions, monuments and literature of the period appeared in various journals, some of these being contributed by Mr. Gopinatha Rao on 'the Ganga-Pallavas,' Mr. K. V. Subramanya Aiyar, on 'the Ancient History of Conjeevaram' published in the *Madras Christian College Magazine*, 'the Literary History of the Pallava Age' by Mr. Rangaswami Sarasvati in the *Journal of the Mythic Society* and the 'Antiquities of Mahabalipuram' by Dr. S. Krishnaswami Aiyangar. Some of the historical portions of the district manuals contain accounts of varying value about the Pallavas, while more recently accounts have also been published in Tamil, the most notable of these being that of Mr. P. T. Srinivasa Aiyangar, entitled *A History of the Pallavas.*

Sources of History

Epigraphy.—Of the sources of information for writing the history of the Pallavas, epigraphy occupies a prominent place compared with the other sources. Dr. Fleet has pointed out, 'We are ultimately dependent on the inscriptions in every line of Indian research.' This is especially true of the history of the Pallavas, for without the inscriptions it is practically impossible to know anything about these kings and their times. We may

[1] vol. ii, pp. 20–66.

divide the Pallava inscriptions[1] conveniently into three classes. To the first class belong records written entirely in Prakrit. The second class of records comprises Sanskrit inscriptions, while the third class consists of those in Sanskrit and Tamil. Of these, the records of the first class probably belong to the earliest period, as it is now recognized that Prakrit was superseded by Sanskrit about the fourth century A.D., while the earliest 'Grantha-Tamil' records of the Pallavas have been assigned to the seventh century. Most of these records are of a donative character. Their object was to record the gifts of lands or money to temples or Brahmans. The most important portion of the records was the specification of the details of the names of the donor, the donee and the donation of the particular gift. From very early times the records give a certain amount of genealogical information and a recital of events was introduced to magnify the glory and importance of the donors. Thus, for instance, the Prakrit charters such as those of Sivaskandavarman contained hardly any allusion to historical events connected with the donor. Gradually however we find a change. The Sanskrit charters beginning from about the fifth century not only enumerate the father and the grandfather of the donor, but some of them, such as the Kūram, Kaśākkuḍi, the Vēlūrpāḷayam and the Bāhūr plates, give a long account of the names of previous kings and their achievements. 'Thus,' as Fleet says, 'not with the expressed object of preserving history, but in order to intensify the importance of everything connected with religion and to secure grantees in the possession of properties conveyed to them, there was gradually accumulated almost the whole mass of epigraphic records from which chiefly, the ancient history of India is now being put together.'[2]

Stone Inscriptions.—Stone inscriptions beginning from the seventh century, so far as this dynasty is concerned, form a distinct class by themselves. These records which are fairly abundant for the later Pallava period are for the most

[1] *Vide* Appendix (A).
[2] Fleet, *Bom. Gaz.*, vol. i, pt. ii, p. 62.

part, donative in character, though one or two of them such as the Vāyalūr pillar inscription of Rājasimha, and the Panamalai inscription of the same king give a genealogical account. Some are short, and record gifts to religious or other institutions, and they are invariably dated in the regnal year of the contemporary king without reference to any era. They are mostly in prose, though a few of these are to be found also in verse such as the inscription at the Pallava rock-cut temple at Daḷavānūr [1] of King Mahēndravarman I. The earliest of these are those written in some of the rock-cut temples believed to have been excavated by Mahēndravarman I, such as the one at Vallam.[2] Many of these rock-cut temples such as those at Pallāvaram, Trichinopoly, Manḍagappaṭṭu, Māmanḍūr contain Grantha and Grantha-Tamil inscriptions some of which are contemporaneous with the caves and have for their object the simple recording of the excavation of these monuments. The copper-plate charters taken along with these stone inscriptions furnish valuable information as regards the history and chronology of the Pallava kings. In spite of the serious disadvantage that these records are not dated in any of the known eras but only in the regnal years of the king, a careful study of the palæography of these inscriptions makes it possible to fix their age more or less accurately. The facts obtained from these records, coupled with those of the contemporary kings with whom the Pallavas came into contact enable us to reconstruct to a great extent the history of the age of the Pallavas. The most important of these contemporary records are those of the Western-Gangas, the Western Chāḷukyas, the Pānḍyas as well as the minor dynasties such as those of the Muttaraiyan and the Bāṇa subordinates of the later Pallava kings.

Pallava Monuments.—Side by side with the inscriptions we have the Pallava monuments themselves. According to one set of scholars whose enthusiasm for their subject hampers them from taking a dispassionate view, the study of architec-

[1] *Ep. Ind.*, vol. xii, p. 225. [2] *S. I. I.*, vol. ii, p 34.

ture constitutes an even more important instrument for fixing dates than the study of palæography and inscriptions. According to Mr. A. H. Longhurst for instance, 'the present method of relying entirely on inscriptions for fixing the dates of ancient monuments adopted by Dr. Hultzsch and others is open to objection because when this method of investigation is employed alone, serious mistakes may occur. It is possible that inscriptions on a monument may have been inscribed long after it was erected. In such cases the inscription would not only give no information about the original author of the monument but may even lead us into error. Then again if the study of architecture is neglected, how is the epigraphist going to determine the age of the monument that does not possess any inscription?'[1] This is a reply to the point of view of Prof. Hultzsch who in his paper on the 'Inscriptions of the Seven Pagodas'[2] wrote:—'The important question of the authors and the dates of these excavations can be answered *only* by a careful study of their inscriptions engraved on them.' Prof. Jouveau-Dubreuil is inclined to agree with Mr. Longhurst, and attaches greater importance to the study of architecture for the determination of dates than to that of the inscriptions. In his work on the *Pallava Antiquities* the author enters into a minute examination of the evolution of the Pallava style in the course of the Pallava age, and distinguishes various styles even during comparatively short intervals of time.

During the last thirty years a large number of Pallava monuments have been discovered at Mahēndravāḍi, Daḷavānūr-Śīyamangalam, Pallāvaram, Trichinopoly, Kīḻmāvilangai, Śingavaram, Tirukkaḻukkuṅṟam, Vallam, Māmanḍūr, Maṇḍagapaṭṭu, Mēlachēri, Sittannavāsal and Mahābalipuram. Some of these consist of rock-cut caves and bear Pallava inscriptions. Others consist of structural temples such as the Kailāsanātha temple at Kāñchīpuram and the Shore temple at the Seven

[1] *M.A.R. for 1918-19*, p. 20.
[2] *Ep. Ind.*, vol. x, p. 2.

Pagodas. Many of these monuments were brought into existence by the Pallava kings and contain their inscriptions. The inscriptions on the Rathas of Mahābalipuram contain some specific references in the shape of the names and surnames of some of the kings. The most important of this class of epigraphs are those on the Dharmarājaratha and the Kailāsanātha temple at Mahābalipuram and Conjeevaram respectively. These temples are dedicated to the Hindu Triad; while the cave temples are dedicated to Śiva or Vishṇu, the presence of representations of Brahma the other member of the Hindu Triad, forms a peculiar feature of these monuments which distinguishes them from later temples. The Ādivarāha temple at the Seven Pagodas contains statues of the celebrated kings Simhavishṇu and Mahēndravarman I in bas-relief. Similarly the rock-cut temple at the top of the Trichinopoly rock appears to have originally contained a statue of Mahēndravarman I, a fact which seems to be alluded to in the inscription discovered there.[1] But the statue is not to be found there now, and may have been destroyed subsequently. Recently Mr. Longhurst has been fortunate in discovering at Bhairavakoṇḍa [2] (Nellore District) a large group of temples attributable to the Pallava age, all of them cut out of rock and closely resembling the Mahēndra caves. There are also a large number of Pallava monuments in South India without bearing any inscription. Further study and research may help in establishing their actual age.

Literature

Next to inscriptions we might consider the testimony of literature and literary tradition. For the earliest period of the history of the Tamil land we are almost entirely dependent on a class of Tamil works known as the Śangam classics and attributable to the first and second centuries of the Christian era. The age of the Śangam has been the subject of keen

[1] *S. I. I.*, vol. i, pp. 28–30. [2] *M. A. R. for 1920–21*, pp. 29–32.

discussion among scholars, and attempts have been made to bring it to the seventh and the eighth centuries. The late Mr. Swamikannu Pillai working from the astronomical details in the eleventh *Paripāḍal* arrived at the conclusion, in his *Indian Ephemeris*,[1] that the author of the piece must have lived in the seventh century. But the generally accepted date, namely, first and the second centuries A.D., seems established on satisfactory grounds, and the new dates have so far not been proved to be beyond doubt correct. The orthodox estimate of the Śangam age expounded by the late Mr. Kanakasabhai Pillai and more fully by Dr. S. Krishnaswami Aiyangar has been followed here.

The Śangam works although they mention several kings and chieftains in the Tamil land contain no mention of the Pallavas (even where they actually describe Kāñchī), or of any member of the various Pallava dynasties known to us from inscriptions. The inference seems, therefore, to be fully justified that the Pallava kings reigned after the age of these Śangam works. Otherwise it is difficult to understand the silence of these works about the dynasty of the Pallavas of Kāñchī especially as we learn from them that the region around Kāñchī was ruled over by Toṇḍamān-Iḷaṁ-Tiraiyan, one of the Chōḷa viceroys. The Śangam works however mention a people known as the *Toṇḍaiyar* among others who are sometimes considered to be the same as, or closely related to, the Pallavas.[2] But the available evidence does not seem sufficient to warrant our identifying the Toṇḍaiyar with the Pallavas as the former term appears to be a tribal name like the Aruvāḷar, Vaḍavar, etc., while Pallava looks more like a family name than that of a tribe. One Śangam work called *Peruṁbāṇāṟṟupaḍai*, written by Rudran-Kaṇṇanār who has also celebrated the Chōḷa king Karikāla and his capital town Kavēripaṭṭinam, is mainly devoted to a description of the condition of Kāñchī during the rule of Toṇḍamān-Iḷaṁ-Tiraiyan who appears to have preceded the

[1] vol. i, p. 108. [2] *Ind. Ant*, vol. lii, pp. 75-80.

Pallava kings at Kāñchī and who, according to certain scholars, was an early Pallava king. With the exception of this poem the other pieces in the Śangam works do not contain any reference either to Kāñchī during the age of the Pallavas or about the Pallavas themselves. Suggestions have been put forward that the Pallavas were foreigners to the south, that the Pallava power was superimposed upon the Tamil land, and that the Tamils therefore scrupulously omitted to mention them, and, even when they did so, mentioned them with contempt. As an illustration the definition in the *Pingalandai* which gives us the synonyms for the Pallavas, includes terms such as *Kayavar*, *Patakar* and *Nīśar*. But against this it must be said that this reference does not apply to the Pallava kings who are referred to in the *Tēvāram* hymns and in the works of some of the Vaishṇava Āḻvārs of the eighth century in terms of praise.[1]

In addition to the references in the hymns of the Śaiva and Vaishṇava saints about these kings new light is thrown on the age of Simhavishṇu in one of the recently-discovered Sanskrit works entitled the *Avantisundarikathāsāra* which, in its historical introduction, not only contains an important synchronism between Simhavishṇu of Kāñchī, Vishṇuvardhana, the early Chāḷukya, and Durvinīta, the early Ganga.[2] This work also gives valuable particulars relating to the literary history of the Pallava age and the patronage of the Pallava kings. The association of Daṇḍin as well as Bhāravi with the Pallava court at Kāñchī, which this work establishes, is very important for understanding the nature of Pallava culture during this period.[3]

Of a similar nature is the discovery of the work *Mattavilāsa-Prahasana*, a burlesque written by the Pallava king Mahēndravarman I, which depicts vividly the contemporary life of religious sects such as the Śākyabikshus and Kāpalikas

[1] *Periya-Tirumoḻi*, ii, 9.
[2] Special note by Editor.
[3] See the Age of Bhāravi and Daṇḍin, *Q.J.M.S.*, vol. xii, p. 10 and the Second All Ind. Ori. Conf., 1922, Proc., pp. 194, 306-7.

in the city, and of which glimpses are obtainable in the hymns of the Āḷvārs and the Nāyanmārs in some of the *Prabandha* and the *Tēvāram* hymns. This work has recently been published by the Travancore Government.[1] There seems to be no doubt that the author of this play Śrī Mahēndravikramavarman is identical with the Pallava king. Mahēndravarman known, from inscriptions and copper-plates, to have reigned in the first quarter of the seventh century. A recently-discovered panel in the Ādivarāha temple in the Seven Pagodas represents him with his two queens, their identity being placed beyond question by the inscriptions over the reliefs.[2] Some of his titles such as *Avanibhājana*, *Guṇabhara*, *Śatrumalla*, *Mattavilāsa*, found in the various cave temples excavated by him, occur in the course of the play. Detailed reference will be made to the work in the section on the literature of the Pallava age.

Among literary works that throw light upon the Pallava age in Tamil, *Nandikkalambakam* deserves prominent mention. This work which consists of about a hundred and odd verses is devoted to a description of the exploits of Nandivarman III, whose death the author laments in the course of the work. A number of verses in the poem describe the martial exploits of this sovereign, his patronage of letters, his capital cities, the extent of territory, and other particulars which together give a detailed record of his reign. The author is regarded by tradition as one of the younger brothers of the king himself although this is considered doubtful. The work has been for a long time out of print and is noticed in some detail in the section dealing with literature of the Pallava age.

To these may be added the Digambara Jaina work called *Lōkavibhāga*[3] discovered and noticed by R. Narasimhacharya till recently Director of the Mysore Archæological Department. It furnishes us with an important chronological datum from which the initial year of one of the early Pallava

[1] Trivandrum Sanskrit Series, No. LV.
[2] Special note by Editor.
[3] *Mys. Archl. Rep. for 1909–10*, p. 45.

kings Simhavarman may be fixed. The work consists of eleven *prakaraṇas*, the last being *mokshabhāga*. The opening verse is in praise of Jinēśvara. The second verse gives, *kshētra*, *kāla*, *tīrtha*, *pramāṇa-purusha* and their *charita* as the five divisions of a *purāna*; and in the third verse the author begins his subject, namely, the description of the world. All the MSS. of this work contain four stanzas which are important to Pallava chronology. The first stanza tells us that the science was first taught by Vardhamāna to Sudharma and others, that it was handed down in succession through a series of teachers, and that it was translated into Sanskrit by Rishi Simhasūri. The second stanza says that at a particular period, corresponding to certain planetary positions, Śarvanandi copied the work in the village named Pāṭalika of the Pāṇarāshṭra. The third stanza gives us Śāka 380, corresponding to the twenty-second regnal year of Simhavarman, king of Kāñchī, as the year in which the work was completed. The fourth stanza informs us that the work consists of 1536 *anushṭub ślokas*. Śaka 380 is apparently the year in which the copying work was completed by Śarvanandi, and the author of the work Simhasūri probably flourished at an earlier period. Calculation shows that there cannot be any doubt about the correctness of the date. Pāṭalika, the village in which Śarvanandi copied the work, is identical with Pāṭalipura in South Arcot District at which, according to the *Periyapurāṇam*, there was a large Jaina monastery in the seventh century A.D.

In addition to these sources we have the account given about the Tamil land, and the city of Kāñchī in particular, by the celebrated Chinese pilgrim and the Master of the Law, Hiuen Tsang, whose work has the advantage of being a contemporary account The pilgrim appears to have visited Kāñchī about A.D. 640. The city having had the reputation of being a seat of Buddhistic learning and the city of birth of the celebrated Dharmapāla who preceded Śīlabhadra at the Nalanda University, the pilgrim spent a considerable time in it. Although he does not mention anything about the contemporary king or court, he has given an account of his impressions relating to the character of the people, soil, climate, temples and the state of Buddhism in the city.

To these sources must be added the *Mahāvaṁsa*, the Ceylon Chronicle written in Pāḷi and giving the earliest known account of the kings of the island. This work is particularly useful for settling the chronology of early South Indian history as it describes the relations and the contact that existed between the kings of Ceylon and those who ruled in the Tamil land. So far as the Pallavas are concerned we find that in the days of Narasimhavarman I as well as in the closing days of the Pallava empire invasions of the island were undertaken by Pallava kings either on behalf of the ruling sovereign or actuated by love of conquest merely. Chapter 47 of this work is particularly interesting as it gives a glimpse into Pallava oversea enterprise in early times.

Next comes tradition, living tradition, about the Pallavas and their age. It is surprising that the memory of the Pallava kings, although perpetuated in the names given after them to dozens of temples such as Paramēśvaravinnagaram, Rajasimhēśvara, Kshatriyasimhapallavēśvara, Śatrumallēśvarālaya, Mahēndravishṇugṛha and to many places, has been forgotten and their good work lost sight of. Names of places such as Pallāvaram, Pallavanīchharam, Nandipuravinnagaram, Paramēśvaramangalam, Mahēndramangalam, Mahēndravāḍi, Mahāmallapuram clearly indicate that these were either founded or named after the kings bearing these names in the Pallava dynasty. In view of all this it is surprising that the memory of the dynasty has not survived to any appreciable extent in living tradition. The Mackenzie Manuscripts collected about a century ago by the indefatigable Surveyor-General, Col. Colin Mackenzie, although containing many accounts of the early history of the Pāṇḍyas, Chōḷas, Gangas, Mahrattas and others do not contain any account relating to the dynasty of the Pallavas. But some of the accounts professing to give the Ancient History of Toṇḍamaṇḍalam and the exploits of Ādonḍaichakravarti seem to preserve a distant reminiscence of what the people of the early part of the nineteenth century believed to have been the ancient condition of Toṇḍamaṇḍalam, by which name the region immediately around Kāñchīpuram was known. This class of traditional accounts preserved in the Mackenzie collection appears to depict the condition of Toṇḍamaṇḍalam prior to the days of Pallava advent. Some of them, such as the account of Toṇḍamān-chakravarti, relate to the conquest of the region from a rude and uncivilized tribe known as the Kuṛumbas and to the introduction of civilization by Ādoṇḍai-chōḷa. There seems to be warrant for presuming that this person was no other than Toṇḍamān-Iḷaṁ-Tiraiyan who is immortalized in the *Perumbāṇāṟṟupaḍai* by Rudran-Kaṇṇanār. If so the Mackenzie collections may be taken as lending support to the view that the region of the Pallavas was under Chōḷa occupation before the Pallavas came from the north. The circumstances under which the Pallava conquest of the Chōḷa region was brought about are not known.

CHAPTER II

THEORIES OF THE ORIGIN OF THE PALLAVAS: PRE-PALLAVA HISTORY OF KĀÑCHĪPURA

THE age of the Pallavas in South India may be taken to extend roughly from the third century A.D. to the end of the ninth. Many facts connected with their origin and early history are, in the existing state of historical research, uncertain. Their chronology is yet in the process of construction, and the genealogical order of succession, in spite of the comparative abundance of copper-plate characters, cannot be regarded as having been finally settled. The question of their origin has baffled investigators, European and Indian alike. Ingenious suggestions and theories have been offered for the solution of this enigma by various scholars who occupied themselves with this work.

VARIOUS THEORIES

The theory that held the field until recently, almost undisputed, is known as the Persian or Parthian origin of the Pallavas, and was adopted by the late Vincent Smith in the first edition of his *Early History of India.*[1] According to the late Mr. Venkayya, who developed this theory elaborately :—

'The Pallavas . . . may, until their origin is satisfactorily established by indisputable evidence, be supposed to be identical with the Pahlavas, Palhavas, and the Pahṇavas of the Purāṇas. This identification is based on etymological grounds and supported by the fact that the Palhavas formed a distinct element in the population of Western India early in the second century. Their movement from Western India to the

[1] *E.H.I.* (1904), p. 348.

East Coast is not only possible but rendered likely by known historical facts.'[1]

This theory, however fascinating to the imagination, rests altogether on the superficial verbal resemblance of the words Pahlava and Pallava.[2] There is no evidence whatever, as Mr. Venkayya himself admits, that the Pahlavas of the west coast moved into the east anytime during the second century A.D. At any rate there is no reference or reminiscence whatever in the large numbers of Pallava copper-plate inscriptions of any such migration. Mr. Venkayya presumes that it was the war of the Western Satrap Rudradāman, A.D. 150, with the Andhra king Gautamīputra-Śātakarṇi and his successor, that probably brought about in some manner, now unknown, the eastward movement of the Pahlavas in his service. It is indeed true that the minister of Rudradāman is called Suviśāka and described in the Junagadh inscription as a Pahlava. But no evidence of a positive character is available to connect him or his descendants with the Pallava kings of Southern India. For one thing this Pahlava minister of Rudradāman was not a ruling king. He is not moreover mentioned in any of the ancestral genealogical lists of the Pallava kings. In the second edition of his *Early History of India* Vincent Smith gave up this theory of Pahlava origin which he had adopted in the earlier edition of *Early History of India*, with the remark that it is more likely that the Pallavas were a tribe, clan, or caste which was formed in the northern part of the Madras Presidency, possibly in the Vengi country.[3] Mr. Venkayya's objection against this view of indigenous origin of Pallavas is the apparent improbability of two tribes, the Pahlava in Western India and the Pallava in the delta of the Godavari, bearing the same name. Some of his other arguments against the indigenous origin of the Pallavas are

[1] *A.S.R.*, 1906-7, p. 221.

[2] It is to be noted however that in Sanskrit orthography Pahlava with a *h* can never be confounded with the word Pallava. In the Purāṇas, as well as in Persian and even in Prakrit the *h* is distinct. The two words appear to indicate two distinct people.

[3] V. A. Smith, *E.H.I.* (1908 ed.), p. 423.

ingenious and may be stated here. One is that the Pallavas never refer to themselves in their records as belonging either to lunar or solar race like other dynasties of South India such as the Chōḷas, Pāṇḍyas, Chāḷukyas, etc. Another is that none of the kings mentioned in the Purāṇas are to be found in the Pallava genealogy such as Manu, Śibi, Ikshvāku, etc. All these facts according to him, raise a presumption that the Pallavas of Southern India were not an indigenous tribe in the sense that the Chōḷas, the Pāṇḍyas and the Cheras were.[1]

Views of L. Rice.—This view of foreign origin was also shared by L. Rice. In his *Mysore and Coorg from Inscriptions* he points out that the Pallava kings of South India were identical with the Pahlavas who, with the Yavanas and Śakas, were destroyed by Gautamīputra-Śātakarṇi and that the word Pahlava is a Prakṛit form of Parthava meaning Parthian, especially the Arsacidan Parthians.[2] As we have already pointed out this conjecture that the Pallavas of the south are identical with the Pahlavas of the west and ultimately with the Parthians and the Persians is based entirely on the similarity of the words Pahlava and Pallava, whereas everything known about the Pallava kings of the south, inscriptions, traditions and monuments indicate that they were a peninsular race; they are probably identical with the class of people described as Toṇḍaiyar in Tamil literature and also familiar as Kāḍavas or foresters. Vincent Smith totally rejected this theory of foreign origin in the third edition of his *Early History of India*, and has expressed his conclusion on the subject in the following terms :—

'The name Pallava resembles Pahlava so closely that most writers have been disposed to favour the hypothesis that the Pallavas and the Pahlavas were identical, and that consequently the southern Pallava dynasty of Kāñchī should be considered as ultimately of Persian origin. But recent research has failed to adduce any historical facts in support of

[1] *A.S.R.*, 1906–7, p. 219, foot-note.
[2] *Mysore and Coorg from Inscriptions*, p. 53.

that notion, and it seems more likely that the Pallavas were an indigenous tribe, clan, or caste.'[1]

One important piece of evidence among others[2] which strongly militates against this theory of the foreign origin is that furnished by the poet Rājaśēkhara, the great critic, in his account of the geographical division of the people of his times.

This is brought out in full relief by Dr. S. Krishnaswami Aiyangar in his dissertation on the Pallavas, wherein discussing the origin of the Pallavas he observes as follows :—

Rājaśekhara on the Pallavas.—'The words "Pahlava" and "Pallava" are philologically one, but we have good authority for taking it that the two terms refer historically to different peoples, thereby illustrating that the partition that separates philology from history is not always very thin. The poet Rājaśēkhara lived in the courts of the Gūrjara sovereigns Mahendrapala and Mahīpāla about the end of the ninth and the commencement of the tenth centuries A.D. just the period when the Pallavas were passing out of existence as the dominant South Indian power. He is the author of a geographical work named *Bhuvanakōśa* to which he actually refers for further information in ch. xvii of his *Kāvyamīmāṁsa*. In this work he makes a division of India into five, and allots to each division, the peoples, towns and rivers that belonged to it. In that section he allots the Pallavas to the southern division, or Dakshiṇāpatha, lying beyond Mahishmatī, while the Pahlavas he allots to the division Uttarapātha lying beyond Prithūdaka.[3] This last name the "great water" probably stands for the Indus, and the people Pahlava are found associated with the Huns, Kambhoja, Bahlika, etc. In the estimation, therefore, of Rājaśēkhara who seems a much travelled man, and has really much interesting information to give of different parts of India in respect at any rate of the cultivation of Sanskrit learning, the Pahlavas and the Pallavas were distinct peoples, one of them belonging to the south and the other to the frontier on the other side of the Indus. Rājaśēkhara, no doubt is a late authority, but undoubtedly

[1] *E. H. I.* (third edition), p. 469.

[2] Cf. C. V. Vaidya's views, *Mediæval Hindu India*, vol. i, p. 380.

[3] This has been since satisfactorily identified with Pehoa in the Panipet District, and this is in complete accord with the details given in Rājaśēkhara.—*Ed.*

gives expression to the prevailing opinion of his time in regard to these two peoples.'[1]

Prof. Jouveau-Dubreuil's Views.—The view held by Prof. Jouveau-Dubreuil is only slightly different. Although he does not go the whole extent of advocating the theory of a Parthian origin of the Pallavas he is inclined to connect the early Pallava kings of Conjeevaram with the Pahlavas of Western India. We read for instance in his chapter on the Pallavas in his latest work, *The Ancient History of the Deccan*.

'Up to the present day we have not found any document which proves a Parthian invasion of Southern India. We may say that this theory makes the Pallava mystery still more mysterious.'[2]

According to him the Pallavas were alien to South India and the early members of this dynasty were not kings. They were neighbours of the Nāgas and Chūṭu-Nagas in the days of Rudradāman in the second century. The first Pallava king inherited the throne of Kāñchī on marrying the daughter of a Nāga chief by name Śivaskanda-Nāga. On pages 55-56 he elaborates this view and establishes a connection between the Pahlavas of the west coast with the Pallavas of Kāñchī. On page 55 of this work he says :—

'. . . . We learn from the Girnar inscription that Suviśāka who was the minister of Rudradāman in A.D. 150 was a Pahlava.'[3]

Thus the word which was written Palhava in A.D. 78 was written Pahlava in A.D. 150 and we note when we see the Girnar inscription, that the compound letter 'hla', resembles the double 'll'. Besides in Mayidavolu plates written in Prakrit this question of letters has been solved in a very simple manner, they wrote Pālava. This can correspond to Pallava for in Prakrit the consonants are not doubled. In the Hirahadagalli plates it is written as Pallava though they are also in Prakrit. Later on when the documents were written in Sanskrit the word Pallava would be understood to mean 'sprout'.

[1] *J. I. H.*, vol. ii, pp. 25-26.
[2] *Ancient History of the Deccan*, p. 47.
[3] Junagadh Insc., *Ep. Ind.*, vol. viii, p. 37, plate line 19.

From all this the following conclusion is drawn :—

'The identity of names leads us to think that the ancient kings of Kāñchī belonged to the same family as the minister of Rudradāman. He lived in A.D. 150 and we know Pallava kings of Kāñchī reigning about A.D. 225.'

Objections to the Theory.—This theory which connects the Pallavas of Kāñchī with the Pahlavas of the west coast presents difficulties, some of which have already been pointed out before. In the first place it was seen that there is no evidence whatsoever of an eastward movement of the Pahlavas. There is moreover no evidence of a Pahlava prince marrying the daughter of a Nāga chief on which Prof. Jouveau-Dubreuil relies for his theory of the attainment of political sovereignty by the Pahlavas. The Vēlūrpāḷayam plates which mention a Nāga alliance [1] do not say that it was the first Pallava king who so attained power. In this record which belongs to the ninth century, he is called Vīrakūrcha and not Śivaskanda. Then again this record mentions many earlier kings such as Aśokavarman who ruled before the days of Vīrakūrcha a fact which militates strongly against the view of Prof. Jouveau-Dubreuil. The theory does not explain why they came to be called Pallavas. It fails to take into consideration the existence of a people known as Toṇḍaiyar, synonymous with the Sanskrit Pallava. Moreover early Tamil literature does not support the view that the Pallavas originally emigrated from Surāshṭra. Finally there is no mention in any of the numerous charters of the Pallava kings and other contemporary kings in South India of Suviśāka the supposed ancestor of the Pallava kings who lived in Rudradāman's court. If he was really connected with the Pallava family of Kāñchī how is it that he does not figure even in one of the lists of their ancestors contained in the Pallava records? It is not again definitely known whether the authority of Śivaskandanāga extended as far south as Toṇḍaimaṇḍalam. No inscription or copper-plate of this chief or others have been found proving that his authority extended

[1] *S.I.I.*, vol. ii, Part 5, p. 510, *verse* 6.

in this region. These considerations make us hesitate to accept the theory of Prof. Jouveau-Dubreuil that the kings of Conjeeveram were descended from the Pahlavas of Rudradāman's time, and that the first Pallava king obtained the throne of Kāñchī by a marriage alliance with the Nāgas.

Yet another View.—Mr. Rasanayagam who does not agree with the views and conclusions arrived at by the Professor seeks to find the home of Pallavas in the south in the region known as Maṇipallavam to the early Tamils.[1] According to him Kiḷḷi's son Iḷaṁ Tiraiyan through the Nāga princess mentioned in the early Tamil work *Maṇimēkhalai* was really the first Pallava king. In this work he is described as the son of Kiḷḷi by Pīlivaḷai, a daughter of Vaḷaivaṇan, the Nāga king of Maṇipallavam. He was lost in a ship-wreck and was found washed ashore with a coil round his ankle of a twig of the Toṇḍai-creeper (*Caphallandra Indica*). Hence his name Toṇḍamān-Iḷaṁ-Tiraiyan. Iḷaṁ-Tiraiyan was therefore the first to become an independent king and progenitor of the Pallava dynasty. His period is fixed as the third quarter of the second century A.D. The dynasty was called the Pallava designated after the mother's native place Maṇipallavam. The titles, such as Ankura, and Pōttaraiyan which were assumed by Pallava kings are synonymous with the word Pallava and remind us of the origin of the name from Maṇipallavam.

Consideration of the Theory.—According to this theory the Pallavas were of Chōḷa-Nāga origin and were indigenous to the southern part of the peninsula and Ceylon. They had nothing to do with Western India, Persia, the Chūṭu-Nāgas, Suviśāka and others. But there are certain difficulties in accepting this view as correct. The earliest members of the Pallava family that we know from copper-plate inscriptions do not include either Toṇḍamān-Iḷaṁ-Tiraiyan or any member of the Chōḷa-Nāga dynasty. On the other hand, they describe themselves as members of the Bhāradvāja-gotra and as the performers of Aśvamēdha, Vājapēya and other sacrifices.

[1] *Ind. Ant.*, vol. lii, pp. 75–80.

Moreover they addressed their charters invariably in Prakrit and Sanskrit, and never in the Tamil language. Such of the charters that contain any allusion to the Nāga marriage mention neither a Chōḷa ancestry nor Maṇipallavam their alleged original home. Their records on the contrary show that they are different from the southern Tamil rulers, and hailed from the north as representatives of Aryan or Sanskrit culture. The hostile relationship of the early Pallavas with the early Tamil rulers, one of the Pallava kings being called the 'submarine-fire to the oceanlike army of the Chōḷas,' [1] seems to be opposed to this Chōḷa-Nāga origin of the Pallava dynasty. For these reasons it looks as if that Toṇḍamān-Iḷam-Tiraiyan had no connection with the Pallava family of Kāñchīpura known to us from charters, and probably was a Tiraiyar-chief [2] who preceded the Pallavas and was a subordinate of the contemporary Chōḷa ruler in the second century A.D.

Other Views.—A more or less similar view is expressed by Mr. M. S. Ramaswami Aiyangar in his recent work *Studies in South Indian Jainism.*[3] According to him the early Pallavas, especially those kings in the fourth century A.D., were called Tiraiyar only and not as Pallavas. In support of this view he mentions the reference [4] to Vishṇugōpa in Samudragupta's

[1] *S.I.I.*, vol. ii, Part 5, p. 510.

[2] He is actually described as given the name of Tiraiyan because he was brought over by the waves of the sea. This seems but a learned attempt at explaining an obscure folk-name Tiraiyar.—*Ed.*

[3] *Studies in South Indian Jainism*, p. 143.

[4] 'The Allahabad pillar inscription of Samudragupta merely speaks of Vishṇugōpa as the ruler of Kāñchī. The name Pallava does not occur there. From this it is evident that in the fourth century A.D. the word Pallava was little used by them. . . . In Saṅgam literature the rulers of Kāñchī are spoken of as Tiraiyan and Toṇḍaimān. . . . Vishṇugōpa, who was ruling Kāñchī at the time of Samudragupta's invasion must therefore be a Tiraiyan.

"The *Toṇḍamanḍalapaṭṭayam* gives an account of the various branches of the Tiraiyar. This has been noted by Kanakasabhai Pillai in his book, *Tamils 1800 Years Ago.* As one of the main branches of Tiraiyar we have Pallava Tiraiyar showing thereby the connection between Pallavar with Tiraiyar. It is therefore natural to suppose that the Pallavas were known to the early Sangam literature by their group name of Tiraiyar but as their power and influence increased in the land

Allahabad pillar inscription as king of Kāñchī only (*Kāñchēyaka Vishṇugōpa*) and not as the king of the Pallavas.

This explains according to him that in the fourth century A.D. the word Pallava was little used by them. Another ingenious suggestion made on similar lines is that of Mr. Swaminatha Aiyar, based upon the apparent similarity of the words Tiraiya, Draya and Darya in Persian. 'Draya' and 'Darya' according to this writer mean the sea in Persian, and Tiraiyar is apparently a Persian-derived name meaning seamen. He would thus ascribe to the Tiraiyar a Persian or Pahlava origin. As the fact seems to accord with the Persian origin of the Pallavas held by certain scholars it was thought by the author as giving the most satisfactory solution of the question. But as was already stated, the Persian origin of the Pallavas rests on the doubtful philological resemblance of words to which the additions of Tiraiya and Draya are now sought to be added. Apart from the resemblance of the words, is there anything positive which supports the identification of these different people Tiraiyar and the Pallavas? The evidence at our disposal on the other hand is wholly against it, and in the existing state of research it is not possible to regard the identification as established. The Pallava kings of the copper-plate charters must therefore be looked upon as different from the Tiraiyar, and the early members of the family such as Śivaskaṇdavarman, Budhavarman, etc., have very little to do with the kings and chiefs known as Tiraiyan and Iḷaṁ-Tiraiyan figuring in early Tamil literature. Another consideration which militates strongly

their branch name Pallava-Tiraiyar assumed greater importance. Hence the absence of the word Pallava in the fourth and the fifth century literature and the greater frequency with which this name occurs in such works as *Nandikkalambakam*."

There is no evidence to prove that the Tiraiyar of the early Tamil literature were the same as the Pallavas, and the testimony of *Toṇḍamaṇḍalapaṭṭayam* is invalidated as the work is only a work of comparatively modern times. It is not correct to say that in the fourth century the word Pallava was little used by them. In the copper-plate charters of the fourth century as well as the following centuries they are called only as Pallavas and never as Tiraiyan. If Vishṇugōpa was a Tiraiyan it is strange that he is not mentioned as such in the Allahabad pillar inscription.'

against the identification of the Tiṟaiyar chiefs and the Pallava kings is the attitude of these kings towards Tamil literature and poets. While we find, that the chiefs of the Tiraiyar like Toṇḍamān-Iḷaṁ-Tiraiyan not only encouraged and fostered Tamil poets but are actually reputed to have been poets themselves. We do not find that any of the early Pallavas were similarly devoted to the encouragement of Tamil. That Toṇḍamān-Iḷaṁ-Tiraiyan was himself a poet is evident from *Puṟanānūṟu* 185, and verses 94, 96 and 106 of *Naṟṟiṇai.* The explanation is that the Pallavas were essentially a northern rather than a Tamilian race, steeped in Aryan or Brahmanic culture which through their encouragement took the leading place in the Tamil country. They were aliens to the Tamil land in this sense that their culture and outlook were totally different from those of the Tamils, and hence did not give themselves to actively patronizing Tamil literature like the Tamil kings of the south. Throughout their history we find them almost exclusively encouraging Sanskrit culture and literature. With the exception of the Āḷvārs and Aḍiyārs and the author of *Nandikkalambakam,* no Tamil poet appears to have enjoyed the patronage of the Pallavas. On the other hand, Sanskrit was actively fostered at the Pallava court, and a number of Sanskrit poets found hospitable reception in the Pallava court such as Bhāravi, Daṇḍin, etc., and some of the kings themselves were noteworthy writers in Sanskrit.[1] When all these considerations are taken into account it becomes difficult to sustain the identity of the Tiraiyar chiefs with the Pallava kings.

Kuṟumba-Pallava identification.—Certain writers are inclined to consider that the Pallavas were the same as the people described as Kurumbar figuring in some of the accounts of the Mackenzie manuscripts. As regards these people there

[1] It has to be noted in this context that Kāñchī was famous as a centre of Sanskrit learning and was noted as 'a *Ghaṭikā* of the Brahmans' in the Velūrpālayam Plates. It was a notable centre of Sanskrit learning when the Kadambas were coming into the view of history as in the story of Mayūra Śarman.—*Ed.*

is a great deal of vague and misleading ideas in the minds of most writers. Who are the Kuṛumbas? According to one of the Tamil *Nigaṇṭus*[1] certain hill chiefs known as *Kuṛunila-mannar* were known as the Kuṛumbas. But in the Mackenzie accounts these people are described as the earliest inhabitants of Toṇḍamaṇḍalam and said to have been given the name for their cruel ways. They are also in some of the accounts believed to have been responsible for the division of the region into twenty-four *kōṭṭams*, most of which figure in Pallava and Chōḷa inscriptions. The story of the conquest of the region by Ādoṇḍaichōḷa, which will be described later on, is believed by Sir Walter Elliot, Sewell and others to have been accomplished in the eleventh century in the days of Kulōttunga Chōḷa, a supposition for which there is no evidence. It is believed by some that these Kuṛumbas were the same as the Pallavas. But there seems to be absolutely nothing which supports such a notion. There is no reference in the numerous inscriptions of the Tamil land that there was at any time a dynasty of the Kuṛumbas, or that the Pallava kings are identical with the Kuṛumbas. Hence it appears to be preposterous to accept the identification.

Still another View.—According to Alexander Rea the references making the Pallavas 'hold the sprout' are pedantic Pandit's puns, or a play upon the double meaning of the word 'Pallava'. 'I would suggest,' he says, 'that it might be derived by somewhat free translation from the two Tamil words *Pāl* and *Aviḻ* (to pull)? referring to their being agri-culturists or milk-drawers like the Gopalas of the northern Dekkan.'[2] He also throws out another suggestion: 'the masculine singular termination in Tamil is *avan*, and the plural *avar*; now prefixing the word *Pāl* (milk), would give Pālavan; or Pālavar as the honorific plural. Pālavan in that case would mean milkman.' Both these suggestions, however appear more fanciful than possible as the derivations have not even grammatical justification in their favour.

[1] *Divākaram.*

[2] Rea, *Pallava Architecture*, p. 2, foot-note 5.

In the present state of research definite conclusions on the question seem unattainable. It is, however, quite plain that the theory of foreign origin of the Pallavas, especially that which gives them a Parthian or Persian home, is without foundation. The theory that contents itself with connecting the Pahlava minister with the Pallavas of Kāñchī although having an air of plausibility is hardly acceptable as no evidence is forthcoming of the eastward migration of the Pahlavas in the second century. The next alternative is to regard them as indigenous to the country. In doing so we have to establish first whether the Pallavas should be regarded as a family or a tribe. Those who contend that the modern Kallar and the Pallis are descended from the Pallavas are labouring under the impression that the Pallavas constituted a big tribe; there seems to be little evidence for the assumption. In the Pallava inscriptions themselves we scarcely come across with the word Kuṛumba as a dynastic surname of any of the Pallava kings. It is therefore improbable that the identification of the Kuṛumbas with the Pallavas postulated by certain scholars rests on sound foundation.

That the rule of the Pallavas of Kāñchī was preceded by that of the Chōḷas is made clear not only by the evidence of Tamil literature, but also from the testimony of the Mackenzie manuscript accounts to which reference had been made already. These accounts although belonging to the early part of the nineteenth century, being the traditional account furnished by the village elders in the days of Col. Colin Mackenzie, profess to relate the early history of the region known as Toṇḍamaṇḍalam which corresponded to the region ruled over by the Pallava kings. 'According to the *Ancient History of Toṇḍamaṇḍalam*, one of the accounts in the Mackenzie collection, the region was occupied by the Kuṛumbas who are said to have been responsible for the erection of the twenty-four forts, and the division of the region into twenty-four districts. These are also said to have carried on a sea-trade with the merchants of Kāvēripaṭṭinam. It is from these Kuṛumbas that one Āḍoṇḍachakravarti, said to be an illegitimate son of the contemporary Chōḷa king, is described as having conquered the region and acquired it for the Chōḷas setting up his own rule at Kāñchī after uprooting the Kuṟumbas. The region which was till then known as Kuṟumbabhūmi is said to have been renamed Toṇḍamaṇḍalam after the name of the conquering Chōḷa prince. If we properly interpret the traditional account in the light of the facts regarding the occupation of the region around Kāñchīpuram by Iḷam-Tiraiyan, it is easy to understand that in this account we find preserved the earliest reminiscence of the conquest of the region around Conjeevaram by the Chōḷas. When did this happen? Early scholars who noticed the account have been misled into thinking that this conquest was made in the eleventh century.[1] They have been led to think so by the reference that the contemporary Chōḷa king in these accounts was Kulōttunga, and there was a Kulōttunga ruling in the eleventh century. But all the other details in the account are against this date. The conditions of the territory and the state of civilization at the time of Ādoṇḍaichōḷa, the first Chōḷa representative, are too primitive to apply to a period like the eleventh century by which time the region had become fully civilized under the Pallavas who are known to have beautified Toṇḍamaṇḍalam, and whose sway over the region had already lasted for eight centuries. It looks therefore probable that the traditional account has mistaken the actual name of the contemporary Chōḷa king at the time of the subjugation of the Kuṟumbas which must have been made by some member of the family of the early Chōḷa Karikāla in the second century A.D.

Pre-Pallava History of Kāñchī.—Kāñchī which is one of the seven great holy cities of India is believed to have had a history much anterior to the beginning of the Christian era. From the Chinese pilgrim Hiuen Tsang we learn that in the days of Buddha in the fifth century B.C. he frequented the region around Kāñchīpuram and made conversions. From the

[1] Sewell, *Lists*, vol. i, p. 177.

same source we learn also that Aśokarāja built several stupas none of which has survived to the present day. It would be remembered that Dharmapāla, the celebrated Buddhist savant and scholar at Nalanda, hailed from Kāñchīpuram. Whether Buddhism made any progress at Kāñchī at the time of Buddha is doubtful as there is not much evidence that Buddhism had advanced into the heart of the Tamil land in this period. Whether Aśoka ordered stupas to be built at the city of Kāñchīpura or not, it is not possible to say. The presumption that he might have done so gains strength in view of the discovery of Aśoka's inscriptions as far south as Siddāpura in the region of Mysore, and from the fact that his inscriptions mention the Chōḷas, the Pāṇḍyas and the Kēraḷaputras. At any rate Hiuen Tsang says that he noticed a stupa about 100 feet high built by Aśokarāja.[1]

During the reign of Karikāla who has been assigned, with acceptable authority by several scholars to the age of the Tamil Śangam in the beginning of the Christian era, Kāñchīpuram appears to have been one of the northern outposts of the kingdom. At any rate it is probable that one of Karikāla's exploits, or those of his generals, must have been the transfer of power from the Āndhra-Śātavāhanas, whose ascendency in this region is indicated by the discovery of ship-coins in profusion in the region between the Pennar and Pālar into the hands of the Chōḷas. At any rate in the period immediately following the city of Kāñchī is found in the possession of Toṇḍamān-Iḷaṁ-Tiraiyan as stated in the *Perumbāṇāṛṛuppaḍai* of Rudran Kaṇṇanār. According to the Mackenzie MSS. one of the achievements of Ādoṇḍachōḷa, by whom probably we are to understand Toṇḍamān-Iḷaṁ-Tiraiyan, is the uprooting of the the Kurumbas by which term the unruly chiefs of the region were probably known. Under the rule of Toṇḍamān-Iḷaṁ-Tiraiyan of Kāñchī, presumably as the Chōḷa viceroy, the city appears to have been in a flourishing condition. The *Perumbāṇāṛṛuppaḍai* of Rudran Kaṇṇanār,

[1] Beal, *Rec.* II, p. 230.

the contemporary of Toṇḍamān-Iḷaṁ-Tiraiyan gives some idea of the city as it was in those days :—' In the heart of the town were the Brahman quarters, where neither dog nor the fowl could be seen. They were flanked on the one side by the fishermen's streets, and on the other by those of the traders, and these were surrounded by the Cheris of the *Maḷḷas* and the toddy-drawers. Then far removed from them were situated at one extremity of the city the *paḷḷis* of the Iḍaiyans, and beyond these lay the isolated *paraichēris* of the Eyinas. Next to the *Maḷḷa* streets were the temple of Tiruveḥkä and the palace of King Iḷaṁ-Tiraiyan.'[1]

The history of Kāñchīpuram is lost in obscurity almost from the days of Karikāla to its occupation by the Pallava kings under Śivaskandavarman. It is probable that during this period it was in the hands of the Chōḷa princes some of whom are mentioned in the *Maṇimēkhalai* to have built Buddhist temples.[2] It is here mentioned that there were Buddhist *chaityas* in Kāñchī constructed by Kaḷārkiḷḷi and Iḷaṁ-Kiḷḷi whose actual position in the Chōḷa family of this period is not known. It would be an interesting study to examine the evidence contained in the Tamil works regarding the connection of the early Chōḷa princes with Kāñchīpuram. There are several members of the Chōḷa family bearing the name of Kiḷḷi mentioned in early Tamil literature. One of these is Kuḷamuṟṟattu-tunjina Kiḷḷivaḷavan, Kiḷḷi who died at Kuḷamuṟṟam, of whom many poets have sung. Then again Kovūr-Kiḷār mentions in *Puṟam* 44 and 45 a certain Kāriyaṟṟu-tuṇjina (who fell or died at Kāri River) Neḍumkiḷḷi of Uṟaiyur and of his friend Iḷaṁ-Tattan. Elsewhere we find the poet singing of Kurāpaḷḷi-tuṇjina (who died at Kurāpaḷḷi) Kiḷḷi-vaḷavan,[3] one of whose exploits was the destruction of Karuvūr. His Pāṇḍyan contemporary was apparently the Ugrapperuvaḷudi who died at Veḷḷiyambalam. Other pieces

[1] *Tam. Stud.*, p. 76.
[2] See chap. 28, Account of Maṇimēkhalai's visit to Kāñchī.
[3] *Puṟam* 373.

in the same collection speak of Sōlan Ilavandigaippaḷḷi-tuṇjina Nalangiḷḷi Śētchenni, Ēnādi (General) Tirukkiḷḷi, etc.

According to the account of *Maṇimēkhalai*, the Chōḷa King Veḷvēṛkiḷḷi, who is probably one of the Kiḷḷis enumerated above, married a Nāga princess called Pīlivaḷai, the daughter of Vaḷai-Vaṇan, and became the father of the prince known afterwards as Toṇḍamān-Iḷam-Tiraiyan whom certain scholars look upon as the ancestor of the Pallavas of Kāñchī. This account although it seems to set up a connection between the Chōḷas and the Pallavas has not been corroborated by the evidence of the Pallava charters.

Śengaṇṇan.—Among the successors of the Chōḷa king Karikāla, one of the most important was Ko-Śengaṇṇan who is mentioned not only in the early, Tamil classics[1] but also in the *Tēvāram* hymns of the Śaiva saints Appar and Sambandar.[2]

We learn from Tamil literature that he defeated his Chera enemy at a place called Kaḻumalam, took his enemy prisoner and confined him at a place called Kuḍavāyil-koṭṭam variously identified with Koḍavāśal and places in the Cochin State. Śengaṇṇan's sway must have extended throughout Toṇḍa-maṇḍalam. The *Kaḷavaḻi-Nārpadu*, a poem celebrating the powers of this king as a warrior, gives a picturesque account of the battle of Kaḻumalam and early Tamil modes of warfare. The age of Śengaṇṇan may be ascertained if we know the correct date of Poygaiyār who was his contemporary. According to certain scholars Poygaiyār is identical with Poygai-Āḻvār the Vaishṇava saint whose age is that of the third Śangam or somewhere near it. According to others Poygaiyār is assignable to the sixth or the seventh centuries A.D. This latter date is impossible if we bear in mind that Śengaṇṇan is mentioned already in the seventh century A.D.

[1] வெள்ளி வெண்ணாஞ்சிலான் ஞால முழுவணைபோல்
எல்லாக் களிறு நிலஞ்சேர்ந்த பல்வேற்
பிணை முழங்கு போர்த்தானைச் செங்கட் சினமால்
கணைமாரி பெய்த களத்து—

Stanza from 'Kaḷavaḻi.'

[2] Appar, Tev. *Tirukuṛukkai Patikam*; Sambandar, *Tiruvānaikkāval Patikam*.

by Appar as a well-known Śaiva saint. He is said to have worshipped at Tirunaraiyūr near Kumbhakonam by Tirumangai Āḻvār, the Vaishṇava saint who also notes that he built as many as seventy temples dedicated to Śiva. If Ko-Śengaṇṇan could become so popular as early as the seventh century to be mentioned by the Śaiva saints of the period in their hymns a considerable time must have elapsed between his period and the period of the Śaiva saints. It would not be wrong to assign him to the period succeeding the age of Karikāla (third century A.D.) and immediately preceding the advent of the Pallavas of Kāñchīpuram.

CHAPTER III

EARLY PALLAVAS OF THE PRAKRIT RECORDS

THE materials for the reconstruction of the early history of the Pallavas are far from adequate. We are entirely dependent upon the few copper-plate charters in Prakrit and Sanskrit for our knowledge of the political history of the Pallava kings of Conjeevaram until about the seventh century when we are on more certain ground. As more than one scholar has remarked the copper plate charters of the early period are more useful for constructing a genealogical list than for writing the political history of the period. The facts contained in the records enumerate the names of the great-grandfather, the grandfather and the father of the donor of the grant and the details of the object of the grant. They do *not furnish many particulars on the political condition of the* period. It is too much to expect much information concerning the period from these charters as their professed object was merely to record donations to certain individuals. As we have already pointed out, it is only from the seventh century that the habit of recording the exploits of the ancestors of the king who made the grant came to be popular in South India.

The Pallava inscriptions and copper charters are divisible as already indicated into three sections. To the first group belongs the Prakrit charters which though bearing no date in any known era have been on palæographical grounds assigned to the third and the fourth centuries of the Christian era. It is well known from the history of the Āndhras that they continued to be powerful in the southern region almost till the first quarter of the third century A.D. We know from the Allahabad pillar inscription of Samudragupta that about the middle of the fourth century A.D. there reigned in the region extending to the banks of the Krishna, a Pallava king named Vishṇugopa. The contemporaneity of Samudragupta with

Vishṇugopa of Kāñchī, who was undoubtedly one of the early kings of the Pallava dynasty of Conjeevaram, leads to the conclusion that Vishṇugopa must have reigned some time about A.D. 340 to 350. But a recent attempt has been made to fix the initial date of the Gupta era at A.D. 200–201 which would put back Samudragupta's period to the middle of the third instead of the fourth century. But this theory rests at present on Jāin tradition merely and has serious objections against it. If this date be accepted, Vishṇugopa of Kāñchī would have to be placed in the middle of the third century, the period of the Pallava kings of the Prakrit charters, and this would necessitate the putting back of the kings of the Prakrit charters to the second century—a position which would be difficult to accept in the present scheme of Āndhra chronology. Without taking up this matter we may proceed to put together the order of succession for the earliest period, which may be styled the age of the kings, of the Prakrit charters, circa A.D. 200–350. The three important Prakrit charters which are the earliest of the Pallava charters—the Mayidavōlu plates, the Hirahaḍagalli plates and the British Museum plates have been published in the *Epigraphia Indica* with text, translation and valuable notes by Bühler, Hultzsch, Leumann and others.

The actual order of succession of the Pallava kings of the Prakrit charters is uncertain, but the following represents the most probable one so far as we could make out from the Prakrit copper-plates that are available :—

Bappa Dēva
|
Śivaskandavarman
|
Buddhy (ankura)
|
Vīravarman
|
Vishṇugopa (A.D. 340).

The earliest of the Prakrit charters that we have is dated from the capital city of Kāñchīpuram issued by Śivaskaṇdavarman while he was yet a crown-prince and dated in the

5

tenth year of his father.[1] Śivaskandavarman is described as a Yuvamahārāja and affiliated to the Bhāradvāja-gotra of the Pallava family. The grant is addressed to the Viceroy at Dhānyakaṭa (Dharaṇikoṭṭa near Amarāvati) in the *Āndhrapathā*. It is thus plain that the kingdom of Śivaskaṇḍavarman's father, who is called Bappa Dēva merely, included Āndhrapathā and Toṇḍamaṇḍalam. The capital of Āndhrapathā the Telugu region, appears to have been Dhānyakaṭaka, while Conjeevaram was the Imperial as well as the local capital of Toṇḍamaṇḍalam, their Tamil dominion. The next in point of time is the grant recorded in the Hirahadagalli plates found in Hirahadagalli in the Bellary District. The king who issued this grant is regarded by all scholars as the same as the Prince who issued the Mayidavolu grant. This is also issued from the city of Kāñchīpuram, and is dated in the eighth year of the king and refers to a grant of the village of Chillerēkakoḍumka in the Śātāhaniraṭṭa probably identical with the Satanani-Āhāra of the Myakadoni record[2] dated in the eighth year of king Puḷumāvi. The plates, besides recording the details connected with the gift, mention the fact that Śivaskaṇḍavarman performed the *Aśvamēdha, Agnishṭōma* and *Vāiapēya* sacrifices. Of these, if there is any truth in the claim of the first we may reasonably presume that Śivaskaṇḍavarman made extensive conquests and that he had some subordinate kings under his rule. There is no means by which we could at present check the accuracy or otherwise of this claim.

Next in order of time comes the Guṇapadeya or the British Museum plates of Chārudēvi.[3] This record gives in genealogical order the names of Vijayaskaṇḍavarman, his son Yuvamahārāja Buddhavaraman and his son Buddhyankura. This record is dated in some unknown year of Vijayaskaṇḍavarman's reign and records an order of the Queen of the heir-apparent consisting of the gift of land to the

[1] *Ep. Ind.*, vol. vi, p. 84ff. and plates.
[2] *Ibid.*, vol. xiv, p. 153.
[3] *Ibid.*, vol. viii, p. 143.

temple of Nārāyaṇa at Dālūra. At present it is difficult to say what relation the Vijayaskaṇdavarman of this record bore to Śivaskaṇdavarman of the first two Prakrit charters. It has been attempted by certain scholars to identify the Śivaskaṇdavarman of the Prakrit charters with the Vijayaskaṇdavarman of the British Museum record as the prefixes Vijaya or Śiva are too insignificant to matter much. But as this relationship is not given in any of the numerous genealogical lists of later times we cannot be sure whether the members of the Prakrit charters and the members of the Sanskrit charters were connected with one another in this manner. One striking fact which is a decisive consideration in this identification is the close similarity of the palæography of the Hirahadagalli and the British Museum copper-plates. As regards the period of these kings we have alredy indicated that it is the age which followed the decadence of the Andhra power, that is, the period from about the middle of the third century to the middle of the fourth century. If we calculate back from the known date of Vishṇugopa the contemporary of Samudragupta, allowing about 25 years for each generation we arrive at A.D. 215 for the reign of Bappa the earliest known Pallava sovereign of Kāñchī. This calculation is only approximate as it is unlikely that the reign-period of all the kings was the same and is based upon the supposed contemporaneity of Samudragupta and Vishṇugopa, and the probability that Vishṇugopa of the Samudragupta pillar inscription was a Pallava king.

The History of the Period.—As we have already pointed out it is not apparent who was the first member of the Pallavas who established the Pallava power in Conjeevaram. So far as we know Toṇḍamān-Iḷaṁ-Tiraiyan and Bappa are the earliest known names associated with the rule of the ancient city of Conjeevaram. The relation of the former with the latter is not known although certain scholars have advocated the view that he was the first member of the Pallava family. The entire absence of his name, and the name Tiraiyan itself or its equivalent in the Prakrit and Sanskrit records of the Pallavas lead us to reject this view. Our knowledge of this ruler is derived from Tamil literature and from tradition embodied in the Mackenzie MSS. The state of the city of Kāñchīpuram during the reign of this ruler is fully described in the early Tamil work, the *Perumbanārrupadai*, by the Śangam poet Rudran-Kaṇṇanār. How the region passed from the hands of Iḷam-Tiraiyan into the hands of the Pallavas remains unknown. It is presumable that about the middle of the first quarter of the third century A.D. there was an invasion of the region from the north led by the Āndhra-Satavāhana rulers or generals in the wake of which the first member of the Pallava family must have acquired sovereignty over the region. A faint recollection of this invasion is recorded in the Mackenzie MSS. accounts concerning Toṇḍaman Chakravarti and Visvāvasurāja. Whether this was brought about by an immediate ancestor of Bappa or Bappa himself is not known. We may roughly fix the period of the passing of Toṇḍamaṇḍalam from the Chōḷa feudatories into the hands of the Pallavas about the closing years of the third century A.D.

Mahārāja Bappa.—It is not clear whether the immediate ancestor of Śivaskaṇdavarman of the Prakrit charters, who is called Bappa in the record found at Mayidavolu, was the actual founder of the rule of the Pallavas at Kāñchīpuram. In all probability he was not. Because, if this had been so we may reasonably expect the mention of such an achievement in the record issued by his son and heir-apparent, and dated in his own reign. The kingdom over which Bappa ruled included in addition to the districts around Kāñchīpuram known as Toṇḍamaṇḍalam or Tuṇḍākarāshtra, the Telugu country on both banks of the Krishna which had Dharanikoṭa or Dhānyakaṭaka for its capital. It may be presumed that during this age the Pallava kingdom was divided into two parts, the northern part comprising the Telugu districts with Amarāvati as capital, and the Tamil districts around Kāñchī with Kāñchīpuram for its capital. Thus the region bounded by the Pālār on the south and the Krishna on the north formed the kingdom of the Pallavas during this period. The close resemblance of the

Mayidavolu plates with the Koṇḍamuḍi plates of Jayavarmaṇ which again resembles the Karle inscription of Gautamīputra Śātakarni and the Nasik inscription of Vasishtīputra-Pulumāvi, fixes the period of Bappa and Śivaskaṇḍavarman approximately as the early part of the third century A.D.[1]—Prof. Jouveau-Dubreuil supposed, in his *Pallavas*, that Yuvamahārāja Śivaskaṇḍavarman of the Mayidavolu record was the grandson of the Āndhra king Śivaskaṇḍavarman.[2] But as he himself admits, this is based entirely on similarity of names such as those of Yuvamahārāja Śivaskaṇḍavarman and Śivaskaṇda Śātakarni.[3] Apart from this there is no positive evidence to prove that the Pallavas were directly connected with the ruling Śatavāhana royal family or descended from them.

Bappa is said to have given away as free gift numerous gold coins as well as a hundred thousand ox-ploughs to increase the prosperity of the Pallava family. This was presumably intended to bring under cultivation vast areas of uncultivated forest tracts in the Telugu country.

Śivaskaṇḍavarman.—The Mayidavolu grant was issued while this sovereign was yet the heir-apparent. From the Hirahadagalli grant dated in the 8th year of his reign we learn that he had the title of Dharmamahārāja. This was evidently assumed after extensive conquests. We do not know with any definiteness what were the regions which he brought under the sway of Pallava rule. But from the fact that this record says that Śivaskaṇḍavarman was a performer of the *Aśvamēdha*, *Vājapēya* and *Agnishṭoma* we may reasonably infer that his suzerainty must have been recognized by several kings. Otherwise the performance of *Asvamēdha* would lose any significance attaching to it unless it is regarded as a false boast. It is not apparent which was the southernmost limit of the Tamil part of his kingdom, but it is presumable that his sway extended as far as the South Pennar while in the north his kingdom included the Telugu districts between the Godavari and Krishna. His capital was Kāñchīpuram while Amarāvati

[1] *Ep. Ind.*, vol. vi, p. 315. [2] *Pallavas*, pp. 8, 9. [3] *Ibid.*, p. 9.

in the north appears to have continued as a flourishing seat of the Buddhists and their monasteries. The records of Śiva-skandavarman give us a glimpse into the Asokan nature of the organization of government during this period. The kingdom was divided into divisions known as *Vishaya*, *Raṭṭha* and *Grāma*. The officers entrusted to rule these areas were known as Vishayikas, Raṭṭhika (Rashṭrikas), and Dēsādikata (Dēsadhikṛtas). These officers were chiefly recruited from the members of the royal family and the commanders of armies. The persons who were consulted by the king on administrative matters were the prime-minister and the private secretary (*Amatya* and the *Rahasyātikata*). It is significant that the names of the various heads of departments are all in Prakrit. It is probable that the Pallava kings continued the administrative system of Asoka on the lines of the Dharmaśāstras and Arthaśāstras. The taxes collected by these kings from their subjects are in accordance with the Sanskrit Dharmaśāstra rules. The taxes and other dues that these kings were entitled to are known as the eighteen kinds of taxes (*Aṭṭārasajāti-Parihāra*). Some of these included the taking of milk and curd from the subjects, the supply of cattle to the officers touring in the villages on royal duty, the supplying of lodging facilities and utensils, fire-wood, vegetables, flowers, menial servants, etc. A complete list of these is furnished in the later charters enumerating the exemptions secured by certain donees to whom free gifts of land were made.[1] During this period the manufacture of salt and jaggery were royal monopolies, and special license had to be obtained for private manufacture.

Inland and foreign commerce must have been in a flourishing condition during this period if we may judge from the writings of the classical writers which mention several sea-port towns such as Kamara, Poduka, Sopatma, Melanga, Kodura, etc. Of these Kodura has been identified with Kudur and Melangus was obviously Malanka or Mavilangai probably

[1] Compare the Kāśakkuḍi and the Vēḷūrpāḷayam plates. *S.I.I.*, vol. ii, p. 346ff. and 507.

Mahābalipuram or Seven Pagodas.[1] Sea-borne trade must have been flourishing at these various ports, and the presence of large numbers of ship-coins and Roman coins of an early period fully lend support to this view. So far as the port of Mahäbalipuram is concerned it is clear, from the evidence of Tirumangai-Āḻvār, that in the early part of the eighth century the place was a busy harbour. This probably was the case in the days of Śivaskaṇdavaraman also. The ship-coins discovered extensively between Cuddalore and Madras have been attributed by some to Pallava kings although it looks probable that they were issued under the auspices of the Śātavāhana kings of the Dakhan.

Vijayaskandavarman, circa A.D. 280.—The order of succession of the Prakrit plates is not known. But we may presume from palæographical indications that Vijayaskaṇdavarman of the British Museum copper-plates succeeded Śivaskaṇdavarman in the interval between A.D. 275 and 340. All that we know about this sovereign and his times is the information given in this record.[2] From this we learn that his queen was called Chārudēvi, and that the heir-apparent to the throne was called Buddhyankura, and that the father of Vijaya-Buddhavarman was called Vijayaskaṇdavarman who is presumably identical with Śivaskaṇdavarman of the earlier charters. The record registers a grant of land to the temple of Nārāyaṇa at the village of Dalūra in the division called Kūlimaharaṭha. This is, so far as we know, the earliest Pallava record mentioning a royal gift to the temples. We do not know anything about the political events during the reign of Buddhyankura who flourished in the years immediately following the death of Vijaya-Buddhavarman. The next member of the Pallava family is Vishṇugopa well known as the Pallava contemporary of Samudragupta.

The connection of the Pallava kings of the Prakrit charters and those of the Sanskrit charters is not clear. According to

[1] *Ind. Ant.*, vol. xlvi, p. 72.
[2] *Ep. Ind.*, vol. vi, p. 88 and vol. viii, p. 143.

some scholars the dynasties of the Prakrit charters and the Sanskrit charters are distinctly different, and not directly connected. According to others[1] all the members of the copper-plates and the stone inscriptions whether they are written in Prakrit, Sanskrit or Tamil are to be connected with one dynasty only the most ancient member of which was Bappa. Future research and the discovery of fresh copper-plate charters or other records alone can solve this question finally.

[1] Jouveau-Dubreuil, *Pallavas*, pp. 72-3, Genealogical Table.

CHAPTER IV

EARLY PALLAVAS OF THE SANSKRIT RECORDS

Sources of Information and Their Nature.—We may now proceed to construct the order of succession of the Pallava kings mentioned in the various copper-plate charters inscribed in Sanskrit in their genealogical order. This is the period ranging from about A.D. 350 to 600. The most important copper-plate records of this period are those addressed from Tāmrāpa, Palakkada, Mēnmātūra, Daśanapura, Pikīra, Ōngōdu (I and II), Darśi, Rāyakota, Chandalūr, Udayēndiram, Uruvappalli, and the stone inscriptions of Vāyalūr and Amarāvati. These charters have for their object the recording of gifts of land to learned Brahmans or temples, and only incidentally mention the ancestral history of the ruling sovereign who issued the grant. Like the earlier charters they are not dated in any known era such as the Śaka which might enable us to fix their date with precision; but they are merely dated in the regnal year of the ruling sovereign. These records are almost all of them written in the Sanskrit language in the early Grantha-Pallava script peculiar to the Pallava records, and have been assigned on purely palæographical grounds to the fifth and sixth centuries A.D. The practice of inscribing a part of the record in Tamil was adopted only from the seventh century onward, the Kūram plates of Paramēsvaravarman being the earliest known Pallava Sanskrit-Tamil charter. To these we may also add the four or five important copper-plate charters of this variety belonging to the seventh, eighth and ninth centuries A.D. which also furnish, in the donative part of the gift, a long genealogy of the earlier sovereigns in the Pallava dynasty. These are the Kaśākkuḍi, Vēlūrpāḷayam, Koṟṟanguḍi, Taṇḍantōṭṭam, and the Udayēndiram plates. These records enable us to check the accuracy of the information contained in the earlier grants.

The Nature of these Records and some Important Synchronisms.—The actual chronological position and the genealogical order of the Pallava kings of this period are, in the present state of knowledge, bound to be tentative and far from strictly accurate. Fortunately an element of certainty in the case of certain of the sovereigns of this period has become possible by two or three important synchronisms. The most valuable of these is contained in the Penugoṇḍa plates of the Western Ganga king Mādhava II, which, unlike most other early Ganga plates, has been accepted to be a genuine record.[1] By stating that Arivarman (equivalent of Harivarman or Āryavarman) and Simhavarman and Skandavarman were installed on the Ganga throne by Simhavarman and Skandavarman of the Pallava family this record gives the valuable information that Āryavarman and Simhavarman of the Western Ganga dynasty were contemporaries of the Pallava kings Simhavarman and Skandavarman, and in all probability their feudatories as well. Dr. Fleet, who has made a special study of these plates, has given it as his opinion that the period when these kings flourished must have been about the last quarter of the fifth century A.D., and that A.D. 475 is a very good date for the record.

The 'Lōkavibhāga' Datum.—The next important work which introduces some certainty in the early Pallava chronology is the Digambara Jain work known as *Lōkavibhāga* which is dated in Śaka 380, i.e. A.D. 458.[2] This date, we understand from the work, corresponds to the twenty-second year of Simhavarman, the king of Kāñchi. Dr. Fleet, who was generally suspicious of early Śaka dates, examined this date carefully, and making a few corrections, arrived at the conclusion that it was equivalent to A.D. 458. As this year corresponded to the twenty-second year of Simhavarman the initial year of his reign may be calculated back as the year A.D. 436. This datum, which was first brought to the notice of

[1] Fleet, *J.R.A.S.*, 1915, pp. 471–85.
[2] *Mys. Archl. Rep. for 1909–10*, para 112.

scholars by Mr. R. Narasimhacharyar of the Mysore Archæological Department, helps us to fix the period of two of the Pallava kings Simhavarman and his son Skandavarman in the second and third quarters of the fifth century. Prof. Jouveau-Dubreuil however underrates the value of this testimony[1] and regards it as rather suspicious especially as it does not say which Simhavarman it was and to what branch of the Pallava family he belonged.

Avantisundarikathāsāra.—Another valuable synchronism which has been discovered recently, is obtained from the Sanskrit manuscript known as *Avantisundarikathāsāra* the historical introduction of which gives an account of Bhāravi and Daṇḍin. We learn from this that Bhāravi visited the courts of Vishṇuvardhana, Durvinīta, and Simhavishṇu. From the fact that the poet is described to have visited these three kings we may infer that these kings were contemporaries. As it is known that Durvinīta belonged to the later part of the sixth century, and as we also know that Vishṇuvardhana is assignable to the same period, we may feel certain that the members of the Pallava kings of the Sanskrit charters belong to a period anterior to the seventh century. From the seventh century onward there is not much uncertainty either in the actual order of succession of the Pallava kings or their dates. The light thrown by the *Avantisundarikathā* upon the political history of South India and chronology is discussed both in the Proceedings of the Oriental Conference Second Session (1922) and in the *Mythic Society's Journal*, by Messrs. M. Ramakrishnakavi and A. Rangaswami Sarasvati.[2]

We have already pointed out that the connection of the Pallava kings referred to in the Prakrit charters such as

[1] *The Pallavas*, p. 18.

[2] Another MS. of the original prose *Avantisundarikathā* by Acharya Daṇḍin has been discovered by Pundit G. Harihara Sastri at Trivandrum. This confirms the contemporaneity of Bhāravi, Vishṇuvardhana I, Durvinīta and Simhavishṇu. It makes however Daṇḍin the great grandson of Damodhara, a friend of Bhāravi, and not Bhāravi himself, the modification being due to a slight error in reading. Summary of papers, Fourth Oriental Conference, pp. 44-7. *Ed.*

Śivaskandavarman, Vijaya-Buddhavarman, etc., with those of the Sanskrit charters such as Skandavarman, Simhavarman, Simhavishṇu, etc., is not definitely known. But the fact that in both the sets of copper-plates the kings are spoken of as belonging to the Bhāradvāja-gotra, and the general resemblance of the names in both lead us to conclude that these kings were members of one family.

Vishṇugopa. Circa 340.—The next point concerns Vishṇugopa, the contemporary of Samudragupta. A perusal of the genealogical portion of the early Pallava charters shows that there were several members bearing this name such as Yuvamahārāja Vishṇugopa, Vishṇugopavarman of the Uruvapalli and the Pikīra plates, besides a Mahārāja-Vishṇugopa who figures twice in the Chura plates.[1] Then again we have, in the Vāyalūr pillar inscription, the name of Vishṇugopa repeated thrice and also the name of Vishṇudāsa. The earliest of these is probably to be identified with the adversary described in the Allahabad pillar inscription of Samudragupta. It has been suggested recently that the orthodox estimate of Samudragupta's southern expedition has been considerably exaggerated and that the Allahabad inscription has been misinterpreted. Thus for instance Prof. Jouveau-Dubreuil in his *Ancient History of Deccan*[2] says :—

'After all these rectifications that we have just made the expedition of Samudragupta presents itself before our eyes in quite another form. It is no more a new Alexander marching victoriously through South India ; it was simply the unfortunate attempt of a king from the north who wanted to annex the coast of Orissa but completely failed. About A.D. 340, Samudragupta left his capital Pāṭalīputra and marched directly towards the south. First he conquered Southern Kosala where the king Mahēndra was reigning in the vicinity of Sirpur and Sambalpur. He then crossed the forests that are to the south of Sonpur and found there the small kingdom of Mahākāntāra which means the "great forest" and where

[1] *Ep. Rep. for 1914.* [2] Jouveau-Dubreuil, *Anc. His. Dec.*, p. 60.

Vyāgrarāja the "Tiger-king" was reigning.[1] Then he reached the coast of Orissa. Manṭarāja, king of Koṛala, Mahēndra of Pishṭāpura, Svāmidatta of Koṭṭura, a citadel on the top of a hill and Damana of Erānḍapalle tried to stop him but were captured. Samudragupta now prepared to make new conquests when he was opposed by a confederacy of all the kings that reigned near the mouth of the rivers Godavari and the Krishna, the most powerful of them being Vishṇugopa the Pallava king of Kāñchi. The other kings were Nīlarāja of Avamukta, Hastivarman of Vengi, Ugrasēna of Pālakka, Kubēra who reigned in Dēvarāshṭra and Dhananjaya whose capital was at Kusthalapura. Samudragupta being repulsed by the kings of the Eastern Deccan abandoned the conquests he had made in the coast of Orissa and returned home.'

Thus according to this view the Allahabad pillar does not speak of Pollachi, Palghat, Mahēndragiri, Colair lake, Ērandol and Mahārāshṭra. The identification of Āiranḍapalla with Ērandol appears in the light of the facts known from the Siddhāntam plates of Dēvēndravarman to be near Chicacole.[2] Similarly Dēvarāshṭra which has been hitherto identified with Mahārāshṭra, thus misleading scholars into the impression that Samudragupta went to Mahārāshṭra, figures in an Eastern Chāḷukya grant.[3] discovered in the Vizagapatam District. All the kingdoms mentioned in the inscription are situated in the east coast of the Dakhan. Again according to the same authority Samudragupta did not advance as far south as Kāñchi to defeat Vishṇugopa, but was effectively subjugated by him on the banks of the Godavari or the Krishna. This is merely a hypothesis which has not been proved; there is no evidence against the orthodox view that Samudragupta did advance against Kāñchīpuram and most scholars are inclined to accept

[1] About the identification of this Vyāgra see *Ind. Ant.*, vol. lv, pp. 103ff and 223ff. *Ed.*

[2] *Ep. Ind.*, vol. xii, p. 212.

[3] *Ep. Rep.*, 1908-1909, p. 109. These identifications cannot yet be regarded as final. Places in East Khandesh have vestiges which would support Fleet's identification yet. See *J. I. H.*, vol. v, p. 399. A note on Vakāṭakas by Y. R. Gupte. *Ed.*

this view. There is nothing to sustain the view that the defeat inflicted upon Vishṇugopa and his collegues have been exaggerated as presumed by Prof. Jouveau-Dubreuil in his *Ancient History of the Deccan.*[1] The distinction made in the Allahabad pillar inscription in regard to the various groups of states Samudragupta came into contact with, is clear evidence of an actual invasion and conquest in regard to these trans-Vindhyan states.

A doubt has been raised[2] whether the Vishṇugopa mentioned in the Allahabad pillar inscription is to be regarded as a member of the Pallava dynasty or otherwise. The Vishṇugopa, described as belonging to Kāñchi, could be no other than a member of the Pallava dynasty although he is not described as a Pallava affiliated to the Bhāradvāja-gotra as the kings of the copper-plate charters are. The consideration which makes the surmise almost certain is that the name is a characteristic Pallava name in the same manner as Nandivarman may be regarded as peculiar to the Pallava dynasty. The name does not occur in any other royal dynasty so far known to us. There is moreover no probability of any other royal dynasty having ruled at Kāñchīpuram just at the period of Samudragupta's raid, other than the Pallava. All these considerations taken along with the fact that the chieftains mentioned in the Allahabad pillar inscription are associated only with the capital city of their kingdoms and not with their dynastic or family names, lead to the conclusion that Vishṇugopa of Kāñchi, the adversary of Samudragupta, was a member of the Prakrit or early Sanskrit charters. We are not at present in a position to know anything more about him except his encounter with Samudragupta, and the probability of his being devoted to Vishṇu as is apparent by the name. No copper-plate, which may be expected to throw light on his reign, has been brought to light yet. But the passage in the Allahābad inscription makes it plain that in the middle of the fourth century A.D., there reigned on the banks of the Godavari and

[1] Ch. iii, pp. 58–61. [2] *South Ind. Jainism*, p. 143.

the Krishna and in their vicinity a number of powerful chieftains such as Hastivarman of Vengi, presumably identical with the Sālankāyana king of that name, Nīlarāja of Avamukta, Ugrasēna of Palakka and others.

Vishṇugopa to Simhavishṇu. A. D. 340 to 550.—This period covers roughly 200 years and is commonly spoken of as the age of the Pallava kings of the Sanskrit charters, as the records of this period are invariably in Sanskrit and not in Prakrit as hitherto. The effects of the invasion of Samudragupta on the Pallava dynasty must have been far-reaching. One of these was probably to weaken the authority of Vishṇugopa, and, after his death, to promote dynastic quarrels among his successors. It is very difficult to establish the exact order of succession of kings enumerated in the historical portion of the copper-plates of this period. Nor is it possible to say definitely whether all the kings, whose names figure in these records, actually ruled or occupied the Pallava throne. The extent of the territory over which their rule probably extended is also uncertain. We have already pointed out that it is possible to establish some connection, at present unknown, between the Pallava kings of the Sanskrit charters and those of the Prakrit records. (A. D. 215–350). We do not know who the first member of the Pallava dynasty of the Sanskrit charters was. In this respect the Vēlūrpāḷayam copper-plate charter ascribed to the later Pallava king Nandivarman III of the ninth century and the Kaśākkuḍi plates of Nandivarman Pallavamalla throw some light on the manner in which the first member of the Pallava dynasty acquired sovereignty.[1]

The historical portion of the Vēlūrpāḷayam grant which supplies a detailed genealogy of the Pallava kings after giving the legendary origin of the Pallavas from Vishṇu to Pallava, through Brahma, Aṅgīrasa, Bṛahaspati, Śamyu, Bhāradvāja, Drōna, Aśvatthāman, etc., proceeds to enumerate certain quasi-historical names such as those of Aśokavarman, Kalabhartṛ

[1] Vēlūrpāḷayam plates, *S. I. I.*, vol. ii, p. 507.

and Chūta-Pallava. The break after the king Aśokavarman indicated in the record (verse 5)[1] suggests that the Pallava kings of the Prakrit charters—Śivaskandavarman, Vijaya-skandavarman, Buddhavarman have to be included here. The omission of these names is probably attributable to the fact that the writer of the document had only a foggy notion of the kings of the early period, living as he did several generations after these kings, when their memory had almost faded away. The historicity of Kalabhartṛ, Chūta-Pallava and Vīrakūrcha is confirmed by the mention of these names in the Vāyalūr pillar inscription of Rājasimha apparently in the order of succession. This latter contains many repetitions and should be used with much care. For example, although it is one of the earliest known list of Pallava kings and belongs to the seventh century, it is impossible to regard that all the kings mentioned in it were ruling kings. On the other hand it appears to have been a list made up in the reign of Rājasimha by a writer, who was obviously labouring under the difficulty of accommodating a number of real and quasi-real kings that tradition and copper-plates had preserved, and who, in doing so, was unable to allow for similarity of names. Being in these difficulties he put together all the names he got at, in an order of his own. This seems to be the only explanation for the repetitions that one notices in the list on the Vāyalūr pillar when compared with other genealogies. Prof. G. Jouveau-Dubreuil in his *Pallavas*[2] expresses the opinion that the Vāyalūr inscription gives a complete list of the Pallava kings in the order of their succession. In the portion earlier than Mahēndravarman I, the Vāyalūr record includes names like Vimala, Konkaṇika, which occur exclusively in Western Ganga lists of kings. Vishṇugopa is mentioned three times, Kumāra-vishṇu twice, which is just possible. However Skandavarman is mentioned five times and Simhavarman four times which appears less probable. But the record is doubtless of great

[1] *S. I. I.*, vol. ii, part 5, p. 508.
[2] p. 18 ff.

value to us as establishing a connection between the members of the Prakrit, Sanskrit, and Simhavishṇu dynasties which have been hitherto looked upon as different dynasties. As we have seen it is impossible to agree with those who hold that the Vāyalūr list[1] gives a complete list of forty-two names of the Pallava kings in their order of succession.

The Vāyalūr Pillar Genealogy

Brahma
Aṇgīrasa
Bṛahaspati
Śamyu
Bhāradvāja
Drōna
Aśvatthāman
Pallava
Aśoka
Harigupta
Āryavarman
Vimala
Koṇkaṇika
Kālabhartṛ
Chūta-pallava
Vīrakūrcha
Chandravarman
Karāḷa
Vishṇugopa
Skaṇdamūla
Kumāravishṇu
Buddhavarman
Skaṇdavarman
Vishṇugopa
Vishṇudāsa
Skaṇdavarman
Simhavarman
Vīravarman
Skaṇdavarman
Simhavarman
Skaṇdavarman
Nandivarman I
Simhavarman
Simhavarman
Vishṇugopa
Simhavarman
Simhavishṇu
Mahēndravarman I
Narasimhavarman I
Mahēndravarman II
Paramēsvaravarman I
...
...
...
...
...
Rājasimha

A careful study of the Vēlūrpāḷayam plates shows that the members represented in this record from Kālabhartṛ, who is

[1] Cf. list of fifty-four names given in *Ep. Ind.*, vol. xviii, p. 151 and the whole epigraph as edited in pp. 145–152, *ibid.*—ED.

7

called Kāṇagopa in the Kāśakuḍi plates, belonged to what we have called the period of Sanskrit charters. As it is clear from this record the members mentioned in verses 5 to 8 as Aśokavarman and others in whose family Kālabhartṛ is said to have been born, included the members of the Prakrit charters such as Bappa, Śivaskaṇdavarman, etc. We cannot rely very strictly upon the order of succession in this record as there are several breaks and gaps in it. We may therefore proceed to make one or two observations regarding the kings of this period.

Vīrakūrcha and His Period.—Of Kālabhartṛ and Chūta-pallava very little is known excepting their names. Of these the first appears to have been the first member of the Sanskrit dynasty. Of Vīrakūrcha, however, the grandson of Kālabhartṛ, we learn from the Vēlūrpāḷayam plates (verse 6) that 'simultaneously with the hand of the daughter of the chief of serpents he also grasped the complete insignia of royalty and became famous.' This means in plain language that Vīrakūrchavarman became king on marrying the daughter of a Nāga chief. As to the actual period of this marriage there is some amount of disagreement among scholars. The marriage of Vīrakūrcha which, according to the Vēlūrpāḷayam plates, gave him a kingdom, according to certain authors, has reference to the first member of the dynasty of the Sanskrit Pallavas. According to Prof. Jouveau-Dubreuil the Nāga marriage of Vīrakūrcha has reference to the first king of the Prakrit charters Śivaskaṇdavarman's father.[1] Verse 6 of these plates therefore has reference clearly to the first member of the Pallava dynasty Vīrakūrcha.

Was Vīrakūrcha the First Pallava king?—This conclusion of Prof. Jouveau-Dubreuil does not appear to be quite correct. In the first place it is possible that the names of Aśokavarman, etc., as we have already pointed out, and others referred to in verse 5 of the Vēlūrpāḷayam record, stand for the names of the members of the Prakrit dynasty. If so, it is difficult to accept the view

[1] *Pallavas*, p. 29.

that Vīrakūrcha was the first Pallava king. In the second place it is possible that Vīravarman's immediate ancestor, presumably his father or grandfather, might have lost hold of the sovereignty of the Pallava kingdom owing to some unknown cause, one of which might have been the invasion of Samudragupta. If this were so, his date would have to be sought somewhere after Vishṇugopa. Again, in the Vēlūrpāḷayam plates it is not stated that Vīrakūrcha who married the Nāga princess, was the first member in the family of the Pallavas or the first to acquire a kingdom and a kingly position in that family. This view is also in agreement with that of Dr. S. K. Aiyangar [1] who in his account of the Pallavas ascribes the marriage of Vīrakūrcha to the period immediately following the invasion of Samudragupta into the south and the consequent disruption. According to his interpretation, 'Put in plain language this (the Nāga marriage) would mean that he married a Nāga princess and thereby acquired the title of sovereignty of the region over which he ruled. This obviously has no connection with the birth of Toṇḍamān-Iḷaṁ-Tiraiyan, who, according to tradition embodied in the classical poem *Perumbāṇaṟṟupaḍai*, was the son of a Chōḷa king through a Nāga princess . . . . Neither the detail of the marriage nor the acquisition will agree with the story of Iḷaṁ-Tiriayan. . . .'

What were the circumstances, political and otherwise, which brought about the matrimonial alliance of Vīrakūrcha, a member of the Pallava family with the daughter of a Nāga king which gave him virtually a wife and a kingdom ? To this question no definite answer is possible in the present state of our knowledge relating to the political condition of the Dakhan in the fourth century A.D. Dr. S. K. Aiyangar has however attempted to solve the problem. In the course of his valuable contribution on the *Pallavas* he identifies[2] the Nāga family with which Vīrakūrcha became connected with the family of Skaṇḍanāga, the Śātavāhana viceroy of the region round Adoni and who probably belonged to a clan of the family of Śātavāhanas other than that which

[1] *Origin and Early History of the Pallavas*, p. 43. [2] *Ibid.*, p. 44.

ruled in the Dakhan but connected by blood, and perhaps even by alliance, with that clan. 'At one time under the rule of the later Śātavāhanas these Nāgas appear to have extended their territory and even acquired a considerable portion of the kingdom of the Śātavāhanas themselves. If the Pallava chieftain in the neighbourhood made himself sufficiently distinguished, a marriage alliance with these Nāgas, from whom came the early Śātavāhana queen Nāganika, would have been possible for him. The hint, vague as it is, in the inscription seems to let us into the secret of the rise of the dynasty of the Pallavas to power.'

As regards the probable period when this happened, he indicates that this must have happened at a time when the Śātavāhanas as a ruling dynasty had passed away, and the attempt at the assertion of the Gupta power over this region under Samudragupta had in a way shaken the authority of the older dynasties to allow of a new dynasty to spring into prominence. The character of the invasion of Samudragupta itself makes it clear that the whole of the western portion or the empire of Āndhras was in the hands of a power whom for some good reason Samudragupta did not attack. One such reason might have been that they held possession of the territory with some power, such as the Vākāṭakas in Berar and Central India. It is likely that their authority was not readily acquiesced in by the smaller chieftains, feudatories of the Śātavāhanas, along the east coast. If this surmise should turn out correct it is possible to conceive that the south-western portion was held by a powerful family of the Nāgas, relatives of the Śātavāhanas, and the Pallavas were among the feudatories who showed a ready inclination to throw off the Śātavāhana yoke. When Samudragupta had come and gone, the western power, whatever that was, might have entered into a marriage alliance with the Pallavas and recognized them in the position to which they had already risen by their own efforts.

Skandasishya (*Skandavarman*).—From the Vēlūrpāḷayam plates again (verse 7) we learn that the son of Vīrakūrcha, who is probably identical with Vīrakūrchavarman of the Darśi copper-plate fragment, was Skaṇdaśishya. He is described in this record as the 'moon in the sky of this family' and is said to have seized the *ghaṭika* of the twice-born from King Satyasēna. This achievement of his enables us to fix his period more or less definitely, although the identity of Satyasēna has not been completely worked out. The reference to a *ghaṭika* at this early period is interesting. There is also a reference, in the Tāḷaguṇḍa inscription of Kakutsthavarman, ascribed to the first half of the sixth century, to Kāñchī being called a *ghaṭika*. But no one has attempted to identify the King Satyasēna mentioned in the Vēlūrpāḷayam plates. In his introductions to these plates published in the *South Indian Inscriptions*, Mr. H. Krishna Sastri says that he remains unidentified.[1] Dr. S. Krishnaswami Aiyangar suggests the possibility that the Satyasēna here referred to may be Mahākshatrapa Svāmi Satyasēna of the coins whose time would be the ninth decade of the fourth century A.D.[2] It is uncertain whether the power of the Kshatrapas extended sufficiently southward so as to make them come into hostile contact with the Pallava kings. The probability is that the Pallavas co-operated with the dynasty of Western Dakhan, the Vākāṭakas, in inflicting a defeat on the Kshatrapas and this interpretation of the situation, therefore, seems to be in accordance with the general trend of Vākāṭaka history as this is the period to which the conquest of Kuntaḷa by the Vākāṭaka-Prithvīsēna I is ascribable. 'Such an advance,' as has been pointed out, 'is possible only by the overthrow of the Kshatrapas, and other successors of the Āndhras in this region.'

The Probable Period of Skaṇdaśishya (*Skaṇdavarman*).—This identification of Satyasēna with Svāmi Satyasimha, father of Mahākshatrapa, Svāmi Rudrasimha III, whose date according to Prof. Rapson, is somewhat anterior to A.D. 388, enables us to fix the dates of Skaṇdaśishya as well as his father

[1] *S.I.I.*, vol. ii, part v, p. 502.
[2] 'The Pallavas,' *J. I. H.*, vol. ii, part i, p. 39.

Vīrakūrcha of the Vēlūrpāḷayam record. Allowing a period of about thirty years for these two kings we arrive at about A.D. 358 for the date of the accession of Vīrakūrcha. According to Mr. Krishna Sastri, this Skaṇdaśishya is perhaps identical with the Skaṇdaśishya of the Tirukkaḷukkuṉṟam inscription,[1] who made a grant to the *Mūlasthāna* temple at the above-mentioned village and spoken of as a former king. The late Mr. Venkayya in his article on this inscription suggested that Skaṇdaśishya is identical with Skaṇdavarman; but as there are several Skaṇdavarmans in the Pallava record it is difficult to identify the exact individual mentioned in the Tirukkaḷukuṉṟam inscription.

The Sanskrit Charters.—We may now proceed to examine in detail the genealogical portion of other copper-plate charters of this period. We have already pointed out that these charters have been assigned on palæographical grounds to the fifth and the sixth centuries of the Christian era. One peculiarity of the charters of this period is that they do not furnish any genealogical list prior to the great grandfather of the ruling sovereign who is the donor. The habit of including a mythical and quasi-historical pedigree, along with the immediate ancestral line, appears to have originated only in and after the seventh century in the Pallava family. About six of these Sanskrit charters have been discovered mostly in the northern districts, and have been edited with text and translations in the *Epigraphia Indica.* Four of these refer to royal camps from which the respective grants were issued, viz. Palakkada,[2] Daśanapura, Mēnmatūra, and Tāmrāpa. Almost all these grants furnish four generations of kings including the donor. There is considerable difference of opinion as to the order in which these kings are to be chronologically represented. In other words the relative position of the kings mentioned in these records and the chronology to be adopted

[1] See Venkayya, *Ep. Ind.*, vol. iii, p. 276.

[2] An unsuccessful attempt is made to identify Pālakka and Palakkada with Nellore in the *Madras Christian College Magazine for January 1927*, p. 42.

for them are uncertain and far from settled. There exists also considerable difference of opinion among scholars as regards the identification of the various royal camps from which these charters were issued. None of these places Tāmrāpa, Palakkada, Daśanapura, or Mēnmatūra has been identified definitely although a suggestion had been made by the late Mr. Venkayya[1] that they are to be looked for in the vicinity of the region comprised by the modern Nellore District. According to certain scholars the fact that the charters of these Pallava kings are addressed from these camps, and not from the capital city of Kāñchīpuram, indicates that the Pallava kings who issued these charters had lost hold of Kāñchīpuram through some cause now unknown, and retired to the Telugu districts bordering on Nellore where they continued their rule. This line of argument was adopted by the late Mr. Venkayya,[2] and is still maintained by some of the officers of the Epigraphy Department.[3] They advocate what has been called the theory of a Chōḷa interregnum during the Pallava rule according to which the Pallava kings soon after the period of the members of the Prakrit charters were driven away from Kāñchi by the Chōḷa king Karikāla. According to the exponents of this view the Pallavas would appear to have taken possession of the city only in the days of Kumāravishṇu who is described in the Vēlūrpāḷayam plates to have captured Kāñchi. We shall revert to this theory of a Chōḷa interregnum a little later.

Various Orders of Succession.—According to Prof. Jouveau-Dubreuil the series of kings Skaṇdavarman—Kumāravishṇu—Buddhavarman I—Kumāravishṇu (donor) of the Chandalūr plates, ruled in Kāñchi before the series, Simhavarman (mentioned in the Uruvappalli plates) Skaṇdavarman and Naṇdivarman, and that, owing to the resemblance of the Chandalūr plates and the Uruvappalli plates, Kumāravishṇu I would have been the immediate predecessor of Simhavarman of Kāñchi. But a close examination of the copper-plates

[1] *An. Rep. Ep. for 1905*, p. 47. [2] *A. S. R. for 1906-7*, p. 224.
[3] *S.I.I.*, vol. ii, p. 503.

of this period shows that the Chandalūr plates are by no means the most ancient of these, as in the opinion of M. Jouveau-Dubreuil. The style and the language employed, from the use of numerical symbols and the citation of date after the manner of the earlier Prakrit charters and the spaces marked between words, almost clearly suggest proximity to the Āndhra period.[1] If such be the case the Ōmgōḍu grant (No. 1) is the most ancient of the Sanskrit charters that we have.

We have already seen that the Vēlūrpāḷayam plates supply the following names among the early members of the Sanskrit period :—

Kālabhartṛ
|
Chūta-pallava
|
Vīrakūrcha
|
Skandaśishya
|
Kumāravishṇu, etc.

The Ōmgōḍu (No. 1) charter gives the following order :—

Kumāravishṇu
|
Skaṇdavarman
|
Vīravarman
|
Vijayaskaṇdavarman

Mr. Krishna Sastri identifies Vīravarman of this charter with the Vīravarman of the published copper-plate charters and with the *Vīrakūrchavarman of the Darśi record.* 'If Vīravarman's identity is thus established, it must be easy to see that his father Skaṇdavarman would be the first king of that name mentioned in the published copper-plate grant and that Vijayaskaṇdavarman, his son, would be identical with Skaṇdavarman II. Kumāravishṇu, the first king mentioned, and the father of Skaṇdavarman I, is probably to be

[1] See *Ep. Ind.*, vol. xv, p. 251, footnote 2.

identified with Kālabhartṛ of the Vēlūrpāḷayam plates[1] though there may be very little in common between the two names.' Thus Mr. Krishna Sastri would identify the first four kings mentioned in the Vēlūrpāḷayam plates with those mentioned in the Ōmgōḍu (I) copper-plates which may be represented as follows :—

Kālabhartṛ	...	Kumāravishṇu
Chūta-pallava	...	Skaṇdavarman
Vīrakūrcha	...	Vīravarman
Skaṇdaśishya	...	Vijayaskaṇdavarman
Kumāravishṇu	...	Kumāravishṇu.

Before examining the view of Mr. Krishna Sastri let us state the genealogical information from the other charters for his period. The Uruvappalli plates,[2] dated in the eleventh year of Simhavarman, although the donor was Yuvamahārāja-Vishṇugōpavarman, give the following genealogy :—

Skaṇdavarmaṇ
|
Vīravarman
|
Skaṇdavarman
|
Y. M. Vishṇugopa (donor)

From the fact that the Uruvappalli plates are dated in the eleventh year of Simhavarman it was held by the late Dr. Fleet that Y. M. Vishṇugopa was a younger brother of Simhavarman, and that he probably never reigned at all.

The Mangaḍūr grant[3] gives the succession in the following order :—

Vīravarman
|
Skaṇdavarman
|
Y. M. Vishṇugopavarman
|
Dharmamahārāja Simhavarman

[1] *S.I.I.*, vol. ii, p. 503.
[2] *Ind. Ant.*, vol. v, p. 51.
[3] *Ibid.*, vol. vi, p. 155,

The Pikīra plates[1] furnish us with the accompanying order which is almost similar to the previous one :—

Vīravarman
|
Skaṇdavarman
|
Vishṇugopavarman
|
Simhavarman (donor)

Thus these three plates together supply five generations of kings ; the Chandalūr plates, which, as we already mentioned, appear to be posterior to these records in point of antiquity give three further generations of kings from Skaṇdavarman, who, we might regard, was identical with Skaṇdavarman II. The Chandalūr[2] plates, we saw, supplies the following names in the order noted below :—

Skaṇdavarman
|
Kumāravishṇu I
|
Buddhavarman
|
Kumāravishṇu II (donor)

The Udayēndiram plates[3] supply the series :—

Skaṇdavarman
|
Simhavarman
|
Skaṇdavarman
|
Nandivarman (donor).

The Vāyalūr pillar inscription becomes acceptable from No. 29, and agrees with the Vēlūrpāḷayam grant thus

[1] *Ep. Ind.*, vol. viii, p. 159.
[2] *Ibid.*, vol. viii, p. 233.
[3] *Ibid.*, vol. iii, p. 142.

continuing the succession to the time of Simhavishṇu as will be seen by the following :—

Simhavarman (Vāyalūr list 29)
|
Vishṇugopa
|
Simhavarman
|
Simhavishṇu
|
Mahēndravarman I

The whole series of Pallava kings from the beginning to the days of Simhavishṇu may be represented by the following table :—

Bappa
|
Śivaskanda (*Circa.* A.D. 220)
|
Buddhavarman
|
Vishṇugopa (A.D. 340)
|
Kālabhartṛ (Ōmgōḍu-Uruvapalli plates)
(Kumāravishṇu)
|
Chūta-pallava
(Skaṇdavarman) (Ōmgōḍu-Uruvapalli plates)
(Married Nāga princess)
|
Vīrakūrcha (Vīrakūrchavarman)
|
Skaṇdaśishya (Donor, Ōmgōḍu Plates)
|

Simhavarman	Y. M. Vishṇugopa or Vishṇugopavarman	Kumāravishṇu I
|	|	|
Skaṇdavarman	Simhavarman II	Buddhavarman
|	|	|
Nandivarman I (Udayēndiram)	Vishṇugopavarman	Kumāravishṇu II.
	|	
	Simhavarman III	
	|	
	Simhavishṇu	
	|	
	Mahēndravarman, etc.	

The above table is only tentative and subject to alteration if necessary on other more satisfactory interpretation of the charters, or when the discovery of new inscriptions, or copper charters should call for such. It is just possible that there might not be any direct connection between the members of the Prakrit charters, those of the Sanskrit charters and the members of the Simhavishṇu dynasty, as is assumed here. But this arrangement is based on the evidence of the Vāyalūr pillar record and that of Vēlūrpāḷayam plates strengthened by the consideration that the Pallava kings of these charters style themselves in these records as members of the Bhāradvāja-gotra. The position of Vishṇugopa, the adversary of Samudragupta in the table, is uncertain. We have already hinted the possibility of his being identical with the first of the Vishṇugopas mentioned in the Vāyalūr pillar record of Rājasimha's reign. We have also alluded to the date suggested by Mr. Shama Sastri in his new light on the Gupta era which at the present state of discussion need not be regarded as having been established beyond doubt.

The earliest member of the Sanskrit charters figures as Kālabhartṛ in the Vēlūrpāḷayam plates, a name which along with his son's name Chūta-pallava, sounds more eponymous than real. Kālabhartṛ is presumably identical with Kāṇagopa of the Kaśakkuḍi plates.[1] In the above arrangement we have indicated the possibility of Kālabhartṛ being identical with the Kumāravishṇu I of Ōmgōḍu No. 1 and Chūta-pallava with Skaṇdavarman I. Mr. Krishna Sastri who also makes this identification says that there is nothing in common between Kālabhartṛ and Kumāravishṇu.[2] The description of Kālabhartṛ as the 'head-jewel of the family' and as Vishṇu the husband of Indira (Lakshmi) in verse 6 of the Vēlūrpāḷayam plates lends support to the identification of this king with

[1] *S.I.I.*, vol. ii, p. 307.

[2] *Ep. Ind.*, vol. xv, p. 251. Also vol. xviii, p. 149, where he definitely gives up the identification. This is hardly justified as the writer of the Vāyalūr pillar inscription has merely put the lists one after the other without attempting to find out actual relationship between the different succession lists. *Ed.*

Kumāravishṇu of the Ōmgōḍu grant which suggests that his other name was a synonym of Vishṇu. It is even possible that this Kumāravishṇu whom we identified with Kālabhartṛ was the same person as Vishṇugopa, the adversary of Samudragupta. This identification has not been made hitherto, although there is nothing unreasonable in this view.

As was already indicated, the actual dates and the duration of the individual reigns of the Pallava kings of this period are approximate so far. Obviously it is not possible for all the sixteen kings and more to have been on the Pallava throne within the short period of about 200 years (A.D. 350 to 550). It is evident from the charters themselves that certain members of the dynasty referable to this period were simply *Yuvamahārājas* or princes only, as in the case of Vishṇugopa—the prince of the Uruvapalli plates. We have already indicated the facts known regarding Kālabhartṛ (Kumāravishṇu) and Chūta-pallava (Skaṇdavarman) from the copper-plates of this period. We have shown that Chūta-pallava *alias* Skaṇdavarman might have been the chief who married the Nāga princess and acquired simultaneously a wife and a kingdom. His son was Vīrakūrcha, identical probably with Vīrakūrchavarman of the Darśi fragment.[1] His son was Skaṇdavarman (II) the donor of Ōmgōḍu plates who is described in this record as one 'who was true to his word, who day by day increased religious merit by gift of cows, gold and land, and who always desired to serve Gods and Brahmaṇs, and ably understood the purport of all *Śāstras*.' From the date of the engraving of the grant which is mentioned as the *Vijayasamvatsarē-trayatrimsē* (that is in the victorious year thirty-three which was the third fortnight of the winter and the thirteenth day) we may conclude that Skaṇdavarman's reign lasted at least for thirty-three years.

Siṁhavarman.—The next Pallava king was Simhavarman in whose eleventh year the Uruvapalli plates of Y. M. Vishṇugopa is dated. It is not apparent why Y. M. Vishṇugopa should

[1] *Ep. Ind.*, vol. i, p. 397.

have addressed the grant in the reign of Simhavarman. The probability is that he did not reign and therefore dated the record in the reign of his elder brother, or possibly in that of his. In the latter case this Simhavarman becomes identical with the donor of the four grants, the Ōmgōḍu plates dated in the fourth year of his reign in the month of Vaiśāka Śuklapaksha-panchami addressed from Tāmrāpa, the Pikira grant dated in fifth year and issued from Mēnmātura, the Uruvappalli plates dated in the eleventh year of his reign, and issued from Palakkada, and the Mangalūr grant issued from Vijaya-Daśanapura and dated in the eighth year of Simhavarman II. Thus we have for this king at least four different copper-plate charters dated in the different years of the reign and issued in different places which were obviously the places where the king happened to be in camp just when the grants were issued. It has been already pointed out that these places Vijaya Tāmrāpasthāna, Mēnmātura, Daśanapura and Palakkada have not been identified though the suggestion has been made that they should be looked for in the Nellore District. The late Mr. Venkayya writes in his *Ancient History of the Nellore District*,[1] 'that it is not impossible that Daśanapura was the ancient name of the modern village of Darśi. It is called Darśī and Dariśi in inscriptions of the fourteenth century found as the place.' He also thinks that the place might have been the capital at the time that the Mangaḍūr grant was issued in the eighth year of Simhavarman. If this is so why is it not possible to hold Palakkada, Tāmrāpa, and Mēnmātura also at the capital of Simhavarman? But such an assumption does not seem to be justified unless we have good reason for regarding that this period was one of constant warfare, and that the kingdom of Simhavarman was frequently threatened, with the result that he had to be continuously changing his capital from one seat to another. But there is no definite evidence to prove that this was a fact. It is assumed by certain scholars that the Pallava kings of this period had lost

[1] *Ind. Ant.*, 1908, p. 283.

their possession of Kāñchi and retired to the Telugu districts in and around Nellore, wherefrom they continued to rule and issue their copper-plates. This explains according to them the charters of Simhavarman and others during this period being addressed not from Kāñchīpuram as in the case of earlier copper-plates but from places in the Telugu districts. For instance Mr. Krishna Sastri says :— . . . ' About A.D. 350 the Pallavas,—perhaps on account of the disturbances caused by the victorious campaign of Samudragupta from the north or owing to the rise of the Kadambas mentioned in the Tālgunḍa inscription[1] were dispossessed of their territory round Kāñchi and pushed back further into the interior.' Again the same authority says[2] :—

' Thus we get from several copper-plates published so far, six generations of Pallavas, with names of nine Pallava kings who called themselves Pallava-Mahārājas and Pallava-Dharma-mahārājas, of the Bhāradvāja-gotra until one of them, Kumāravishṇu I (II ?) reconquered Kāñchīpura, evidently from the Chōḷas, who had taken possession of it sometime subsequent to Vishṇugopa the contemporary of Samudragupta and had established themselves in the Toṇḍa-country.' Thus according to this view there was a Chōḷa interregnum at Kāñchi and a break in the line of Pallava kings during the period of the Sanskrit charters.

Is the Chōḷa Interregnum Possible?—This interregnum according to which a number of Pallava kings in the fourth and the fifth century are supposed to have lost possession of Kāñchi some time in the fourth century has become a favourite notion among the epigraphists which however does not appear to be supported by the historical facts of the period known to us. Even the late Mr. Venkayya has expressed himself in favour of the theory of a Chōḷa interlude in the midst of the Pallava rule. In his ' Ancient History of the Nellore District '[3] for instance, dealing with the Pallava kings of this period he says, ' The

[1] *Ep. Ind.*, vol. viii, p. 28.
[2] *Ibid.*, vol. xv, No. 11, p. 249.
[3] *Ind. Ant.*, 1908, p. 284,

extent of Pallava dominions during this period from the fourth century to the end of the sixth century A.D. cannot be ascertained. At any rate they appear to have been in possession of the modern Nellore District or at least a portion of it. In fact four of the above-mentioned grants are from that district. Kāñchi which was the capital during the reign of Śivaskandavarman and Vishṇugopa, figures as such only in the last two [1] of the above-mentioned grants which are evidently later than the rest.' 'If this is not due to a mere accident it may be that the Pallavas had to retreat from Conjeevaram owing, perhaps to a coalition among the Chōḷa, Pāṇḍya and the Chera kings, or to the domination of one of them. In this case, the Pallavas, had probably to confine themselves to the Nellore District or to a portion of it, where the villages granted in two of the copper-plate inscriptions may be traced.'

Some Objections.—But as against this mere supposition, there are serious difficulties in the way of our accepting the assumption of any break in the main line of Pallava kings from the earliest times. At any rate the mere fact of certain copper-plates being addressed from places situated in the Telugu districts far away from the capital city cannot be held to support the view that the king or kings who issued them should necessarily have lost possession of Kāñchi. Such at any rate is not the indication that we get from the large numbers of copper-plates and stone records of the Pallava kings obtained in various parts of the country. In these records there is not the remotest suggestion that the Pallava kings at any period in their rule lost possession of the city of Conjeevaram for any appreciable length of time. A reference in the Vēlūrpāḷayam plates[2] of Nandivarman III to the capture of Kāñchi has curiously been interpreted as meaning that Kumāravishṇu for the first time after the capture of the city by the Chōḷas in the days of Karikāla, recaptured it. Such an assumption appears however to be

[1] Chandalūr and Udayēndiram records.
[2] Verse 8, *S.I.I.*, vol. ii, p. 508.

unwarranted. In the first place it is just possible that the capture of Kāñchi alluded to in the Vēlūrpāḷyam plates is a reference to his having obtained possession of the city from a collateral cousin, or some other foreign power, such as the Kadambas, which had obtained possession of the city for a short period. In the second place if the fact of the capture of Kāñchi from the Chōḷas is at all true, it is strange that the Vēlūrpāḷayam plates should not have made mention of the fact in recording such a distinguished achievement, more especially as Buddhavarma another king is mentioned as the 'submarine-fire to the ocean-like army of the Chōḷas' *Chōḷa-sainyārṇava-vāḍabhāgni* (verse 8). But the insuperable difficulty in postulating a Chōḷa occupation in the interval between the Pallava kings of the Prakrit charters and those of Simhavishṇu, based merely upon the stray reference to the recapture of Kāñchīpuram by Kumāravishṇu and on the fact of the charters of the Pallavas for some period being dated from places outside the capital at Kāñchi, lies in the impossibility of accommodating the reign of Karikāla and all the events connected with the history of his reign to this period. According to any rational scheme of chronology it is very difficult to find a place for Karikāla and his successors midway between the Pallava kings of the Prakrit charters and those of the Sanskrit charters as suggested by the epigraphists. The facts relied upon by them as evidence for this position for Ḳarikāla are derived from late Eastern Chāḷukya copper-plates some of the facts being incredible in themselves.[1] Altogether the data for the Chōḷa occupation of Kāñchi during the Pallava rule are too meagre and unsatisfactory to be seriously considered as justifying the assumption of a Chōḷa interregnum.

We have already referred the four Sanskrit charters issued respectively from Ōmgōḍu, Pikīra, Daśanapura and Palakkada between the fourth and the eleventh years of Simhavarman to this reign. The probable date of this king is derivable from purely epigraphic and palæographic evidence as the middle of

[1] *A.S.R.*, 1906–7, p. 225.

the fifth century. But the discovery of the *Lōkavibhāga*, a Jain manuscript, has gone a great way towards fixing the actual period of rule of this king.

The 'Lōkavibhāga' Datum.—This leads to the initial date of the Pallava king Simhavarman as A.D. 436. According to the *Digambara*, Jain manuscript, *Lōkavibhāga*, Śaka 380 corresponded to the twenty-second regnal year of Simhavarman, king of Kāñchi, the year in which the work was completed. "The reference makes it clear that the first year of this king must have been A.D. 436, and that this king continued to rule for at least a period of twenty-two years.

Śaka 380 is apparently the year in which the copying work was finished by Sarvanandi and the author of the work Simhasūri, probably flourished at an earlier period. The twenty-second stanza was sent to Mahamahopādyāya Sudhākara Dvivedi, Benares, for favour of calculation. There is no question about the correctness of the date. Pāṭalika, the village in which Śarvanandi copied the work, is perhaps identical with Pāṭalīpura in South Arcot District, at which according to *Periyapurāṇam* there was a big Jaina monastery in the seventh century A.D. . . . Pāṇarāshṭra may be identified with *Perumbāṇappāḍi* (the Bṛhad Bāṇas laid under tribute by Mayūra Śarman, Kadamba) the province over which the Bāṇas ruled.

As regards the actual period of Simhavarman (II) we have already pointed out that being probably identical with the king of the name referred to in the Penugoṇḍa plates of the Western Ganga king Mādhavavarman II, his reign must have been at the same period as that of Harivarman the Ganga prince whom he is said to have installed on the throne. Judged palæographically the characters of the Penugoṇḍa plates point to their having been inscribed in the fifth century A.D. Dr. Fleet was also of opinion[1] that 'A.D. 475 seems a very good date for it.' If the plates which are dated in the reign of Mādhava II, are dated about the year A.D. 475, Simhavarman the

[1] See *J.R.A.S.*, 1915, p. 482.

contemporary of Ayyavarman whom he installed on the Ganga throne must have flourished immediately before. Hence it is not improbable that Simhavarman II began his rule sometime about the third decade of the fifth century which is also the date that we arrive at by the *Lōkavibhāga* datum, equating the twenty-second year of Simhavarman with the Śaka year 380. This yields for Simhavarman, as we saw, the year A.D. 436 as the initial year, which tallies both with the palæographical indications of Penukoṇḍa and the Ōmgōḍu plates as well as the other considerations relating to the date of the Pallava kings who followed him. A calculation backward from the known date of Simhavishṇu also leads us to the same period.

An attempt made to belittle the value of this datum furnished by the *Lōkavibhāga* for the initial date of Simhavarman II requires careful consideration. Mr. H. Krishna Sastriar, relying upon what he interprets as a reference to an eclipse in the Ōmgōḍu plates, lines 31–32, dated in the fourth year of his reign, considers the datum of the *Lōkavibhāga* invalidated. The fourth year of Simhavarman II, according to the *Lōkavibhāga*, corresponds to the year A.D. 440 in which year there happens to be no solar eclipse during the month of Chaitra. But this objection of Mr. Sastriar is based upon a wrong interpretation of the object of the grant of the Ōmgōḍu plates and of the expression *grahaṇanimittam* in line 31. In the first place the plates are dated in the fifth day of the bright fortnight, of Vaiśāka, whereas if the occasion of the grant had been the solar eclipse the record would have been dated on the new moon day. This difficulty Mr. Krishna Sastriar gets over by supposing that the grant which was actually made on the new moon day of Chaitra, a possible day for the nearest solar eclipse, was actually engraved 'on the plates five days later.'[1] The explanation does not appear to be at all satisfactory. The expression '*grahaṇanimittam*', appears to convey, as has been pointed out, the meaning of 'for the sake of acceptance' rather than 'on account of the eclipse',

[1] *Ep. Ind.* vol. xv pp. 252–55.

as it looks strange that the copper-plate record should not mention the character of the eclipse and other circumstances connected with it. 'It is very unusual,' says Prof. Krishnaswami Aiyangar to indicate an eclipse in this manner, without saying what eclipse it is, and otherwise defining the *Puṇyakāla*. What is worse in the interpretation of the epigraphist is that the date of the grant is actually specified in the concluding portion. "*Sa vijayarājya-Samvatsarē-Chaturthē-Vaiśāka-Śukla-paksha-Panchamyām dattam.*" This is quite unequivocal. In the face of this it would be difficult to prove that the grant was made on an eclipse day from the document. The difficulty and inconsistency are the results of the interpretation, and neither the author nor the scribe could be held responsible for the blunder which is not theirs.'[1]

Successors of Simhavarman II.—Very little is known about the successors of Simhavarman II till we come to the accession of Simhavishṇu. The Vāyalūr pillar inscription which is relied upon by Prof. Jouveau-Dubreuil for this period gives the names of the following kings in the order of succession mentioned below :—

Simhavarman II (A.D. *c.* 436–460).
Vishṇugopavarman II.
Simhavarman III.
Simhavishṇu (A.D. *c.* 575–600).

The Vēlūrpāḷayam plates give the following names for this period. After a host of kings passed away with Vishṇugopa, came Nandivarman who is reported in this record to have caused a 'powerful snake' to dance. Then followed Simhavarman who is said to have wiped off the pride of his enemies. After him came Simhavishṇu. As we already saw there is a slight discrepancy in the order of succession herein stated and those given in other plates. The probability seems to be that soon after the reigns of Simhavarman II and Skaṇḍavarman II the contemporaries of the Western Ganga kings Ayyavarman and Mādhavavarman II about the close of the fifth

[1] *J. I. H.*, vol. ii, p. 56.

century A.D., the Pallava kings Kumāravishṇu II who captured Kāñchi, Nandivarman I, Simhavarman III, occupied the Pallava throne before Simhavishṇu, about the last quarter of the sixth century, commenced to rule at Kāñchīpuram. Practically nothing is known of the reign of these kings from the copper-plates and inscriptions of this period until we arrive at the reign of Simhavishṇuvarman, or Mahēndravarman I, his son and successor, whose accession marks the commencement of the age of the Great Pallavas which lasted for two centuries and a half from about A.D. 600 to 850.

CHAPTER V

CONTEMPORARY POLITICAL POWERS. THE SALANKAYANAS, KADAMBAS, ETC.

THE most important among the contemporary royal dynasties that ruled in the Dakhan during this period, contemporaneous with the Pallava kings of the Sanskrit charters, were the Kadambas, the Vākāṭakas, the Sālankāyanas, the Western Gangas, the Vishṇukuṇḍins, and the chieftains of various places in the region around the mouth of the Krishna and the Gódavari figuring in the Allahabad pillar inscription already noticed, one of whom was probably a Sālankāyana-Hastivarman of Vengi. It is unnecessary to give here an account of all these powers from the available records. A short account of the Sālankāyanas, the Kadambas and the Vishṇukuṇḍins who appear to have come into close contact with the Pallavas are given here as far as the information from the records permits.

The chronology of the Kadambas cannot be regarded as having been definitely fixed. The period of the earliest of the Kadamba kings Mayūraśarman who is described as a Brahman in the Tāḷguṇḍa pillar inscription has been fixed by scholars from internal evidence and palæographical indications as the middle of the fourth century, though Mr. Shama Sastriar in his *Mysore Archæological Reports* is inclined to carry back his period considerably earlier.[1]

The Tāḷguṇḍa pillar inscription of Kakutsthavarman gives a glimpse into the circumstances leading to the establishment of the political power of this Brahman dynasty in the Dakkan. This record in graphic language describes how the first member of this dynasty Mayūraśarman, a Brahman belonging to the Mānavyasa-gotra, and a native of Sthāṇukuṇḍūr came

[1] See the *Mys. Arch. Report*, 1923.

to the city of Kāñchīpuram for completing his Vedic studies, how he had a quarrel with a Pallava horseman, and how not bearing to be told that the Brahman caste was inferior to that of the Kshatriyas he put himself at the head of a band of adventurers and attacked the Pallava sovereigns in the inaccessible forests of Śrī-Parvata. Then with the aid of the Bṛihaṭ-Bāṇas and others he founded the Kadamba kingdom of which Banavasi was the capital. The Pallava kings had to admit his claims as a ruling power and had to effect a temporary compromise. Now we must try to find out what was the probable period of Mayūraśarman and who his Pallava contemporary was. As we have already suggested, this dismemberment of the Pallava kingdom must have followed the confusion which resulted from the invasion of Samudragupta about A.D. 340. The Kadamba Prakrit inscription of Maḷavaḷḷi [1] written as it is in Prakrit, though it does not mention the name of the king, may be taken to refer to the most ancient king of the Kadambas presumably Mayūraśarman. In regard to his Pallava contemporary only the vaguest guess can be made. As we have assigned Mayūraśarman to about A.D. 350 his Pallava contemporary must have been either Vishṇugopa or his immediate successors Vīrakūrcha or Skaṇdavarman I.

Of the successors of Mayūraśarman, Kangavarman and Bhagīratha attributable to the second half of the fifth century A. D., probably carried on hostile operations against the Pallava kings of the period. Of the others it appears that Raghu, Kakutsthavarman, Śāntivarman and his two sons Mṛigēśavarman and Mandhātrivarman ruled during the sixth century A.D. and were evidently contemporaneous with Vīravarman, Skandavarman II, Simhavarman, and Skandavarman III of the Pallavas. The southern conquest of Prithvīsena, the Vākāṭaka king, who, according to the Ajanta inscription[2] is described as having defeated the

[1] *Ind. Ant.*, vol. xlvi, p. 154.
[2] Cave No. 16, *Arch. Sur. W. Ind..*, vol. 4, p. 53 ff.

Kuntaḷas, i.e. the Kadamba king, probably took place about the period, A.D. 350–360 and the Kadamba king must have been Kangavarman who is described in inscriptions as having been engaged in 'lofty exploits and in terrible wars.' Of the others we know that Kakutstha, who is ascribable to the first quarter of the fifth century, was the donor of the Tāḷgunḍa inscription. The marriage of Narēndrasēna, the grandson of Prabhāvati Gupta with the daughter of the king of Kuntaḷa named Ajjhitabhaṭṭārika is probably to be attributed as Prof. Jouveau-Dubreuil suggests to Kakutstha's reign. Thus it turns out that Kakutsthavarman's boast, in the Tāḷgunḍa inscription, that he gave his daughter to Guptas and other kings would be correct if the Gupta-Vākāṭaka king, Narēndrasēna, was the son-in-law of this king. According to our arrangement of Pallava chronology he must have been a contemporary of Simhavarman II and it was probably during this period that the installation of the Western Ganga kings Ayyavarman and Mādhavavarman must have taken place. Of Śāntivarman who succeeded Kakutsthavarman on the Kadamba throne very little is known. Of his sons Mṛigēśavarman and Mandhātrivarman who together ruled for the rest of the fifth century we have some records. According to the Halsi plates dated in the eighth year of his reign Mṛigēśa uprooted the Gangas and was a very fire of destruction to the Pallavas.[1] We learn from another record[2] that his queen was called Prabhāvatī who was born in the Kaikeya family. Almost contemporaneous with the reigns of Śāntivarman, Mṛigēśavarman and Mandhātrivarman, A.D. 450–500, the younger branch of the Kadamba family Krishṇavarman I, the son of Kakutstha and the elder brother of Śāntivarman with Prince Dēvavarman as Yuvamahārāja ruled at Triparvata. Soon after the death of Mandhātrivarman the throne of the Kadambas passed to Ravivarman who, according to the Halsi plates, is said to have acquired regal power by the strength

[1] Halsi plates, *Ind. Ant.*, vol vi, p. 24.
[2] *Mys. Arch. Rep. for 1910-11*, p. 35.

and prowess of his own arm which means that there was some trouble in his succession and that he had to fight for the throne. According to another record,[1] he is said to have slain Vishṇuvarman, presumably a collateral cousin and descendant of Krishṇavarman, and uprooted Chaṇḍadaṇḍa of Kāñchi. Records dated in the fifth year of Ravivarman, and the thirty-fifth year have been discovered. He was followed by Harivarman at Vaijayanti till about A.D. 550 when the rise of Pulakēśin I probably put an end to, or obscured, his power. The subsequent history of the Kadambas does not concern us here. Krishṇavarman, his son Ajavarman, Bhogivarman and Vishṇuvarman are known to have ruled as kings from recent records. That the Kadambas continued to be powerful as late as the end of the eighth century is seen from the mention in the Vēlūrpāḷayam plates[2] that the Pallava king Dantīvarman married Aggalanimmati, 'the daughter of the celebrated king and a crest-jewel of the Kadamba family.'[3]

Sālankāyanas, circa A.D. 350 to 500.—Almost contemporaneously with the Pallava kings of the Sanskrit charters, may be placed the Sālankāyana dynasty. The word Sālankāyana appears originally to have been the name of a Vedic Rishi. There are nearly five grants for this dynasty that are available to us. If Hastivarman of Vengi, who figures among the adversaries of Samudragupta in the Allahabad inscription, was a Sālankāyana (identified by Vincent Smith as a Pallava) he may be regarded as the earliest member of this family known hitherto. The Ellore Prakrit[4] plate the alphabets of which closely resemble the Pikīra, Mangalūr and Uruvapalli plates, are dated in the thirteenth year of Māhāraja-Vijayadēvavarman, and were issued from Vengipuram. These plates describe Vijayadēvavarman as the performer of the *Aśvamēdha* the fervent Māhēśvara and the devotee at the fect of the Holy Chitrarathasvāmi. The grant is addressed to the villagers of Ellora which may be identified with the modern town of Ellore.

[1] *Ind. Ant.*, vol. vi, p. 30.
[2] *S.I.I.*, vol. ii, part v, p. 511.
[3] *Ibid.*, verse 18.
[4] *Ep. Ind.*, vol. ix, p. 56.

Another grant[1] of the Sālankāyanas written in Sanskrit and therefore considered to be posterior to the Prakrit charter already mentioned, records that Vijayanandivarman son of Chandavarman issued it in the eighth year of his reign from the city of Vengipura. As regards the popular identification of Vengi with the Pedda Vengi[2] it must be pointed out that, as there are no less than four places bearing the name of Vengi in the Northern Circars alone, it is possible that the usual identification should not be regarded as final on the matter.

Recently two more copper-plates [3] have been discovered by the late Mr. K. V. Lakshmana Rao which, along with the other records, give nearly six generations of the dynasty :—

The following is the order of succession adopted by Mr. Lakshmana Rao :—

C. 350. Hastivarman of Vengi
|
375. Vijayadēvavarman
|
400. Vijayanandivarman
|
425. Buddhavarma
|
450. Chandavarma
|
475. Vijayanandivarman
|
500. Vijayaskandavarman
|

The first of the newly-discovered Kāntēru plates records a grant of Vijayaskandavarman, who is there described as meditating on the feet of the holy Chitrarathasvāmi and as belonging to the family of Sālankāyanas, to one Śivarāya in a village called Chinnapura in the Kudrahāravishaya in the fifth year of the king's reign on the full moon day in the month of Vaiśāka.

The second registers a gift to one Svāmichandra a piece of land in the village of Kuruvāḍa by Mahārāja Śrī Nandivarman.

[1] *Ind. Ant.*, vol. v, p. 175 and plate.
[2] *Mad. Jour. of Lit. and Sc.*, vol. xi, p. 392.
[3] *Viz. Col. Mag.*, October, 1922,

A word may be said about the religious leaning of these kings and their relation with the Pallava kings. As regards the first we can only say that the peculiar cult of the Sālankāyanas who called themselves *Bhagavat-Chitrarathasvāmi-Pādānudyāta* may have reference to their tutelary deity, the God of Chitraratha. This term probably refers to the worship by the Sālaṇkāyanas of the Sun-god, and the representation of the figure of the sun in some of the charters issued by these sovereigns, lends some support to this view.

As regards the other point, namely, the relation of the Sālankāyanas with the Pallavas the following points may be noted. To begin with, there is a close resemblance between the names of the members of the two dynasties such as Skaṇdavarma, Buddhavarma and Nandivarma which also occur in the Pallava copper-plates. The figure of the seated bull which frequently finds a place in the seals of the Pallava charters also figures in the Sālankāyana charters. Finally the fact that for more than six generations the Pallavas and the Sālankāyanas are never known to have come into conflict even once is a significant one, and probably indicates that the Sālankāyanas were on friendly terms with the Pallavas and continued to rule independently along with them in amity. This probably indicates that the two families were in some manner, hitherto unknown, related to one another. It is just possible that the Pallavas and the Sālankāyanas had a common ancestry as Sālankāyana is a *Gotra* belonging to the Bhāradvāja-clan. The Sālankāyanas appear to have exercised political power from about A.D. 340 to about A.D. 480, when the rise of Vishṇukunḍins, and the ascendency of the Vākāṭakas put an end to the political power of these people who are no more heard of in South Indian history.

The Vishṇukunḍins, circa A.D. 450 to 550.—The origin and significance of the term Vishṇukunḍin like that of other dynastic names is buried in obscurity. The conjecture has been put forward that their name is connected with Viṇukonḍa in the Krishna District, which appears to have been the cradle of their power. The first Vishṇukuṇḍin king Mādhavarman I appears to have owed his throne to his marriage with a princess of the Vākaṭakas, though the Chikkula plates [1] which mention the fact do not specify whose daughter the princess was.

The only class of evidence available to us to write an account of the Vishṇukuṇḍins is the inscriptional one. About four records have been discovered. These include the Rāmatīrtham, Chikkula and Pulimboru grants all of which were discovered only in comparatively recent years. The first two of these have been critically edited in the volumes of *Epigraphia Indica.* According to these records, Mādhava I was succeeded on the throne by his son Vikramēndravarman I, then by Indrabhaṭṭārakavarman and Vikramēndravarman II. The last mentioned record takes the line still further and mentions the names of Vikramēndra, Govindavarman, and Madhavavarman II. Practically nothing is known of the first two sovereigns—Madhava I and Vikramēndravarman I. The Rāmatīrtham plates [2] help us to know that Indrabhaṭṭārakavarman must have ruled at least for a period of thirty-seven years as these plates were recorded in that year. This document consists of three copper-plates from Rāmatīrtham written in Sanskrit prose, and record the fact that Indravarman granted to a certain Brahman the village of Peruvāḍaka in Plaki-Rāshṭra (l. 6). The record also mentions that Mādhavavarman performed eleven horse-sacrifices, and hundreds of other sacrifices. Then after mentioning that Vikramēndra was an ornament of both the families, the Vākātakas and the Vishṇukuṇḍins, the record states the important fact that Indravarman encountered 'in hundred-thousands of battles numerous four-tusked elephants' (l. 5) a probable allusion to the fact that this king spent the major part of his reign in fighting with his enemies.[3]

The last of the Vishṇukuṇḍins, known as Mādhava II, is

[1] *Ep. Ind.*, vol. iv, p. 193 ff. [2] *Ibid.*

[3] According to Prof. Jouveau-Dubreuil there was a coalition of kings who attacked this sovereign which probably included Harisēṇa, the Vākātaka. Cf. *Ancient History of Deccan*, p. 91.

credited with the achievement of having crossed the Godavari evidently with a view to extend his dominions. Unfortunately the Western Chāḷukyas under Pulakēsin had grown powerful in this reign, and the advance of the Vishṇukuṇḍin power was not only stopped but their dominion appears to have been annexed to that of the Chāḷukyas.

According to M. Jouveau-Dubreuil the rock-cut monuments of Undavalli, Sittanagaram, Bezwada, and Mogulrazapuram were the work of the Vishṇukuṇḍins.[1] There is, however, considerable difference of opinion on this matter.

Before concluding the account of the Vishṇukuṇḍins, their relationship with the Pallava dynasty may be alluded to. At present this theory of the Pallava-Vishṇukuṇḍin relationship rests almost entirely on the mere resemblance of names of the two dynasties and is open to suspicion. Dr. Jouveau-Dubreuil noticing for the first time the resemblance of the names of the Vishṇukuṇḍin king Vikramēndra and Mahēndravikrama, the Pallava king, was led to postulate an unrecorded marriage relation between the daughter of Vikramēndra I and Simhavishṇuvarman whose son through this Vishṇukuṇḍin alliance was named according to the usual Hindu custom after the name of the grandfather on the mother's side as Mahēndravikrama.[2] According to the same authority the rock-cut temples excavated by Mahēndravarman I, in the various parts of the Tamil country, coupled with the mention of the name of the king Mahēndravikrama in the Trichinopoly cave inscription lend considerable support to this relationship of Vishṇukuṇḍins and the Pallavas. But at present this theory rests purely on the resemblance of names and is unsupported by any piece of positive evidence, literary or other, discovered so far. In none of the published inscriptions is it so much as

[1] *Pallavas*, p. 33.

[2] This is far too fanciful to build such a theory on. Mahēndravikrama means possessed of the valour of Mahēndra. Vikramēndra means an Indra in valour. They may amount to the same in point of sense ultimately; but they are different names and differently formed. The two terms are not without substantial difference of meaning to the Sanskritist. *Ed.*

alluded to that Simhavishṇu, the father of Mahēndravarman and the founder of the line of the great Pallavas of Kāñchi, entered into a matrimonial alliance with the Vishṇukuṇḍins; nor is the mere resemblance of the names[1] alone sufficient for postulating such a relationship as this. Nor is the resemblance between Vikramēndra and Mahēndravikrama quite so close. Finally there is no clear evidence that the style of Mahēndravarman cave temples were borrowed from Vishṇukuṇḍin examples on the banks of the Krishna. The origin of the Uṇḍavalli caves and the actual kings who excavated them cannot be considered as finally settled, and not until this is done is it possible to assert that the art of Mahēndravarman was derived from it. Mr. Sewell thought that these caves were the work of the Chāḷukyas.[2] Mr. Krishna Sastriyar was struck with their resemblance with the caves of Orissa and would take them to the Andhra period.[3] The genealogy of the Vishṇukuṇḍins so far known may be represented as follows:—

Combined genealogy obtained from the Rāmatīrtham Chikkula and Pulimboru grants:

Circa 475.

Mādhavavarman I

|

Vikramēndravarman I

|

Indrabhaṭṭārakavarman

|

Vikramēndravarman II
Vikramahēndra

|

Govindavarman

|

Mādhavavarman II

[1] The similarity does not take us far. They are hardly names but mere descriptive titles. See note on previous page. *Ed.*

[2] *List of Ant.*, vol. i, p. 77.

[3] *Ep. Rep., Madras for 1909*, part ii, p. 75.

CHAPTER VI

THE PALLAVA ASCENDENCY—'THE DYNASTY OF SIMHAVISHṆU,' A.D. 575–900

INTRODUCTORY

FROM the beginning of the reign of Simhavishṇu, also known as Simhavishṇupottarayan and Avanisimha, about the last quarter of the sixth century, a new epoch begins in the history of the Pallava power. From this period onward the Pallava authority begins to penetrate much farther into the Tamil country than before. Again during this period flourished the greatest of the Śaiva and Vaishṇava saints, the majority of the Āḻvārs and the Nāyanmārs who by their memorable religious propagandic work handed down in their hymns, were destined to revolutionize South Indian religious thought and outlook. In another respect also, this period of Pallava history is of special importance in South Indian history. It was during this period that a beginning is believed to have been made in the Tamil land to build temples and other monuments in stone instead of in perishable material such as wood and brick. This important change in the building material was destined in the course of a few centuries to cover the whole of the Southern India with a network of temples dedicated to Śiva, Vishṇu and Brahma. Above all, the active spread of Sanskrit culture and learning in the Tamil country was systematically and sedulously encouraged by the Pallava kings of this period, and recent research seems to support the view that some of the greatest poets and rhetoricians including Bhāravi and Daṇḍin the authors of *Kirātārjunīya* and *Kāvyādarśa*, flourished in this age at the Pallava court at Kañchīpuram.

Sources of Information for this Period.—For the earlier we had to depend almost wholly on copper-plate charters. But during this period (A.D. 575 to 900) inscriptions on stone appear to have become very popular in the Tamil country. We have therefore in addition to copper-plate grants large numbers of these stone inscriptions scattered throughout the Pallava dominions. Though some of these have been critically edited by Messrs. Hultzsch, Venkayya and others, the larger part of these still remain unedited and even unpublished. Of the stone inscriptions so far discovered nearly a hundred records are connected with the members of the Simhavishṇu dynasty and bear the regnal years of these kings. They have for their object the registering of gifts of gold or land for temple services, or endowments for religious and secular learning by the kings, or other persons of distinction. These inscriptions which are for the most part very short, unlike the copper-plate records, do not furnish a genealogy. They mention usually the year of the ruling king when the inscription was put up and the gifts made. They consequently furnish little information either as regards the ancestry of the ruling sovereign or of any of his political achievements. But they give details as regards how the various gifts should be appropriated and furnish valuable glimpses into the social, economic and administrative arrangements of the times.

Apart from the inscriptions and copper-plate records dated directly in the years of the Pallava kings and discovered in the various parts of the Pallava kingdom, we have also records from the other contemporary dynasties such as those of Western Chāḷukyas, the early Pāṇḍyas, the Rāshṭrakūṭas, the Gangas, Kadambas, the Bāṇas and the Muttaraiyans. The records of this period also mention the Pallavas coming into contact with the Maḷavas, Kaḷabhras, Chōḷas, Kēraḷas, Sinhaḷas, Tuḷus and the Konkaṇas; but we do not know much about the political condition of these people during this period.

Many of the inscriptions of the Pallava kings appear in temples and other monuments that they constructed during this age at Kāñchīpuram, and other places. The earliest of these are found in the cave-temples of the South Arcot, Trichinopoly and Chingleput Districts, and are dated in the reign of Mahēndravarman I. The others are found in the structural temples at the Seven Pagodas and at Kāñchīpuram, such as the Kailāsanātha temple. The rest are distributed in various villages.

Literature.—We turn from the inscriptions and monuments to the evidence furnished by literature, both religious and secular. The bulk of the religious literature embodied in the *Tēvāram* of Appar, Sambandar, and Sundarar and the Vaishṇava *Nālāyiraprabandha* belong to this period as also the Sanskrit works *Mattavilāsa* and perhaps *Kiratārjuniya*, etc. These, however, do not compare favourably with the inscriptional records as historical documents. For one thing the hymns of the saints hardly mention contemporary political or other events with exceptions such as those in the poems of Tirumaṇgai-Āḷvār. In the next place there is no secular work in Ṭamil belonging to this period with the exception of *Nandikkalambakam*.

Sanskrit: *Mattavilāsa-Prahasana*

The recently-discovered Sanskrit work entitled *Mattavilāsa-Prahasana*, though mainly devoted to the description of the drunken revelry of a Kāpālikā, incidentally throws much light upon the contemporary religious atmosphere in the city of Kāñchīpuram. Moreover the work having been composed by one of the Pallava kings Mahēndravikrama, has a special interest to the student of Pallava history. Of greater importance, as throwing light on the encouragement of Sanskrit learning under the Pallava kings of this period may be mentioned the recent discovery of Daṇḍin's *Avantisundarikathāsāra* by the officers of the Madras Oriental MSS. Library.

Avantisundari-kathāsāra

This work mentions the Chāḷukya Vishṇuvardhana and the Western Ganga Durvinīta as having been contemporaries of Simhavishṇu, and thus establishes a valuable synchronism in South Indian history hitherto unknown. By mentioning Bhāravi and Daṇḍin as living in the Pallava court, it puts beyond all doubt that Kānchīpuram the capital of the Pallavas was during this age a very important centre in the south for Sanskrit learning and culture. This is independently corroborated by the inscriptional evidence furnished by the Sanskrit charters.

Among Tamil works of the later Pallava period we may mention Perundēvanāṉ's *Bhāratavenbā* believed to be composed in the ninth century. It is believed originally to have consisted of 12,000 stanzas though only about 800 so far have come down to us. The author of this work is supposed to have lived during the reign of Nandivarman III, the victor in the battle at Teḷḷāṟu and is also taken to be the one who edited the classical anthologies. In the invocatory verses prefixed to the *Udyōga-Parva* of the *Bhāratavenbā* the author mentions the victory of this king at Teḷḷāṟu, and we may therefore infer that he was a contemporary of this king and composed his *Bhāratavenbā* in the reign of Nandivarman III. As to his having edited the classical anthologies the identification presents great difficulties.

The *Bhārata-venbā* of Perundēvanār

The only Tamil historical piece, as distinguished from religious works of which as we said, there is a large quantity that has come down to us from Pallava times, is the poetical work entitled *Nandikkalambakam*, which in a hundred and ten stanzas commemorates the martial exploits of a certain Pallava king-Nandi, probably Nandivarman III. This king, as we shall see, lived in the second quarter of the ninth century. The meagreness of purely Tamil literary enterprise, if we except the *Tēvāram* and Vaishṇava *Prabandham*, probably indicate that the Pallava kings were essentially patrons of Sanskrit learning and Brahmaṇic culture. The bulk of Tamil literature known as the Śangam works preceded, as we stated above, the advent of the Pallava kings of Kāñchīpuram.

Nandikkalambakam

Along with these we have the impressions of the Chinese pilgrim and Master of Law—Hiuen-Tsang—regarding the city of Kāñchī about the year A.D. 640. His notes furnish a description of contemporary religious and secular life. We have already noticed the historical value of *Mahāvaṁsa* for this period of Pallava history.

Chinese testimony—Hiuen-Tsang

The Great Pallavas, *Simhavishṇu Dynasty. Simhavishṇu-*

varman, A.D. 575 to 600.—The Kaśakkuḍi plates[1] taken along with the Kūram,[2] and the Vēlūrpāḷayam[3] give us the following genealogy of the Pallavas of this period :—

- Nandivarman
  - Simhavishṇu
    - Mahēndravarman I
      - Narasimhavarman I
        - Mahēndravarman II
        - Paramēśvaravarman I
          - Narasimhavarman II
            - Paramēśvaravarman II
            - Mahēndravarman III
  - Bhīmavarman
    - Buddhavarman
      - Ādityavarman
        - Govindavarman
          - Hiraṇyavarman
            - Nandivarman II
              - Dantivarman
                - Nandivarman III
                  - Nripatungavarman
                    - Aparājita

The genealogy for this period is full, and there is not the uncertainty of the early Pallava history either about the reigns of this period, or about the order in which the kings succeeded one another as most of the documents give the above order without substantial change. It would be noticed that from the days of Simhavishṇu in the third quarter of the sixth century for a period of 125 years the throne remained in the hands of the direct successors of this king. We do not know what position the members of the collateral line, of whom the Kaśakkuḍi plates mention Bhīmavarman, Buddhavarman, Ādityavarman, Govindavarman and Hiraṇya, occupied. They evidently occupied a subordinate position as the

[1] *S.I.I.*, vol. ii, part 3, pp. 346–53.
[2] *Ibid.*, vol. i, p. 152.
[3] *Ibid.*, vol. ii, part 5, p. 508 ff.

viceroys under these kings. Not until we come to the days of Paramēśvara II in the beginning of the eighth century do we find that a descendent of Bhīma, the younger brother of Simhavishṇu, effecting a change of dynasty by succeeding to the Pallava throne.

No inscription or copper-plate ascribable to this king Simhavishṇu has yet been discovered. But his name is perpetuated in the historical introduction to the work already referred to wherein the author says that Bhāravi, one of his predecessors, went to his court by invitation. In the *Mattavilāsa-Prahasana*, written by his son Mahēndravarman I, he is referred to in the prologue in terms of praise.[1]

As regards his achievements we read in verse 10 of the Vēlūrpāḷayam grant that his prowess was widely known on earth, that he quickly seized the country of the Cholas, embellished by the daughter of Kavēra, whose ornaments are the forests of paddy-fields, and where are found brilliant groves of areca.[2] From this we may infer that this king who is called Avanisimha for the first time extended the Pallava territory as far as the delta of the Kaveri. In doing so he had to encounter the individual and united opposition of the southern powers who are referred in the Kaśākkuḍi plates,[3] among the vanquished: the Kaḷabhra, Māḷava, Chola, Pāṇḍya and the Simhala proud of the strength of their arms.

That this conquest of the Tamil regions was no mere formal praise drawn from the imagination of the writer of the document is seen in the absence of reference to any similar achievement in the records of his son Mahēndravarman I, and suggest

[1] पल्लवकुलधरणिमण्डलकुलपर्वतस्य सर्वनयविजितसमस्तसामन्तमण्डलस्य आखण्डलसमपराक्रमश्रियः श्रीमहिमानुरूपदानविभूति परिभूत राजराजस्य श्रीसिंहविष्णुवर्मणः पुत्रः शत्रु षड्वर्गविग्रहपरः परहित-परतन्त्रतया महाभूत सधर्मा महाराजो: श्रीमहेन्द्र विक्रमवर्मा नाम। ९

Mattavilāsa, Sthāpanā, p. 3.

[2] *S. I. I.*, vol. ii, part 5, p. 510. [3] *Ibid.*

clearly that he must have inherited the region around the Kaveri as part of the ancestral dominions which his father had left him. Of the earlier Pallava kings we know of only one king Buddhavarman who is said to have encountered the Cholas, and who is described in the Vēlūrpāḷayam plates as being the submarine fire to the ocean-like army of the Cholas. Whether he conquered the region watered by the Kaveri is, however, not known. We may, therefore, take it that the region was for the first time brought under the Pallavas under Simhavishṇu.

Our knowledge of the Cholas, the Pāṇḍyas, the Kaḷabhras and the Māḷavas [1] whom Simhavishṇu is said to have defeated is very limited, in the present state of our knowledge.

[1] We do not know who these Māḷavas were and whether they are identical with the Māḷavas of the north. They are probably to be associated with the people of Maḷanādu who figure in early Tamil literature.

As regards the Kaḷabhras we find that their history is equally obscure. These people figure also among the kings conquered by the Chāḷukya king Vikramāditya and Vinayāditya. They seem to have invaded the Pāṇḍyan capital and having routed the ruling king established their rule. According to the Vēlvikuḍi plates the Adhirāja was ousted from Power and the country occupied by the Kaḷabhras. (*Tiruviḷaiyādal-Purāṇam*). Mr. Venkayya relying on the evidence of *Periyapurāṇam* where the Karṇāṭakas are said to have invaded and occupied Madura, proposed to identify the Kaḷabhras with the Karṇāṭakas (*Ep. Rep. for 1908*, paras 25–26). Mr. T. A. Gopinatha Rao deriving the word Kaḷabhra from Kaḷavara tries to identify the Kaḷabhras with the Muttaraiyar mentioned in the Seṅ-talai Pillar inscription. (*Ep. Ind.*, 15).

Kaḷabhras cannot be Karṇāṭakas obviously, as the Chāḷukyas themselves must have ruled over Karṇāṭaka and therefore over the Karṇāṭakas. Kaḷabhras must, therefore, be people different from the groups known to us otherwise. There was a people occupying the Pallava territory—the northern part in particular—whose name has hitherto been read as Kaḷvar in the Śangam works. They had a chief by name Pulli with headquarters at Vēngaḍam (Tirupati). It is these people that are called Kaḷabhras in a Sanskritized form. Kaḷvar later Kaḷḷar in Tamil are called *Kaḷamāḷ* in Sanskrit. This seems to indicate a form Kaḷavar in Tamil which would become Kaḷabharu in Kannaḍa, Sanskritized into Kaḷabhra. I am assured by Pandit Mahamahopadyaya Svāminātha Aiyar that the reading of the MSS. is Kaḷavar and not Kaḷvar. It is the irruption of these people into the south through the advance of the Pallava dynasty that brought about a great revolution in the Tamil country. The Maḷavas are a similar ethnic group with almost similar habits. They also occupied the territory on the northern and western border of the Tamil land. Their chiefs took the Tamil title Maḷavaraiyan which has become Maḷavarāyan which is still a common name in the Tamil country of Kaḷḷar families.

Simhavishṇu's religious leanings were towards Vaishṇavism which his very name suggests. It should, however, be remembered that the Pallava kings of Kāñchīpuram were some of them devoted to Śiva and some to Vishṇu as the names of the Pallava kings indicate. Thus for instance, while there are names like Vishṇugōpa and Kumāravishṇu which suggest that the kings who bore such names were devoted to Vishṇu, it is a fact that their sons and grandsons bear names like Skandavarman and Paramēśvaravarman which indicate their devotion to Śiva while names like Buddhavarman possibly indicate the Buddhistic leanings of this Pallava sovereign. But in the case of Simhavishṇu the Udayēndiram plates [1] of Nandivarman II clearly call him *Bhaktyārādita-Vishṇu-Simha-Vishṇu* in terms which leave no possibility of escape from regarding him as a Vaishṇava.[2] None of the temples that this sovereign might have constructed for Hindu gods has been discovered as yet, though Prof. Jouveau-Dubreuil puts forward the suggestion that the Śiyyamangalam cave temple which contains an inscription of Avanibhājana, identified by Hultzsch with Mahēndravarman I, might have been excavated by Simhavishṇu. 'It may not be impossible,' says he, 'that the Śiyyamangalam temple which contains the images of the lion and the inscription of King Avanibhājana belongs to the days of king Simhavishṇu (called Avanisimha in the Kaśākkuḍi plates). It is not impossible, in fact, that the *birudas* such as *Śatrumalla*, *Lalitānkura*, *Avanibhājana* were borne also by Mahēndra and by his father Simhavishṇu.' [3]

It is a remarkable fact that no inscription dated in the reign of this sovereign has come down to us although from the later copper-plates and stone inscriptions as well as the recently discovered manuscript *Avantisundarikathāsāra* we may be sure that Simhavishṇu actually ruled as a king for a

The Tamil Maḻavar changes into Māḻavas by falseanalogy in Sanskrit, Maḻavaraiyan becoming Māḻavarāyan even in Tamil at a later period. *Ed.*

[1] *S.I.I.*, vol. ii, p. 74, ll. 11-12.

[2] *Early History of Vaishṇavism in South India*, p. 95.

[3] *Pall. Ant.*, vol. i, p. 40.

period of time. His name moreover figures in the two records which indicate that his kingdom comprised at least the regions where these records are found. Maṇali, a village near Tiruvoṛṛiyūr (not far from Madras), was called in ancient times Simhavishṇu-Chaturvēdimangalam. Similarly, No. 265 of 1907 calls Kanjanūr in Kumbhakonam Taluk, Simhavishṇu-Chaturvēdimangalam which shows that it must have been so named during the reign of this king. The region from Maṇali to Kanjanūr where this sovereign should have reigned probably constituted the kingdom. It is possible that the discovery of fresh inscriptions will throw new light on the matter.

A Relief of Siṃhavishṇu.—One of the most interesting discoveries of the Epigraphy Department in recent years has been the identification of royal sculptures at the Ādivarāha-svāmi temple at Mahābalipuram.[1] These reliefs relate to two kings cut in bas-relief in the Varāha cave in the village of Mahābalipuram and were noticed as early as 1913,[2] by Mr. Krishna Sastri in his report although no identification had been then attempted by him. This was due to the failure to notice the inscriptional label that is put over the bas-reliefs which have now been copied and read. From these it is now clear that the representations are those of Simhavishṇupōtaraya and Mahēndravarman I. These kings are here represented with their queens in an attitude of adoration. The Archæological Superintendent's Report for 1922–23 says on page 94, 'No. 661 of 1922, is engraved on the portal of the north niche in the Varāha cave, and consists of the name Śrī Simmaviṇṇu-Potādhirājan in the Pallava-Grantha characters. The niche below this inscription contains the seated figure of a king with a high crown (*kiriṭa*), and chest and ear ornaments flanked

[1] These reliefs and the inscriptions at the Ādivarāha temple have been studied by Rao Bahadur H. Krishna Sastri in a recent *Memoir* issued by the Archæological Survey of India.

[2] The figures in the interior of this temple are first mentioned in one of the Mackenzie MSS. accounts and in *The Cave Temples of India* by Fergusson and Burgess (1890) although no identification is attempted.

on either side by a standing female figure representing, by their crowns, his queens . . . No. 662 of 1922 cut on the top of the corresponding niche on the south side of the main cave, and opposite to the image of Simhavishṇu referred to above, consists only of the name Śrī-Mahēndra-potādhirāja. The niche contains the standing image of a king distinguished by his crown and ornaments. His half-raised hand points towards the shrine of the God evidently—whither he appears to be leading the nearer queen by her right hand. The above two inscriptions serve as labels to show whom the images represent. . . .'

One explanation of the presence of the image of Simhavishṇuvarman in the Ādhivarāha temple at Mahābalipuram may be that the monolith was excavated by him. If this is so it shows that some of the monuments of the Seven-Pagodas are as old as the days of Simhavishṇu. This would throw new light on the real age of the monuments of the Seven-Pagodas.[1]

Mahēndravarman I. A.D. 600 to 630.—Mahēndravarman, known also as Mahēndravikrama, and by surnames such as Mattavilāsa, Guṇabhara, etc., came to the throne after Simhavishṇu about the beginning of the seventh century. His reign is memorable in many respects. In the first place he is believed to have given for the first time a real start to excavating temples out of solid stone. In the second place his reign synchronized with the religious activity of Appar, and the literary efforts of Bhāravi in the field of Sanskrit letters. From a purely administrative point of view his government provided the quiet atmosphere for the peaceful pursuit of avocations to his subjects hitherto tormented by wars. From a military point of view his rule witnessed the beginnings of the Pallava-Chāḷukya and Pallava-Pāṇḍya conflicts which were destined to be continued by his successors for over a century and a half. Considerable impetus was given to productions in the fields of drama, music, painting and other arts.

[1] Hultzsch *Insc. of Seven-Pagodas*, *Ep. Ind.*, vol. x, p. 1,

[Page 88.

MAHENDRAVARMAN AND HIS QUEENS

The most powerful contemporary of Mahēndravarman I and his son Narasimhavarman I was Pulakēśin II. The actual causes of the conflict between the Chāḷukyas and the Pallava kings lie buried in obscurity. Among the wild guesses made in this direction the most ingenious is that of Mr. Rice who considers that their (Chāḷukya) name bears a suggestive resemblance to Seleukia, and that they should be probably associated with Seleucidae[1] in which case the Pallava-Chāḷukya conflict would only be a natural sequel to their original warfare on the banks of the Tigris.

It was about the beginning of the seventh century that Pulakēśin II made himself Master of Vengi which till then was under the Pallavas, and established his brother Kubja-Vishṇuvardhana as his viceroy. His descendants afterwards became independent making him founder of the Eastern Chāḷukya dynasty. It was in the course of his southern wars that Pulakēśin came into conflict with the Pallavas at Kāñchīpuram. The Aihole inscription[2] which enumerates his exploits says of his encounter with the Pallavas that 'he caused the splendour of the Lord of the Pallavas who had opposed the rise of his power to be obscured by the dust of his army and to vanish behind the walls of Kāñchīpuram.' This important reference would suggest a defeat and retreat on the part of Mahēndravarman I before his Chāḷukyan adversary, but we learn however from the Kaśākkuḍi plates[3] that Mahēndravarman I gained a victory at Puḷḷalūr which has been identified by Dr. Hultzsch with Puḷḷalūr (Polilore in early British period of Indian history and now Paḷḷūr) in the Conjeevaram taluk in the Chingleput District. This was the scene of two other battles between the English and the French in the British period. It is not stated who the enemies of the Pallavas in this victory were. But it is extremely likely that they were no other than the Chāḷukyas who in a later record described the Pallavas as their 'natural enemies.'

[1] *Mys. Gaz.*, vol. i; also *Mys. and Coorg from Ins.*, p. 62.
[2] *Ep. Ind.*, vol. vi, p. 11. [3] *S.I.I.*, vol. ii, part, 3, p. 343.

Religion.—According to tradition Mahēndravarman I was originally a Jain and was given to persecuting the votaries of other religious denominations. In the *Periyapurāṇam* account his conversion to Śaivism was brought about by Appar otherwise known as Tirunāvukkaraśu. Appar was one of those who is believed to have been thus persecuted, but his wonderfully miraculous powers, especially the manner in which he escaped the tortures to which he was subjected by the Jains, moved the Pallava king to embrace the Śaivism of Appar.

This event which may have taken place in the middle of his reign marks an important epoch in the history of Śaivism. There is probably an allusion to this event in the king's life in the Trichinopoly rock inscription [1] which refers to him as having turned back from hostile conduct to the worship of the *linga* (emblem of Śiva). We have at present no means of ascertaining the exact circumstances connected with this event. It happened presumably sufficiently early in his reign as the number of Śiva rock-cut temples excavated by him are numerous and must have taken many years to come into existence. All these cave-temples as they are styled have a peculiarity in shape and have been discovered at Vallam (Chingleput), Mahēndravāḍi (North Arcot District), Daḷavānūr (South Arcot District), Śiyyamangalam and Pallāvaram. He probably originated the habit of inscribing the surnames of the reigning monarchs in the pillars and walls of the various temples that he built. Among the surnames that this king assumed may be mentioned those of Guṇabhara, Purushōttama, Satyasanda, Avanibhājana, Sankīrnajāti, Vichitrachitta, Narēndra, *Cheṭṭhakāri*, Aluptakāma, Kalahapriyaḥ, Lalitānkura, Śatrumalla, etc. Of these the *biruda* Cheṭṭhakāri, if it is really an equivalent with Chaitya-kāri, would indicate the temple-building propensities of the king. This probably has reference to the rock-cut temples of Mahēndravarman I, all over the Tamil country. The Telugu *birudas* such as

[1] *S.I.I.*, vol. i, No. 33, p. 29.

Nilvilonayambu, Pasarambu, Ventulavittu, etc., occurring in these inscriptions have been taken to indicate the Telugu origin of Mahēndravarman's style. It must not be imagined that this sovereign's zeal for Śaivism blunted his sympathy for other religions, a feature of his character in pre-Śaiva days. Though he may have professed his devotion to Śiva he caused to be cut out in rock a Vishṇu temple called *Mahēndravishṇugṛha* [1] on the banks of Mahēndra Taṭāka in Mahēndravāḍi. This inscription records in Pallava-Grantha that Guṇabhara caused to be cut out of rock the temple of *Mahēndravishṇugṛha* in Mahēndrapura. This place has been identified by Dr. Hultzsch with Mahēndravāḍi, near Arkonam. This catholicity was due to the general tendency of the age when Vishṇu and Śiva had not begun to have their separate followers and were placed in the same temple without distinction as we find in the monuments of the Pallavas at the Seven-Pagodas and elsewhere. The Maṇḍagappaṭṭu inscription of this king for instance records the fact King Vichitrachitta caused to be constructed a temple to Brahma, Īśvara and Vishṇu without the use bricks, timber, metal and mortar. In other words it was a monolithic rock-temple that was excavated.[2]

The Mahēndra Style.—The principles of the style of architecture adopted and popularized by Mahēndravarman I have been studied in full by Prof. Jouveau-Dubreuil in his *Pallava Antiquities* and by Mr. A. H. Longhurst of the Archæological Department. According to the former scholar the monuments of Mahēndravarman's period discovered hitherto are caves excavated in rocks. The pillars are formed of two cubical

[1] *Ep. Ind.*, vol iv, p. 152f.

[2] T. A. G. Rao. *Ibid.*, vol. xvii, p. 14. This short record is of importance inasmuch as it records that before the time of Vichitrachitta bricks, timber, metal and mortar were the common temple-building materials. This falsifies the notion that structural temples were non-existent before the seventh century A.D. in South India, a view based on the absence of the remains of any previous to this period. This statement in the Maṇḍagappaṭṭu inscription warrants the conclusion that such temples were in existence before.

parts separated by a prismatic part. . . . These caves are all of them situated in Toṇḍamaṇḍalam and Tamil land, and are distinguished by (1) Sanctuaries destitute of Śōmaskanda image, (2) Circular *lingams*, (3) Dvārapālas of a peculiar posture, (4) Double-arched Tiruvātchi (*prabhā toraṇas*), (5) Cubical pillars. All of them are, besides subterranean *maṇḍapas*. The Archæological Report for 1918–19, Section 26, says: 'A very characteristic feature about the temples in this style is the type of pillar found in them. These are about two feet square in section and seven feet in height. The upper and lower portions are cubical while the middle portion of shaft has the angles levelled off which makes the middle third octagonal in section. Sometimes the cubical portions are decorated with a conventional lotus flower design similar to the lotus medallions appearing on the stone rails of the Amarāvati stūpa. The capitals of the pillars are simple corbels or brackets supporting the architrave above. . . . Each pillar has a corresponding side pilaster.'

Pallava Painting.—A vestige of Pallava painting has also been discovered in recent times in the Pudukkotta State, at Śittannavāśal. The style of the rock-cut temple at Śittannavāśal is identical with that of Māmanḍūr cave built by Mahēndravarman I. This cave temple seems to have been at one time fully painted but the painting on the upper part of the edifice is alone visible now, namely, the painting on the ceiling, the capitals and the upper parts of the pillars. 'The principal subject that is preserved is a grand fresco which adorns the whole extent of the ceiling and the verandah. This fresco represents a tank covered with lotuses. In the midst of the flowers are found fishes, geese, buffaloes, elephants and three men who surely are Jains holding lotuses in their hands. Their pose, their colouring and the sweetness of their countenance are indeed charming. . . . Therefore the decoration of the capitals of the pillars in the facade is well preserved. It consists of lotuses whose blooming stems intertwine with elegance. The two pillars in the passage are adorned with the figures of dancing girls.'[1] It is presumable, as Jouveau-Dubreuil suggests that the art of dancing was encouraged by Mahēndravarman I who probably wrote a treatise on the subject. The Māmaṇḍūr inscription[2] of this king alludes to the work *Dakshinachitra* probably a treatise on painting and other works on music composed by him.

The Musical Inscription at Pudukkotta.—To this period is also ascribed the musical inscription at Kuḍumiyāmalai[3] in the State of Pudukkotta. The *Epigraphy Report for 1906* says that the inscription was engraved at the instance of an unnamed king who was a disciple of a certain Rudrāchārya who composed the *svaras* for the benefit of the pupils. Relying on the panegyric given in the Māmaṇḍūr record, and the reference to Vālmīki of the *svaras* and *varṇas* of music therein detailed, and to the *Mattavilāsa-Prahasana*, as also the close resemblance between the Kuḍumiyāmalai inscription and the Mahēndravarman inscription at Trichinopoly, scholars[4] have concluded that Mahēndravarman I was an accomplished musician and that the Kuḍumiyāmalai musical inscription was engraved at his order.

Mahēndravarman I as an author.—In the previous paragraphs it was mentioned that the Pallava court in the days of Simhavishṇu was a centre of Sanskrit culture. The occurrence of the name of the work[5] *Mattavilāsa-Prahasana* in the Māmaṇḍūr inscription indicates that there was in existence at the time, a work bearing that name. No one knew of this work until the Oriental MSS. Department of the Travancore State discovered this work some years ago. It has now been published as one of the Travancore Sanskrit Series by

[1] This subject is treated by N. C. Mehta in his 'Studies in Indian Painting' where four of the fresco paintings of this temple have been reproduced. Mr. Mehta, however, doubts that the temple is a Jain one. *Studies in Indian Painting*, pp. 11-12.

[2] *Q.J.M.S.*, vol. xiii, p. 572.

[3] No. 354 of 1904.

[4] G. Jouveau-Dubreuil, *Pallavas*, p. 23.

[5] The work was probably modelled on another early *Prahasana Bhagavadajjukam* recently published and which is attributed to Bodhayana. The name of this prahasana also occurs in the Māmaṇḍūr inscription of Mahēndravarman I in the line preceding the one where *Mattavilāsa* is mentioned. (See *I.H.Q.*, vol. i, p. 263, Note 3.)

Mahamahopadyaya Pandit T. Ganapati Sastri. This work is of great value in enabling us to know the nature of religious and secular life led by people during the days of Mahēndravarman I, in the first quarter of the seventh century.

The Contents of this Work.—The work describes the drunken revelry of a Kāpālika with a female-companion, his falling out with a hypocritical Śākyabikhshu, believing him to have stolen his *Kapāla* (alms-bowl) which had been carried away by a dog, his having recourse to a degenerate Pāśupata for the settlement of the dispute and finally the recovery of the *Kapāla* from a mad man. We have already seen that the titles *Mattavilāsa*, *Avanibhājana*, *Śatrumalla* and *Guṇabhara* were borne by Mahēndravarman I and occur in various inscriptions. Of these the title Śatrumalla is mentioned in the concluding lines of the play; and that of Avanibhājana is referred to in the fourth *pāda* of the *mangaḷa śloka* . . . and Guṇabhara and Mattavilāsa are also found in the words of *Naṭī* in the *sthāpana.* The virtues of the king are eulogized in the opening portion of this work.[1]

Light thrown on Contemporary Life by the Work.—This little play is full of interest to the student of religious history as it affords valuable material regarding the extinct Kāpālika faith, and the vices of the Śākyabikshus and the views regarding the teachings of the Buddha held by the followers of other religions, such as the Kāpālikas. 'From the *Mattavilāsa-Prahasana* it becomes clear that to a Kāpālika, the Kapāla is as essential as is a sacred thread to a Brahmaṇa. If he loses it he should provide himself with another in a stated time. He should cover his body with ashes and make himself hideous, and drink liquor from skull of a human being. . . . One of his articles of

[1] प्रज्ञादानदयानुभावधृतयः कान्तिः कलाकौशलं
सत्यं शौर्यसमायता विनय इत्येवम्प्रकारा गुणाः ।
अप्राप्तस्थितयः समेत्य शरणं याता यमेकं कलौ
कल्पान्ते जगदादिमादिपुरुषं सर्गप्रभेदा इव ॥

Mattavilāsa, p. 3. T. Sans. Ser., No. LV.

faith is that the effect always resembles, to a certain extent, the cause; therefore, from the practice of austerities in this life one cannot obtain bliss in another life since austerities and bliss are of opposite nature. The Kāpālikas carried in addition to the Kapāla, a cow's horn both for blowing during their worship and drinking from. The people of this faith associated freely with women-Kāpālikas. . . . The opinions held by the particular Kāpālika, Bhaṭya-Soma of our play, regarding the Śākyabhikshus are that the Śākyabhikshus indulged freely in animal food and fattened themselves pecuniarily by being the managers of several *vihāras*, and led a comfortable life, against all the rules of their order: they covered themselves only to conceal their foibles. Their teacher Buddha, did nothing more than steal his doctrines from the *Vēdānta* and the *Mahābhārata* of the Brahmans, and compiled therefrom his doctrines.'[1] The mention of Buddhas, Bikshus, Kāpālikas and Pāśupatas, in his burlesque by Mahēndravarman I as among the inhabitants of Kāñchīpuram bear out the surmise that Buddhism flourished there till at least the seventh century A.D., and that the statement of Hiuen-Tsang regarding the existence in Kāñchīpura of a large number of *vihāras*[2] finds support in this work of Mahēndravarman.

The reign of Mahēndravarman I synchronized with the period of decay of Buddhist and Jain religions at Kāñchīpuram and the Tamil land. The Śaiva saints Appar, and Tirugñāna-Sambandar were actually engaged in propagating the Śaiva faith. According to the testimony of these saints, as represented in their references to the Śākyas, we have to infer that the Buddhists and Jains of this period were in a degenerate position then. They are mentioned in the same strain also in several verses in the Vaishṇava work *Nālāyiraprabhandam.*[3]

[1] *M.C.C. Mag.*, vol. 34, p. 413.

[2] Beal's *Rec.*, vol. ii, p. 229.

[3] புலையறமாகிநின்ற புத்தொடுசமணமெல்லாம்
கலையறக்கற்றமாந்தர் காண்பரோ, கேட்பரோதாம். *Tirumālai*, v. 7.

வெள்ளியார் போதியார் என்றிவர் ஓதுகின்ற கள்ளநூல். *P. T.* vol. ix, p. 7, *v.* 8.

அறியார்சமணரயர்த்தார் பவுத்தர்
சிறியார் சிவப்பட்டார். *Nān. Tiru*, *v.* 6.

The reign of Mahēndravarman I is believed to have been the period of the Vaishṇava saint Tirumaliśai and therefore also that of the first three Āḻvārs by certain scholars. Mr. M. Srinivasa Aiyangar[1] in his *Tamil Studies* expresses the view that the Guṇabhara mentioned in the *Nānmugan-Tiruvandādi* is a reference to Mahēndravarman I, and concludes, on this basis alone, that he was his contemporary. But a careful examination of the context and meaning of this stanza[2] shows that the Guṇabhara of the Āḻvār cannot be interpreted as alluding to any mortal man.

[1] *Tamil Studies*, pp. 305-6.

[2] காப்பு மறந்தறியேன் கண்ணனே யென்றிருப்பன்
ஆப்புஅங் கொழியவும் பல்லுயிர்க்கும்—ஆக்கை
கொடுத்தளித்த கோனே! குணபரனே! உன்னை
விடத்துணியார் மெய்த்தெளிந்தார்தாம். (St. 93, *Nān. Tiru.*)

[2] See also *Early Hist. of Vaishnavism in South India*, p. 54.

CHAPTER VII

NARASIMHAVARMAN I (MAHAMALLA) A.D. 630–660

NARASIMHAVARMAN I succeeded Mahēndravarman I on the Pallava throne about A.D. 630. He is called in some of his inscriptions, Vātāpi-Koṇḍa-Narasimhavarman and this alludes to his supreme achievement, namely, the capture and destruction of Vātāpi (Badami in the Bijapur District). He is one of the most remarkable sovereigns of the line of Simhavishṇu, and the Pallava empire must have been considerably enlarged during his reign. His reign is well-known for the following :—(1) Invasion and capture of Vātāpi ; (2) Invasion of Ceylon ; (3) The excavation works at Māmalla-puram ; (4) The visit of the Chinese pilgrim to Kāñchīpuram.

The Chāḷukya-Pallava Relations.—It has already been seen that in about the middle and closing years of his father, Pulakēsin II advanced as far as the city of Kāñchī, forcing 'the lord of the Pallavas to retreat behind the walls of Kāñchīpuram.'[1] The Kūram plates[2] belonging to the reign of Paramēśvara-varman I mention the important fact that Narasimhavarman I inflicted a crushing defeat on Puḷakēśin, in the battles of Pariyaḷa, Maṇimangala and Śūramāra. The exact locality corresponding to these places cannot, at this distance of time, be made out except in the case of Maṇimangala which may be safely identified with the modern village of Maṇimangalam, situated at a distance of only twenty miles from Kāñchī. This reference in the Kūram plates indicates another Chāḷukya invasion early in Narasimhavarman's reign on which occasion the Chāḷukya army would appear to have advanced very near the Pallava capital itself before it sustained the defeat mentioned in the record.

[1] *Ep. Ind.*, vol. vi, p. 11. [2] *S.I.I.*, vol. i, p. 152.

Raid on Vātāpi.—Shortly after the repulse of the Chāḷukya armies from the neighbourhood of Kāñchīpuram, Narasimhavarman I made serious preparations for a counter-invasion into the Chāḷukya territory. This expedition was entrusted to the command of Siṛu-Toṇḍa who was known otherwise as Paranjōti. That this aggressive expedition under the command of Śiṛu-Toṇḍa marched against the Chāḷukya capital, captured it and returned with great spoils to Kāñchi is learnt from the life of Paranjōti,[1] otherwise Śiṛu-Toṇḍar in the *Periyapurāṇam*. The Vēlūrpāḷayam plates refer to this exploit:—'From his son Mahēndra was born Narasimhavarman I famous like Upēndra (Vishṇu) who, defeating the host of his enemies took from them the pillar of victory standing in the centre of Vātāpi.'[2] This is also referred to in a mutilated inscription found at Vātāpi[3] and written in characters of this period, probably put up by Narasimha to commemorate his capture of the city. This record, although mutilated, contains the surname Mahāmalla, and the words *Kshitibhujām-agrēsara Pallava* and (Nara) *simha-vishṇu*. From these it is clear that Narasimhavarman I captured the city of Vātāpi; and probably set up a pillar of victory at this place recording this achievement. There can, therefore, be no doubt regarding the capture of the city by the Pallava king.

Ceylon Invasion.—The circumstances that led to the intervention of Narasimhavarman I in the affairs of Ceylon are gathered chiefly from the *Mahāvaṁśa*.[4] It appears from this account that Mānavamma, a Ceylon prince, having become an exile fled to India, and, arriving at the city of Kāñchīpuram, managed to enter service under Narasimhavarman I with a view to secure his aid and ultimately to gain the Ceylon throne.

[1] மன்னவர்க்குத் தண்டுபோய் வடபுலத்து வாதாவித்
தொன்னகரந் துகளாகத் துளைநெடுங்கை வரையுகைத்துப்
பன்மணியு நிதிக்குவையும் பகட்டினமும் பரித்தொகையும்
இன்னனவெண் ணிலகவர்ந்தே யிகலரசன் முன்கொணர்ந்தார்—

Per. Pur., Life of Paranjoti, *v.* 6.

[2] *S.I.I.*, vol. ii, p. 508, *verse* 11. [3] *Ind. Ant.*, vol. ix, p. 199.
[4] The *Mahāvaṁśa*, ch. 47 (Turnour's translation).

Here he is described as having constantly engaged himself in service of the king and proved his trustworthiness by many an act of bravery and loyalty. The *Mahāvaṁśa* mentions in great detail the various acts of Mānavamma, particularly his services to Narasimhavarman I in his wars against the Vallabha, the Chāḷukya king: how once king Vallabha came to make war against Narasimha and how the Pallava king with a view to test Manavamma left him at his capital city and proceeded to the battle-field alone, and how Manavamma's affection caused him to leave the safety of the fortified capital and join his king in the field of battle in victory, defeat, or death. Such action was bound to increase Narasimha's esteem for him, and it is therefore not surprising that when the Ceylon prince prepared to go back to his country Narasimhavarman I gave him a strong escort and an army with which he was able to secure the Ceylon throne. But this success did not last long. Soon after, his army deserted him and the Prince of Ceylon came back once more to seek the help of Narasimhavarman I. Again Narasimhavarman I gave him an army much bigger than before, and this time the Pallava king himself accompanied his troops as far as the harbour where his men went on board on their voyage to the shores of Ceylon. It is noteworthy that this naval expedition of Narasimhavarman I set sail from the ancient Pallava port, Mahābalipuram, which, according to contemporary account was a harbour at this time. It is worthy of note that Hiuen-Tsang[1] who stayed in the city for a considerable time (*circa* 642) recorded the fact that ships go to Ceylon from Kāñchi, and that it extended by twenty miles to the coast.[2] Tirumaṅgai Āḻvār also records that Mahābalipuram was a busy port in his hymns on this place and particularly notes that in its harbour ride at anchor 'vessels bent

[1] Beal, *Records*, vol. ii, p. 228.

[2] புலங்கொள் நிதிக்குவையோடு புழைக்கைமாகளிற்றினமும்
நலங்கொள் நவமணிக்குவையும் சுமந்தெங்கும் நான்றொசிந்து
கலங்களியங்கும் மல்லைக்கடன் மல்லைத்தலசயனம்
வலங்கொள் மனத்தாரவரை வலங்கொள் என்மடநெஞ்சே.

Peria Tirumoḻi, Kaḍanmallai Hymns, 6.

to the point of breaking laden as they are with wealth, big trunked elephants and nine gems in heaps.'

This second naval expedition was a complete success and must have made a profound impression on the contemporary powers of South India.[1] The Kaśākkuḍi plates which confirm the conquest of Ceylon justly compare this achievement of Narasimhavarman I with that of Rama's conquest of Lanka.[2] Prince Mānavamma was firmly placed on the throne, and not until Narasimhavarman I's death did trouble overtake him again.

Monuments of Narasimhavarman I. Improvement of Mahābalipuram.—Like his father, Narasimhavarman I was a lover of building temples all over his kingdom. Some of his earlier monuments such as the cave temples at Trichinopoly district and Pudukotta were excavated from out of rocks as those of Mahēndravarman I. The peculiar features of the monuments of Narasimhavarman have been described by A. H. Longhurst as follows:—'The cave temples are excavated in the face of the rock in the same manner as those belonging to the earlier period, but their facades are usually more ornamental and contain pillars of a different variety. On plan the interiors are much the same as those of the cave temples of the Mahēndra style, with similar small square shrine chambers cut in the back wall which are usually free from ornament within. The pillared-hall in front of the shrine often contains large panels cut in the side walls filled with sculptural figures in high relief. These are usually of great beauty and executed with

[1] 'It is certainly astonishing that in the inscriptions of the Pallavas and other Southern dynasties no reference whatever is made to the relations which in those days must have existed between Coromandel and the Far East. The explanation probably is that those relations, of which the accounts of the Chinese pilgrims have left us such a valuable record were of a perfectly peaceful nature. Suppose the powerful Pallava princes of Kāñchīpura had equipped armadas and carried their arms to the remote shares of Campā and Java, may we not assume that their conquests on the far side of the ocean would have been extolled in their *praçastis* with no less effusion than we find lavished on their victories over the Chalukyas?'—J. Ph. Vogel—*The Yupa Inscriptions of King Mulavarman.*

[2] *S.I.I.*, vol. ii, p. 343, *verse* 22.

remarkable skill. The interior too of the more ornamental cave temples is provided with cornice and plinth mouldings.

'The most striking feature about the Māmalla style is the curious shape of the pillars.[1] The square heavy pillars with corbel-capitals of the earlier period are replaced by pillars of a more elegant shape and better proportion. The base of the pillar is carved in the shape of a conventional lion sitting very erect and carrying the shaft of the column on the top of its head. This shaft is still octogonal in section but of better proportion and crowned with a bulbous capital having a flat abacus. Between the capital and the architrave is usually a double-bracket supporting the cornice. This latter feature is obviously a stone copy of a wooden-model.' [2]

According to Mr. Longhurst examples of Māmalla style are only found at the Seven Pagodas. 'It will be remembered,' says he, 'that it was Māmalla who founded Māmallapuram naming the town after himself.[3] Although most of the monuments there may be said to be in the Māmalla style it is quite certain that all of them could not possibly have been excavated during his life time, as the work must have taken over a century and even then was never finished. Therefore we may presume that Māmalla's son and successor Mahēndravarman II and also the latter's son Paramēśvaravarman I, carried on the work begun by Māmalla keeping more or less to the original style. . . .'

Dr. Hultzsch on the age of the Seven Pagodas.—About the exact age of the monuments of the Seven Pagodas the views of scholars differ considerably. According to Venkayya[4]

[1] Note by Editor.

[2] *Arch. Report for 1918-1919*, p. 26 ff. Also see same writer's remarks in *Pallava Architecture*, Part i, *Memoirs of the Arch. Surv. India*, No. 17, p. 11.

[3] In the opinion of the late James Fergusson derived from a study of the sculptures and the architecture the date of the Seven Pagodas is somewhat earlier than 700, but their execution may have been spread over half a century or even more and that A.D. 650 or 700 may be safely relied upon as the date at which the rocks were carved into the wondrous forms which excite our admiration. *Cave Temples of India*, p. 110.

[4] *A.S.R.*, 1906–7, p. 234.

Mahābalipuram was founded by Narasimhavarman I, surnamed Mahāmalla,[1] after his own surname and that the earliest of them cut out by him.

The place is ordinarily supposed by most official Epigraphists and Western archæologists to have had no previous history[2] or existence although the mention of this place by the earliest Āḷvārs and the recent discovery of inscribed statues of Simhavishṇu and his son Mahendravarman I clearly goes against such a presumption. According to Dr. Hultzsch the majority of short epigraphs on the monolith now styled Dharmarāja Ratha resemble those of the Mahēndravāḍi and Śiyyamangalam cave inscriptions of the Pallava king Mahēndravarman. Among the names and surnames of the king who excavated the Dharmarāja Ratha, we find twice the name of Narasimha which seems to have been his actual name while the remaining designations look like mere surnames. Among the successors of Mahēndravarman I there are two kings named Narasimhavarman. As the type of the alphabet is more archaic than that of the second of the inscriptions which probably belongs to Paramēśvaravarman I, father of Rājasimha, Narasimhavarman of Dharmarāja Ratha inscriptions may be identified with Narasimhavarman I, the son of Mahēndravarman I. This identification is rendered almost certain by a reference to the published facsimile.[3]

About the year A.D. 642, the celebrated Chinese pilgrim and Master of Law, Hiuen-Tsang, visited the Pallava capital and appears to have stayed there a considerable time. He described the country round the capital by the name of Drāviḍa, and extending about 6000 *li* in extent. The soil was fertile and produced abundance of crops. He found the climate of the

[1] Note by Editor on the age of Mahabalipur.

[2] According to Jouveau-Dubreuil the monuments at the Seven Pagodas do not go back prior to the seventh century, A.D. see his Archaéologie du sud de L'Inde, tome i, pp. 74–102. His theories on the age and the evolution of Pallava monuments are generally followed by A. H. Longhurst, V. A. Smith and Ānanda C. Coomaraswamy in his recent work on *the History of Indian and Indonesian Art*. (pp. 102–104.)

[3] Hultzsch, *Ep. Ind.*, vol. x, p. 1 ff.

region hot, and the character of the people courageous. The people were deeply attached to the principles of truth and highly esteemed for their learning[1] a fact which is also noted by one of the *Tēvāram* hymnists.[2]

As regards Buddhism the pilgrim found some hundred *Saṅghārāmas*, and 10,000 priests all of whom studied the teaching of the *Sthavira* school of Mahāyāna Buddhism. The Hindu, including the Jaina temples numbered about eighty and in other parts around he found that the sect of the Digambaras had many adherents. Hiuen-Tsang also refers to the tradition current then that the Tathāgatha in olden times when he lived in this world frequented this part very much and converted many men. Therefore Asoka the Buddhist emperor is believed to have built a large number of *stūpas* here traces of which the pilgrim was able to notice in many places around Kāñchi. The Chinese pilgrim also refers to the tradition that Kāñchīpuram was the birth place of Dharmapāla, the well-known metaphysician who preceded Śīlabhadra as head of the great University of Nalanda. The pilgrim also visited Molo-kiu-chi (the Pāṇḍya country) where he found some of the inhabitants following the true doctrine, but others impetuous and wholly given to commercial gain. The Buddhist pilgrim also found that in the Pāṇḍya country his religion was in a state of decay though traces of monasteries were found everywhere.[3]

Mahēndravarman II.—About A.D. 655, Narasimhavarman I, the Mahāmalla, died having raised the Pallava power to a glory unprecedented in Pallava history. The exact period of the duration of Narasimha's reign is not known, but from the evidence of the *Mahāvaṃśa*, and the prolonged stay of Mānavamma at the court of this king as well as the military and naval enterprises associated with his reign, his reign must have lasted a fairly long time. He was succeeded by Mahēndravarman II about

[1] Beal, *Records*, vol. ii, p. 228.

[2] கல்வியே கரையிலாத காஞ்சிமாநகர் — Appar, *Tēvāram*, *Tirukaçhchimēṛṛaḷi Patikam*, verse 8.

[3] Beal, *Records*, vol. ii, pp. 228–30,

whom practically nothing is known, except the reference in the Kūram plates that he 'thoroughly enforced the sacred law of the castes and the orders.'[1] This probably indicates a peaceful reign free from disturbances of hostile invasions from outside. According to Mr. M. S. Ramaswami Aiyangar, Mahēndravarman II was the contemporary of Appar.[2] But there is no evidence to show that Mahēndravarman II was a Jain in the earlier part of his reign and that his conversion to Śaivaism was brought about by Appar. On the other hand, as we saw already, Appar was a contemporary of Mahēndravarman I, the son and successor of Simhavishṇu (A.D. 600–630).

Paramēśvaravarman I (circa 600 to 680).—With the accession of Paramēśvaravarman I we once again find ourselves in very stirring times. Invasions and counter-invasions of the Pallavas and the Chāḷukyas become once more the order of the day. His great Chāḷukyan contemporary was Vikramāditya I who, according to the Gadval plates,[3] conquered Kāñchi, defeated Īśvarapōtarāja and destroyed the Mahāmalla family. This grant also gives the very important particular that at the time of the southern invasion, Vikramāditya I was encamped at Uragapura[4] on the southern bank of the Kavēri. These plates furnish the details of date, i.e. the year both of

[1] The Vēlūrpāḷayam plates omit his name altogether from the genealogical list. *Ibid.*, *S.I.I.*, vol. ii.

[2] *Studies in South Indian Jainism*, p. 66.

[3] *Ep. Ind.*, vol. x, No. 22, pp. 100–6.

[4] As regards the identification of Uragapuram the statement in the plates that it was on the southern bank of the Kaveri makes it clear that it must have been the ancient Chōḷa capital Uraiyūr near Trichinopoly. Dr. Hultzsch was inclined to identify it with Nagapatam, taking Uragapura to be a literal translation in Sanskrit of the Tamil word Nāga-Paṭṭinam. (*Ep. Ind.*, vol x, p. 102.) Attempts have been made to identify it with Pāmbūr. But the fact that Peruvaḷanallūr, where a battle was fought between the Pallavas and the Chāḷukyas, lies about twelve miles from Trichinopoly (north-west) shows the camp where Vikramāditya stayed and made this grant could not have been very much farther According to Prof. Jouveau-Dubreuil (*Pallavas*, p. 43) Uragapuram is the 'City of Raṇarasika,' of the Kailāsanātha temple inscription (*S.I.I.*, vol. i, p. 13). But it seems more sound to regard that Paramēśvaravarman I led another invasion against Badami, and that the Kailāsanātha temple inscription has reference to this achievement.

the reign and of the Śaka era. The actual date of the grant as given in the record is the full-moon *tithi* of *Vaiśākha* in the twentieth year of the reign, which was current after 596 Śaka years had passed. According to Dr. Fleet the equivalent may be taken as Tuesday, 25th April, A.D. 674, which fully confirms the correctness of other dates obtained for the reign by Prof. Kielhorn.

The details of the Pallava-Chāḷukya campaign are not clearly known from any records, but it is certain that success did not uniformly attend on the Chāḷukya invader. The Kūram record already referred to, which belongs to this period, after giving an elaborate account of the martial exploits of Paramēśvaravarman I mentions in particular the fact that he made Vikramāditya 'whose army consisted of several *lakshas* take to flight covered only by a rag.'[1] Similarly the Vēlūrpāḷayam record[2] makes pointed reference to Paramēśvaravarman having crushed the conceit of his enemies like the sun destroying the mists. Neither of these grants furnishes any detail which might help us to locate the exact place where the Pallava and the Chāḷukyan forces met in battle. This very important detail is obtained from the Udayēndiram plates[3] which mention the name of the site of battle as Peruvaḷanallūr which we may correctly identify with the village of Peruvaḷanallūr in the Lalgudi taluk of the Trichinopoly District. As we know that the Gadval plates mention the important detail that the Chāḷukya emperor was encamped in Uragapuram, this identification receives added confirmation, especially as this place lies a few miles from this village. The campaign between the Pallavas and the Chōḷas must have been therefore conducted in and around the town of Trichinopoly. A glowing description of the battle is given in the Kūram plates from which we learn that Paramēśvaravarman's war-elephant was called Arivāraṇa and that his horse was known as Atiśaya.[4]

[1] *S.I.I.*, vol. i, p. 144.
[2] v. 11, Vēlūrpāḷayam plates, *ibid.*, vol. ii, p. 508.
[3] *Ibid.*, vol. ii, p. 371.
[4] 'At the head of a battle,—in which the disk of the sun was caused to assume the likeness of the circle of the moon through the mist of the

This king appears to have been a great devotee of Śiva and pleased that God by constructing large numbers of Śiva temples all over the kingdom. From the inscription on the Gaṇēśa temple at Māmallapuram,[1] Dr. Hultzsch has concluded that Atyantakāma after whom the temple is named must have been a surname of Paramēśvaravarman I himself

dust, there was produced by the marching of the countless troops of men, horses and elephants, which was terrible through the thunderlike sound of drums, which teemed with unsheathed swords that resembled flashes of lightning, in which elephants were moving like clouds, and which therefore resembled an unseasonable appearance of the rainy season; in which tall horses looked like billows, in which elephants caused distress on their path, just as sea-monsters produce whirlpools, in which conches were incessantly blown and which therefore resembled the gaping ocean; which was full of swords and shields, just as of rhinoceros, creepers and *vāraṇa* trees, which was crowded with heroes who possessed bows and mighty elephants, as if it were crowded with *Sara* (grass) and which was agitated by a violent wind in which the path of the wind was obstructed by arrows, that flew past each other on the bows, while these were bent by the warriors; in which javelins, pikes, darts, clubs, lances, spears, and discuses were flying about; in which troops of furious elephants firmly impaled each other's faces with the piercing thunderbolts of their tusks; in which squadrons of horsemen were connected by their swords, that had struck each other's heads, in which there were soldiers who were noted for their dexterity in fighting with sword against sword, pulling of hair against hair and club against club; in which the ground was thickly smeared with saffron as the blood was mixed with copious rutting juice of the elephants that issued in consequence of their considering each other as equals, or despising each other; in which both large armies had lost and dropped arms, necks, shanks, thigh bones and teeth; in which, owing to the encounter of the armies, both sides were broken, urged on, put to flight and prostrated on the ground; which was attended by the goddess of fortune sitting on the swing of the doubt about mutual victory or defeat; in which brave warriors were marching on the back of lines of, fallen elephants, that formed a bridge over the flood of blood, in which soldiers stood motionless, if their blows did not hit each other's weak parts; which was covered here and there with shattered banners and parasols with fallen elephants and with dead and half dead soldiers who had done their duty whose strong arms still raised the weapon whose lips were bitten and whose eyes were deep red with fury; in which a multitude of white *chāmaras* was waving; in which tiaras, armlets, necklaces, bracelets and ear-rings were broken, crushed and pulverised, in which the *kūshmāndas*, rākshasas and *piśāchas* were singing, intoxicated with drinking the liquor of the blood; and which contains hundreds of headless trunks, that were vehemently dancing together in a fearful manner according to the beaten time he, unaided, made Vikramāditya, whose army consisted of several *lakshas* take to flight, covered only by a rag.' (Kūram plates; Dr. Hultzsch's Translation, *S.I.I.*, vol. i, p. 153 ff.)

[1] *Ep. Ind.*, vol. x, p. 8.

'The second and very florid alphabet found in the inscriptions of the Pallava king Atyantakāma on the monolith now styled Gaṇēśa temple (No. 20), in the two caves called Dharmarājamaṇḍapa and Rāmānujamaṇḍapa. The same alphabet is employed in the Kāñchī inscriptions of Rājasimha and his son Mahēndravarman III. The Kāñchīpuram inscriptions state that Rājasimha was the son of Ugradaṇḍa the destroyer of Raṇarasika's city and that the epithet Raṇarāśika refers to the Western Chāḷukya king Vikramāditya I (A.D. 655–680). The alphabet of the Atyantakāma's inscription at the Seven Pagodas resembles so closely that of Kailāsanātha temple epigraphs that both must be assigned to the same period. That Atyantakāma's actual name was Paramēśvara is seen from verse 2 of No. 20.' 'I propose to identify this Atyantakāma with either Paramēśvaravarman I, the father of Rājasimha or Paramēśvaravarman II, the son of Rājasimha preferably with the former.'

It thus appears that the rock-cut monument known as the Gaṇēśa temple as well as the Rāmānujamaṇḍapa were probably excavated at the orders of Paramēśvaravarman and that the former one was a Śiva temple. From the eleven *ślokas* in the Gaṇēśa temple inscription we learn that Paramēśvaravarman I had Chitramāya, Guṇabhājana, Śrībhara and Raṇajaya as surnames. Vidyāvinīta Pallava was another title of Paramēśvaravarman I. In the village of Kūram Paramēśvaravarman appears to have built a structural temple to Śiva, called in the plates Vidyāvinīta-Pallava-Paramēśvaragṛha. The object of the Kūram grant is a gift of the village of Paramēśvaramaṅgaḷam (evidently named after the king) made to the temple of Śiva which had been built at Kūram by Vidyāvinīta Pallava. The village was probably named after the king himself and divided into twenty-five parts of which three were to be enjoyed by two Brahmans Anantaśivāchārya and Pullaśarman who looked after the divine service of the temple. The fourth part was set aside for the providing of water and fire for the temple maṇḍapa, the fifth for the reading of the *Bhārata* at this place while the remaining twenty parts were given to twenty

Chaturvēdins. Kūram is described here as belonging to Mānyavantrarāshṭra of Nīrvēḷūr, a division of Uṟṟukāṭṭukoṭṭam.

Narasimhavarman II—Rājasimha, circa 680–700.—Narasimhavarman II succeeded his father towards the close of the seventh century. His reign appears to have been completely peaceful and free from foreign invasions. Among the temples built by his king may be mentioned the Kailāsanātha temple, called the Rājasimhēśvara after his surname Rājasimha, the Airāvatēśvara temple at Kāñchi, the Shore-temple near the sea at Mahābalipuram, and the Panamalai temple all of which contain his inscriptions. The habit of registering the surnames of the ruling king begun by Mahēndravarman I appears to have become exceedingly popular now and was extensively put into practice by Rājasimha more than 250 of his *birudas* being found in the walls of the Kailāsanātha temple alone.[1]

Some of these are :—'Rishabalāñchana', 'Śrī-Śaṅkara-bhakta', 'Śrīvādyavidyādhara', 'Śrī-Āgamapriya', 'Śrī-Pratimalla', 'Śiva-Chūḍāmaṇi', etc. These titles are suggestive of his personal tastes, his accomplishments and religious inclinations. The inscriptions of the Kailāsanātha temple besides the *birudas* of this king, include those of his son Mahēndravarman III and his queen Rangapatāka whose names are associated with the erection of a part of the temple.[2] This Rangapatāka appears to have been one of Rājasimha's queens and her record consists of three Sanskrit verses in characters similar to Rājasimha's inscription. This inscription registers the fact that the small Śiva shrine was constructed by Rangapatāka[3] the Queen of Narasimhavishṇu, or Kālakāla whose sign was the bull.

[1] *S.I.I.*, vol. i, Nos. 25 and 26, pp. 14–18.

[2] *Ibid.*, p. 23.

देवे जगद्दलयक्षणबद्धदीक्षे निर्भिन्नशत्रुहृदये नरसिंहविष्णौ ॥

वाल्लभ्य मूर्ज्जितमत्रारप्य विराजतेया निर्ज्जित्य गर्व्वमिव पुष्करदेवतायाः

[3] *Ibid.*

निर्म्मापितमिदन्धाम तया चन्द्रशिखामणेः

पताकयेव नारीणां रम्यं रंगपताकया ॥

The Monuments of Rajasimha.—The most important among the temples now existing, built by Rājasimha is that at Kāñchīpuram known as the Kailāsanātha temple. One of the inscriptions in this temple records the construction of this temple by Rājasimha. There is a story in the *Periyapurāṇam* account of Pūśalār Nāyanār [1] which mentions that a Kādava king built a temple to Śiva and heard a celestial voice directing the postponement of the consecration by a day as on the day appointed he had to be present at the temple of the devotee Pūśalār for a similar function. This presumably has a reference to that erected by Rājasimha as it is mentioned that Rājasimha heard a celestial voice in one of the inscriptions the Kailāsanātha temple in itself.[2] The construction of this temple is also referred to in the Vēlūrpāḷayam plates in the following terms :—Verse 13 'His (Paramēśvaravarman's) son's son was Narasimhavarman II who equal to Mahēndra once again organized the *ghaṭika* of the twice-born and built of stone a house for the moon-crested Śiva which was comparable to the Mountain Kailāsa. Among the other temples built during this period we may mention the Śiva temple at Panamalai, the Shore-temple at Seven Pagodas and the Airāvatēśvara temple at Kāñchīpuram. It has been doubted in some quarters whether or not the Shore-temple at Mahābalipuram is a Pallava structure. Recently about six Sanskrit verses in Pallava script have been discovered round the plinths of the two *balipīṭhas* here. The record is not complete but contains an eulogy of a Pallava king whose surnames were Atyantakāma, Aparājita, Śivachūḍāmaṇi,

1 காடவர் கோமான் கச்சிக்கற்றளி யெடுத்துமுற்ற
மாடலாஞ் சிவனுக்காக பெருஞ்செல்வம் வகுத்தல்செய்வா
ளுடபாலறியாதாரைத் தாபிக்கு மன்னுன் முன்னுள்
ஏடலர் கொன்றைவேய்ந்தா ரிரவிடைக் கனவிலெய்தி

நின்றவூர் பூசலன்ப னெடிதுநா ளினைந்து செய்த
நன்றுநீ டாலயத்து நாளைநாம் புகுவோநீயிங்
கொன்றிய செயலைநாளை யொழிந்துபின் கொள்வாயென்று
கொன்றைவார் சடையார்தொண்டர் கோயில்கொண் டருளப்போந்தார்.

— *Per. Pur.* Pūs. Nāy. v. 9 and 10.

2 *S.I.I.*, vol. i, p. 12.

etc., attributes that we now know belonged to Rājasimha. Another verse refers to him as Rājasimha, Raṇajaya, Śrībhara and Chitrakārmukha and is identical with verse 12 of the Kāñchīpuram inscription of Rājasimha. The mention in the record of the king as the ruling sovereign makes it almost certain that he was Rājasimha, son of Paramēśvaravarman I, who bore the surnames Kshatriyasimha and Rājasimha. The two Śiva temples of the Shore-temple Khatriyasimha. Pallavēśvaram and Rājasimhapallavēśvaram were apparently contemporary with Rājasimhapallavēśvaram of Kāñchīpuram, and have been named after Rājasimha I.[1]

Literature and Literary Patronage.—The age of Narasimhavarman II was one of intense literary activity. It has been already pointed out that Sanskrit poets and Sanskrit culture were specially patronized by Pallava kings.[2] It is suggested that Daṇḍin, the well-known Sanskrit writer, probably flourished for some time in the Pallava court at Kāñchīpuram, and references to Kāñchīpura and its rules bave been discovered in his works. In his *Kavyādarśa*[3] Daṇḍin mentions a Śaiva king Rājavarma who judging from the way in which he is spoken of must be regarded as his contemporary and probably was Rājasimha Pallava who according to his inscriptions is known to have been a very devout Śaiva.[4] Prof. M. Rangachariar has also quoted a tradition with reference to chapter v of *Kāvyādarśa*[5] that it was composed by Daṇḍin for giving lessons in rhetoric to a royal prince at Kāñchīpuram who in all probability was

[1] *Mad. Ep. Coll.*, 566 of 1912. Also *see* Antiquities of Mahābalipuram, *Ind. Ant. for 1917*, p. 49 ff.

[2] In the Vēlūrpāḷayam plates Rājasimha is recorded to have revived the *ghaṭika* of the twice-born. The nature of learning acquired at the Brahminical *ghaṭika* is described in the Kaśākkuḍi plates ll. 71 ff (*S.I.I.*, vol. ii, p. 358).

[3] Ch ii, p. 279.

[4] *Tēshāmvaṁśēprasūtāt-Raṇarasikapurōn-mardhanāt Ugradaṇḍāt*
Subramanyakumārō Guha iva Paramādīśvarādāttajanmā
Śaktikshuṇṇārivarggōviditabahunayaś Śaivasiddhāntamārggō.
Śrīmānatyantakāmah kshata Sakalamalō dhūrdharaḥ Pallāvānām.
S.I.I., vol. i, No. 24, 5, 6.

[5] *Ind. Ant.*, 1912, p. 90 ff.

Rājasimha's son.[1] All these references, taken along with the passage in *Kāvyādarśa* where Daṇḍin illustrates a particular form of composition by a couplet[2] which refers to the city of Kāñchi[3] and its rulers the Pallavas and the evidence furnished by the recently-discovered *Avantisundarikathā*, make it clear that Daṇḍin lived for a considerable period at the Pallava court in Kāñchīpuram.

Whether the series of dramas published at Trivandrum as Bhāṣa's, were really composed during the reign of Rājasimha it is not possible to say. But certain scholars hold that *Svapnavāsavadatta* and other works of the series were abridged editions of the works of Bhāṣa prepared for the staging of them before the court of a Pallava king, presumably Rājasimha from the colophons of these plays. These plays bear a close resemblance to *Mattavilāsaprahasana* of Mahēndravarman I. The evidence available seems to favour the view that the Pallava rather than the Pāṇḍya court was responsible for the production of these plays, if these are not Bhāṣa's own.

Paramēśvaravarman II, A.D. 700–710.—About the close of the first decade of the eighth century Rājasimha was succeeded on the Pallava throne by Paramēśvaravarman II. The reign of this sovereign appears to have been shortlived. The Vīraṭṭānēśvara temple inscription of this king is dated in the third year of his reign. The Kaśākkuḍi plates record of him that he 'conquered the coquetish ways of the Kali age, that he led the way of policy, which had been prescribed by Dhishaṇa (Bṛhaspati) and that he protected the worlds.'[4]

[1] It is Rājasimha himself that appears to have been Āchārya Daṇḍin's pupil from the *ślokas* under reference if the altered reading proves to be correct. *Ed.*

[2] *Kav. Dar.*, ch. 3, p. 114.

[3] '*Nāsikyamadyāparitaḥ chaturvarṇavibhūshitā.*
Āstikāchitpurīyasyām-ashṭavarṇāhvayōnṛpāḥ.
Kav., iii, 144.

In commenting on this well-known enigma in Daṇḍin's work Taruṇavāchaspati explains it as meaning Kāñchi ruled over by Pallava kings. (Age of Daṇḍin, *Ind. Ant. for 1912*, p. 91).

[4] *Verse* 26, *S.I.I.*, vol. ii, No. 73, p. 357.

In the Vēlūrpāḷayam plates he is described as the chastiser of the Kali and that he governed according to the laws of Manu.[1] As we have no inscription dated in the years subsequent to his third regnal year we may presume that his reign was very short.

[1] *Verse* 14, *S.I.I.*, vol. ii, part v, p. 511.

CHAPTER VIII

DYNASTIC REVOLUTION. HIRAṆYAVARMAN AND HIS SUCCESSOR PALLAVAMALLA

HIRAṆYAVARMAN I

THE Kaśākkuḍi plates of Nandivarman Pallavamalla pass on from Paramēśvaravarman II to Nandivarman, the descendant of Bhīmavarman, thereby suggesting that the Pallaya throne passed into the hands of Nandivarman II immediately after Paramēśvaravarman II. The circumstances that led to a change in the family are not stated. According to the Udayēndiram plates it appears that Paramēśvaravarman II left a young prince called Chitramāya whose cause was espoused by the Dramila princes. The recently-discovered Koṛṛanguḍi plates dated in the sixty-first year of Nandivarman II Pallavamalla, mention after Vīrakūrcha and others one Hiraṇyavarman who is said to have ruled as king. The Vēlūrpāḷayam plates do not mention this fact. But the Taṇḍantōṭṭam plates [1] record of him that he was born for the good of the world and that he made his enemies settle in forests and was the asylum of those who eagerly desired protection. His place in the Pallava family may be indicated in the following table :—

Simhavarman

Simhavarman	Bhīmavarman
:	|
Mahēndravarman	Buddhavarman
	|
	Ādityavarman
	|
	Govindavarman
	|
	Hiraṇya I
	|
Paramēśvara II	Nandivarman II
:	
Chitramāya	

[1] Taṇḍantōṭṭam plates, v. 1, *S.I.I.*, vol ii, part 5, p. 528.

Sculptures in the Vaikunṭhaperumāḷ Temple at Kāñchi.—The sculptures inside the Vaikunṭhaperumāḷ temple at Kāñchīpuram throw some light upon the history of this period. The original sculptures were considerably mutilated, but the temple authorities have tried to repair them with brick and mortar. The explanatory notes have not been filled in completely but are found on a small portion of the south verandah and explain thirteen compartments of the upper row of sculptures. The first of these notes refers to the death of Paramēśvaravarman of the Pallava family which was descended from the God Brahma and mentions the ministers, the Ghaṭikaiyār, the Mūlaprakṛti and Hiraṇyavarma Mahārāja. It is partially damaged but ends with the word 'place'. The second compartment ends with the words *enru soṇna iḍam*, 'the place where he said that'. The fourth mentions Śrīmalla, Raṇamalla, Sangrāmamalla, and Pallavamalla as Hiraṇyavarma's four sons and ends with the words 'Paramēśvaran *nan povēn eṅru toḷuduniṅra iḍam*', 'the place where Paramēśvara stood in a worshipping posture saying he would go'.[1] Then Hiraṇyavarma Mahārāja and Dharaṇikoṇḍapośar are mentioned; also the Nagarattār i.e., the citizens of Kāñchīpuram, the Mūlaprakṛti and the Kāṭaka-Muttarayar. Mention is also made of the coronation (*Abhishēka*) of young Pallavamalla under the style Nandivarma.[2]

The Probable Interpretation of the Sculptures.—The sculptural representations in these panels taken along with the information contained in the Kaśākkuḍi plates[3] help us to establish that there was a change of dynasty on the death of Paramēśvaravarman, and that Nandivarman II, till then named Paramēśvaran Pallavamalla was chosen to occupy the Pallava throne by the people. In this enterprise Nandivarman II appears to have received considerable help from Hiraṇyavarman I, and his trustworthy general Udayachandra whose exploits for the cause of his master are described in detail in the Udayēndiram plates.[4] The Kaśākkuḍi plates dated in the

[1] The actual text has been published in *S.I.I.*, vol. iv, pp. 10–12.
[2] *Ibid.*
[3] *Verse* 27, *S.I.I.*, vol. ii, part 3, p. 357.
[4] *Ibid.*, *S.I.I.*, pp. 37–72.

twenty-second year of this king records the important fact that 'he was chosen by his subjects'. The sculptures at the Vaikunṭhaperumāḷ temple have been interpreted as indicating a general election to the Pallava throne on the death of Paramēśvaravarman II. 'The Kaśākkuḍi plates[1] of Pallava king Nandivarman Pallavamalla tell us, that, after the death of Paramēśvaravarman II, Nandivarman, son of Hiraṇyavarman, was chosen by his subjects. It may therefore be concluded that this part of the sculptures were intended to represent the various events connected with the succession of Nandivarman who might be the prince referred to in the notes as Pallavamalla. As the Vaikunṭhaperumāḷ temple was called Paramēśvaraviṇṇagaram, very probably after the Pallava king Nandivarman Pallavamalla called also Paramēśvaravarman[2] it may be supposed that both the sculptures and the explanatory notes accompanying them were cut out soon after the temple itself was built.'

It would be more accurate to consider that the sculptures at the Vaikunṭhaperumāḷ temple at Kāñchīpuram taken as a whole represent the whole history of the Pallava family rather than the immediate events connected with the accession of Nandivarman Pallavamalla about the beginning of the eighth century. It is well known that the explanatory notes have not been filled in completely for all the long series of bas-reliefs of which only a small number could be interpreted with the help of inscriptions.[3] It is therefore incorrect to regard all these sculptures as being connected with only the immediate events relating to the accession of Nandivarman II. If we examine the sculptures from the commencement, almost from the first panel which presents Vishṇu, to the following which represent Brahma, Angīrasa, Bṛhaspati, Bhāradvāja, Drōṇa and Aśvatthāman, the birth of Pallava, is found to be graphically represented while the rest illustrate and continue the family history.

[1] *S.I.I.*, vol. ii, part 3, p. 344.
[2] Paramēśvaran Pallavamalla was the name and Nandivarman was the title of Nandivarman Pallavamalla. See *S.I.I.*, vol. iv, No. 135, p. 11
[3] Para 2 of *M.E.R. for 1906.*

Then again it is not necessary to infer that Paramēśvaravarman II should have been either deposed or forced to retire from the throne.[1] The inscription here requires to be thoroughly re-interpreted. The correct explanation of the scene is the selection of Nandivarman Pallavamalla, then called Paramēśvaravarman Pallavamalla, to the throne from among the four sons of Hīraṇyavarman. The details (See footnote below) furnished in the descriptive labels fully confirm the statement in the Kaśākkuḍi plates that he was raised to the throne by the general approval of the citizens and thoroughly falsify the usurpation theory put forward by some writers.

The Position of Hiraṇyavarman.—The only difficulty still facing us is with reference to Hiraṇyavarman who is described in the newly-discovered copper-plates from Koṛṛanguḍi as having actually ruled as king. The Taṇḍantōṭṭam plates make a glowing reference to him and describe his stirring prowess[2] in the field of battle, giving the impression that he was a ruling sovereign of Kāñchī. The Vēlūrpāḷayam plates and the

[1] It has been generally supposed that Nandivarman Pallavamalla usurped the Pallava throne soon after Paramēśvaravarman II. This is not at all supported by the evidence furnished by the Vaikunṭhaperumāḷ temple sculptures which represent the events that took place immediately after the death of Paramēśvaravarman II leading to the accession of Pallavamalla. The inscriptional evidence has been translated thus in the *Epig. Indica* : 'After the death of Paramēśvaravarman II, a deputation consisting of the *Matras*, the *Malaprakritis* and the *Ghatakayar* waited on Hiraṇyavarma-Maharaja and represented the fact that the country was without a ruler and requested him to grant them a sovereign. There upon king Hiranyavarman sent for the chief potentates (*Kūlamullar*) and enquired which among them would accept the sovereignty. All of them refusing, he asked his sons Srimalla, Raṇamalla, Sangrāmamalla and Pallavamalla. Pallavamalla humbly offered to go, but king Hiraṇyavarman was at first unwilling to risk his son, who was then only twelve years of age, in such a perilous undertaking. But Hiraṇyavarman was soon persuaded by Daraṇikoṇdapōsar to give his consent. Receiving the weapons presented to him both by his father and Daraṇikoṇdapōsar, Pallavamalla proceeded to Kānchipuram, crossing on his way several hills, rivers and forests. Hearing of his approach a certain Pallavadi-Araiyar came with a large force, and placed him on an elephant's back and returned to the city where he was received by the feudatory chiefs, the members of the merchants' guild, the *mulaprakritis*, and Kadakka-Muttaraiyar. He was then crowned king under the name Nandivarman and with the insignia of Videlvedugu, *Samudraghōsha*, *Khaṭavānga-davaja* and *Vrishabha lanchhana* by the ministers' feudatories, the *ghatakayar* and the *ubhaiya-gaṇa*.' *Epig. Ind.*, vol. xviii, p. 117.

[2] *Verse* 1, Taṇḍantōṭṭam plates, *S.I.I.*, vol. ii, part 5, p. 520.

Bāhūr plates omit his name alogether. There cannot be any doubt that Hiraṇyavarman mentioned in the Kaśākkuḍi [1] plates as the immediate ancestor of Nandivarman II and the sixth descendant of Bhīmavarman, the brother of Simhavishṇu, is the same as the Hiraṇyavarman figuring in the Taṇḍantōṭṭam plates[2] as well as the bas-reliefs in the Vaikuṇṭhaperumāḷ temple just mentioned. According to Mr. Krishna Sastri, this Hiraṇyavarman was really Dantivarman, the son of Nandivarman II and the Taṇḍantōṭṭam plates belonging to Nandivarman III, the son of Dantivarman, the donor of the Vēlūrpāḷayam plates. He observes [3] :—

'The first plate of the preserved portion begins by referring to a king who conquered the south and states that a certain Hiraṇyavarman was born again "for the welfare of the world.". . . . The father of Vijayanandivikramavarman is here stated to have been Hiraṇyavarman; while the father of Vijayanandivikramavarman is here stated to have been Hiraṇyavarman; while the father of Vijayanandivikramavarman according to the Vēlūrpāḷayam plates was Dantivarman. If the proposed identity of Vijayanandivikramavarman with Vijayanandivarman is accepted, the apparent discrepancy in the name of the father could be explained. The statement that Hiraṇyavarman was born again, evidently indicates a second king of that name and we may suppose that Dantivarman, the father of Vijayanandivikramavarman, was also called Hiraṇyavarman like his grandfather Hiraṇyavarman I, the father of Nandivarman Pallavamalla. If the foregoing surmises are confirmed by future researches the Taṇḍantōṭṭam grant would be fifty-two years later than the Vēlūrpāḷayam grants of the same king.'

There arise, however, many difficulties in accepting this view and regarding that the Hiraṇyavarman of the Taṇḍantōṭṭam plates is the same as Dantivarman, the son of Nandivarman Pallavamalla. For one thing there is no evidence

[1] *Vide* ante *S.I.I.*, vol. ii, p. 520. [2] *Ibid.*
[3] *S.I.I.*, vol. ii, part v, p. 518.

that Dantivarman had the surname Hiraṇyavarman as is supposed by Mr. Krishna Ṣastri. In the second place *Ēkadhira*, a surname that occurs in the Taṇḍantōṭṭam plates for Nandivarman II, also occurs in the Kaśākkuḍi plates of the same king thus proving that the donor of this grant was the same as the grant of Kaśākkuḍi. The palæography of these plates (Taṇḍantōṭṭam) is according to scholars much too archaic to be assigned to the middle of the ninth century A.D. and really belongs to the middle of the eighth century,[1] and are akin to the Kaśākkuḍi plates. The objection to the high regnal year usually given for Nandivarman II by the epigraphists cannot be considered valid any longer as he is known to have succeeded to the throne in his twelfth year[2] and as we have inscriptions and copper-plates of this sovereign dated in the forty-seventh, fiftieth, fifty-second, sixty-first, sixty-second and sixty-fifth years of his reign. Again the Taṇḍantōṭṭam plates describe Nandivarman II as a devout worshipper of Vishṇu, and this is in perfect accordance with all facts known about him and we cannot therefore imagine that he was also a devout worshipper of Śiva as the donor of the Vēlūrpāḷayam plates is said to have been. It is therefore very probable that Hiraṇyavarman mentioned in the Taṇḍantōṭṭam as well as in the Koṟṟanguḍi plates, dated in the sixty-first regnal year of Nandivarman II is identical with Hiraṇyavarman I, the father of Nandivarman II. Whether Hiraṇyavarma Mahārāja was an independent ruler of Kāñchi as hinted in the Koṟṟanguḍi plates and whether he ruled for a long time, cannot be ascertained in the present state of our knowledge. It looks very probable that during Paramēśvaravarman II's reign he wielded considerable power and was possibly placed in charge of a part of the Pallava dominions. The death of this ruler gave him an opportunity to install his son who was very young at the time of his accession as a ruler of Conjeevaram, and who reigned for an exceptionally long period as seen from inscriptions dated in the sixty-fifth year of his reign.[3]

[1] Jouveau-Dubreuil, *Pallavas*, p. 61. [2] *S.I.I.*, vol. iv, No. 135.
[3] *Ep. Coll.*, No. 566 of 1922.

Reign of Nandivarman II Pallavamalla, circa A.D. 710 to 775.—Let us first take up the duration of the reign. There is considerable difference of opinion as to the exact period of his reign. Certain scholars, including the officers of the Epigraphical Department[1] do not believe that Nandivarman Pallavamalla had anything like a length of reign indicated by the Taṇḍantōṭṭam and Koṟṟanguḍi plates, and the inscriptions of Tiruvallam and Seven Pagodas all of which they wrongly assigned to Nandivarman III. It will be recollected that the Tiruvallam record is dated is the sixty-second year and that the inscription discovered at the Seven Pagodas[2] is dated in the sixty-fifth year of Nandivarman. So far as we know this is the longest reign in the Pallava family and this is all the more remarkable because it was followed by another long reign namely that of Dantivarman, one of whose inscriptions is dated in the fifty-first year of his reign,[3] the two reigns together covering 116 years. The officers of the Epigraphical Department however have been continuously attributing the high regnal years to Nandivarman III[4] son of Dantivarman for reasons not altogether convincing or clear. Even in the Epigraphy Report for 1922–23 we come across with the following remarks :—

'From the high regnal years given in the lithic regards[5] of Mahābalipuram and in this copper-plate (Koṟṟanguḍi plates) grant, the kings Nandipotavarman and Ko-Vijaya Nandi-

[1] It is very unlikely, observes H. Krishna Sastri in *Mad. Epig. Rep. for 1912* 'that a usurper like Pallavamalla with so many enemies to oppose and disturb his peaceful rule, could have continued to occupy the Pallava throne for so long a period as 50 years. His latest sure date, however, must be the 22nd year in which the Kaśākkuḍi plates were issued.' This is generally based on the assumption that no stone inscriptions hitherto discovered should be attributed to Nandivarman Pallavamalla. Mr. K. V. Subramanya Aiyar definitely opposed this view as early as 1917 in his *Historical Sketches of Ancient Dekhan* (p. 49) and the discoveries of subsequent records as well as the fresh interpretation of the Vaikuṇṭha-perumāḷ inscriptions above referred to have amply proved the correctness of his inference. He has discussed the matter in detail in the *Epig. Ind.*, vol. xviii, pp. 116–117, while editing the *Pattatattamangalam grant of Nandivarman*.

[2] *Ep. Coll.*, No. 666 of 1922.

[3] *Madras Ep. Coll.*, No. 262 of 1904.

[4] *S.I.I.* vol. ii, p. 518.

[5] No. 666 of App. B.

vikramavarman mentioned in them respectively must be identical with Kovijaya Nandivikramavarman (Nandivarman III) of the Tanḍantōṭṭam plates and the Tiruvallam rock inscription.'[1] But some of the exploits recorded of this king in this record, conquest over the Vallabha, Kaḷabhra, Kēraḷa, Pānḍya, Chōḷa, Tuḷuva and Konkaṇa as well as the invocation to Vishṇu in the commencement of the record militates strongly against the view which attributes this record to Nandivarman III whose sole achievements that we know of were the series of victories ending with that at Teḷḷāṟu mentioned frequently in his inscriptions. It is therefore probable more especially as Nandivarman II is described to have followed Hiraṇyavarman that this record belongs to Nandivarman II.[2] The duration of his reign may therefore be definitely taken as not less than sixty-five years so far as present epigraphic evidence goes and that Nandivarman Pallavamalla lived at least to the age of seventy-seven.

Events of His Reign.—The most important events of his reign may be ascertained from his own copper-plates of which we have no less than four (viz.) the Kaśākkuḍi plates dated in the twenty-second year of his reign, the Udayēnḍiram plates dated in the twenty-first year of his reign, the Tanḍantōṭṭam and the Koṟṟanguḍi plates dated in the fifty-eighth and the sixty-first years of his reign. Of these the Udayēnḍiram record gives valuable information regarding the military achievements of this period while the Kaśākkuḍi and the Koṟṟanguḍi plates furnish details of his personal accomplishments and the culture of the period. The contemporary records such as the Kailāsanātha temple inscription of Vikramāditya II, at Kāñchīpuram the Vakkalēri plates of Kīrtivarman, the Kēndūr plates, as well as the Pānḍya records from Vēḷvikkuḍi and Śinnamanūr throw some light on the relations that subsisted between these powers and the Pallava king. The Vakkalēri plates[3] in particular furnish detailed

[1] *M.E.R.*, 1902–3, p. 95.
[2] Note by Editor.
[3] *Ind. Ant.*, vol. viii, p. 23.

information relating to the invasion of Kāñchi by the Chāḷukyan emperor Vikramāditya II and his exploits there.

The Chāḷukyan Invasion of Kāñchi.—The Pallava-Chāḷukya wars which had been lost sight of since the days of Narasimhavarman I, the Mahāmalla, appear to have been once more renewed. The Kēndūr plates of Vikramāditya II describe an actual invasion into the Pallava dominions (*Tundākarāshtra*) and the capture of the city in somewhat graphic terms:—Being resolved to uproot completely his natural enemy (*prakṛti-amitra*) Vikramāditya II (A.D. 733 to 746) reached Tuṇḍāka-Vishaya, 'beat and put to flight, at the opening of the campaign, the opposing Pallava king named Nandipōtavarman, took possession of particular musical instruments called *Kaṭumukhavāditra*,[1] the *Samudraghosha*, the *khatvānkhadvaja*, many excellent and well-known intoxicated elephants and a heap of rubies which dispelled darkness by the brilliancy of the multitude of their rays . . . entered without destroying the city of Kāñchi, which was as it were a girdle adorning yonder lady, the region of the south . . . rejoiced the Brāhmaṇas, and poor and helpless people by his uninterrupted liberality . . . acquired high merit by restoring heaps of gold to the stone temple of Rājasimhēśvara, and other gods which have been caused to be built by Narasimhapotavarman . . . distressed by the Pāṇḍya, Chōḷa, Kēraḷa, Kaḷabhra and other kings. . . .'[2]

The above extract from the Kēndūr plates distinctly makes it clear that Vikramāditya II actually captured the city of Kāñchi from the Pallava king Nandipotavarman, that is, Nandivarman Pallavamalla, and occupied it for a period of time during which he endowed some of its temples with grants. This occupation of the Pallava capital by Vikramāditya is further confirmed by the discovery of a Kanarese inscription of Vikramāditya engraved on one of the pillars of

[1] These are alluded to in the hymns of Tirumangai Āḻvār in the Paramēśvaravinnagaram verses in expressions which are literal translations in Tamil of the Sanskrit names of the war instruments. They also figure in the mutilated inscriptions at the Vaikunthaperumāḷ temple, Kāñchīpuram.

[2] *Ep. Ind.*, vol. ix, p. 205.

the *maṇḍapa* in front of the Rājasimhēśvara shrine. This inscription which has been published[1] by Dr. Hultzsch records the fact that Vikramāditya Satyāśraya, after his conquest of Kāñchi, did not confiscate the property of Rājasimhēśvara temple, but granted large sums to the same, and ends with an imprecation. The Chāḷukyan attack on Kāñchi was therefore apparently different in character from the raid of the Pallava king Narasimhavarman I on Vātāpi which involved much destruction if the *Periyapurānam* account[2] is to be believed.

When did this expedition on Kāñchi start? Though no definite answer is possible it is presumable that this took place in the earlier half of Nandivarman's reign, in all probability between A.D. 733 to 746, when the Pallava king was preoccupied with wars against the southern powers.[3] In any case the occupation of the city by the Chāḷukyan army does not appear to have lasted for any considerable period. Nandivarman II was not slow in summoning his forces, to drive out the foreign invader from Kāñchīpuram. How this was brought about and when it was brought about are not clearly known. Whether the achievement was effected by the single-handed efforts of his own generals unaided by a coalition of other powers of the Tamil land, it is not also possible to say. It is however clear that Nandivarman Pallavamalla recaptured Kāñchi, and continued to carry on the administration undismayed by the Chāḷukya invasion that took place. It is a mistake to suppose that the Chāḷukyan invasions in the reign of Pallavamalla either exhausted the resources, or cut short his reign. On the other hand in spite of the rude shocks that the raids of Vikramāditya and Kīrtivarman must have caused, Nandivarman II continued in power as ruler of Kāñchi for the unusually long period of

[1] *Ep. Ind.*, vol. iii, p. 359. *Vide* App. A.

[2] *Periapurānam, Siruttoṇḍanāyanār Purānam, v.* 6.

[3] This is confirmed by the presence of an inscription of Vikramāditya (II) in the Kailasanātha temple which records that Vikramāditya after his conquest of Kāñchi did not confiscate the property of the Rājasimhēśvara temple but enriched it by granting large sums of gold. (*Ep. Ind.*, vol. iii, p. 359). Similarly the Vakkalēri plates also make reference to this event (*Ind. Ant.*, vol. viii, p. 23).

sixty-five years as we may safely ascribe the inscription recently discovered at the Seven Pagodas[1] to him.

Other Campaigns of Pallavamalla.—The reign of Nandivarman II appears to have been almost literally crowded with military engagements, sieges, invasions, and counter invasions. It has already been noticed that the Western Chāḷukya invasion of Kāñchi[2] which probably took place early in his reign resulted in the capture of the city by the enemies. The southern campaigns may now be noticed. Although the causes that brought about the conflict with the powers of the south especially the Pāṇḍyas of this period are by no means clear it may be surmised that the southern powers who were somehow dissatisfied with the accession of Pallavamalla to the throne of Kāñchi, in supersession of the regular family, now espoused the cause of Chitramāya a young prince who presumably had some claims by descent from Paramēśvaravarman II. This involved Nandivarman II in a long and deadly campaign against the Dramiḷa (Tamil) powers. In this campaign he seems to have received valuable help from his trusted general Udayachandra, the lord of Villivala, whose services are enumerated in the Udayēndiram plates dated in the twenty-first year of his reign. The victories enumerated in the Vēḷvikkuḍi and Sinnamanūr plates for Arikēsari-Parānkuśa-Māravarman at Neḍuvayal, Kuṛumaḍai, Maṇṇikurichchi, Koḍumbaḷūr, Pūvaḷūr, Tirumaṅgai, Kuḷumūr, and Śankaramaṅgai probably form part of the campaign of Pallavamalla and assigned to this period. Some of these battles such as those of Maṇṇai, Neḍuvayal, Nenmali, etc., are referred to in the Paramēśvaraviṇṇagaram hymns of Tirumaṅgai Āḷvār.[3] Many of these places also occur among the examples quoted in the commentary upon the Tamil work

[1] Ins. No. 666 of 1922. This inscription is wrongly ascribed to Nandivarman III in M. R. 1923. The reference in (verse 7) the Patattalmangalam grant of Nandivarman II that he ruled as King while yet very young and the statement in the Vaikunthaperumāḷ temple inscriptions that the prince was twelve years old at the time of coronation confirm the longevity of this reign.

[2] Raid on the south by Vinayāditya, son of Vikramāditya.

[3] *Per. Tir.* ii, 9.

Iraiyanār-Ahapporuḷ which also mentions many other places not mentioned in the inscriptional records Koṭṭāṛu, Nāraiyāru, Viḻiñam, etc.

Siege of Nandipura.—One of the most important of the achievements of Udayachandra whose exploits are enumerated in the Udayēndiram plates[1] was the release of Nandivarman II from the fortified town of Nandipura which was besieged by his enemies the Tamil kings. Nandipura which is identical with Nandipuraviṇṇagaram of Tirumaṅgai Āḻvār is situated not far from the modern town of Kumbhakonam, and is now-a days known as Nāthan-Kovil. During the later Pallava age especially in the eighth century, this place appears to have served as the seat of Pallava power in the southern districts, and was presumably fortified. It is noteworthy that the hymns to this shrine of Tirumaṅgai Āḻvār, who was a contemporary of Pallavamalla, have a clear reference to Nandivarman.[2] The circumstances that led to the siege of this place by the southern powers are not clear. But it has been presumed that the Tamil powers joined together in a great coalition espousing the cause of Chitramāya, the Pallava prince, and attacked Pallavamalla at a time when he had been staying at Nandipura. The circumstances relating to the release, and list of the other battles are described in the Udayēndiram plates.

Udayachandra's Exploits.—Udayachandra is described in the record as the lord of the River Vēgavati, and of the city Vilvala,[3] the ornament of the whole world. Born of the race of Pūchan, which had been in the uninterrupted hereditary service of the Pallava race . . . 'when he perceived that Pallavamalla was besieged in Nandipura by the Dramiḷa

[1] ll. 37 to 62.

[2] தந்தைமனமுந்த துயர்நந்தஇருள் வந்தவிறல் நந்தன்மதலை
எந்தையிவனென்றமரர் கந்தமலர் கொண்டுதொழ நின்றநகர்தான்
மந்தமுழவோசை மழையாகவெழுகார் மயில்களாடு பொழில்சூழ்
நந்திபணிசெய்தநகர் நந்திபுரவிண்ணகரம் நண்ணுமனமே!

See Nandipuraviṇṇagarapatikam, *Per. Tiru.*, v. 10.

[3] Identified with Vilvaḷanagara-viḷḷivalam in the Chingleput District.

princes, unable to bear this, like the visible death of the crowd of enemies of Pallavamalla, (he) slew with (his) sharp sword which glittered like a petal of water-lily, the Pallava king Chitramāya and others; he defeated the hostile army on the battle-fields of Nimbavana Chūtavana, Śankaragrāma, Nellūr, Nelvēli, Śūravaḷundur, and so forth, and thus bestowed the whole kingdom many times on the Pallava. . . . He split the opposing Śabara king called Udayana, in the terrible battle of Nelvēli, which could hardly be entered by a common man, and seized his mirror banner made of a peacock's tail; who in the northern region also, pursued the Nishada chief, called Prithivi-Vyāgra who desiring to become very powerful was running after the horse of the *Asvamēdha*, defeated him and ordered him out of the district of Vishṇurāja, which he subjected to the Pallava, and seized faultless pearl necklaces of excellent lustre, an immesurable heap of gold, and elephants; and he destroyed the fort of Kāḷidurga, which was protected by the Goddess Kāḷi, and defeated the Pāṇḍya army at the village of Maṇṇaikuḍi.'[1]

Among the localities mentioned wherein Udayachandra achieved victories for his master occurs, Nellore which is identical with the headquarter station of the modern Nellore District. Nelvēli is probably identical with Nenmali mentioned by Tirumangai Āḷvār in his *Periya-Tirumoḷi.*[2] It is identified by Dr. Hultzsch with modern Tinnevelly. If the Śabaras are identical with the modern Sauras of the Ganjam and Vizagapatam District it would not be correct to identify Nelvēli where the Śabara king is said to have been killed (l. 52) with Tinnevelly. It is therefore to be identified with some other place on the border of the Telugu districts. We may identify the Vishṇurāja with the Eastern Chāḷukya king Vishṇuvardhana III who was a contemporary Vikramāditya II. The Śankaragrāma mentioned in the Udayēndiram plates has been identified with Sankaramangai mentioned in the larger

[1] ll. 37 to 62, Udayēndiram plates; *S.I.I.*, vol. ii, part 3, p. 372.

[2] நென்மலியில் வெருவச்செருவேல் வலங்கைப்
பிடித்த படைத்திறல் பல்லவர்கோன்—ii, ௯, 8.

Śinnamanūr plates, while Maṇṇaikuḍi is identical probably with the Maṇṇikurichchi of the Veḷvikuḍi plates where Kō-Śadaiyan claims a victory over the Pallavas. Maṇṇaikuḍi may be identified with the village of Maṇakuḍi in the Arantangi Taluk of the Tanjore District. The battle-fields of Nimbavana, Chūtavana and Śankaragrāma may be similarly identified with Veppangāḍu, Kovilūr (Tiruvūśattānam of the Tēvaram) and Sankaranārkuḍikāḍu.[1] The region in and around these places in the Tanjore District appears to have figured largely in the campaigns of the Pallavas against the Pāṇḍyas, and are evidently alluded to in the hymns of Tirumangai Āḻvār, in the Paramēśvaravinnagarapatikam.

One of the references in the Udayēndiram plates, namely, the *Aśvamēdha* horse which was detained by Prithivi-Vyāgra has been interpreted as containing a reference that Nandivarman Pallavamalla performed an *Aśvamēdha* sacrifice[2] to celebrate his supremacy.

Rāshṭrakūṭa Invasions on Kāñchi.—The Rāshṭrakūṭa kings who were contemporary with Nandivarman Pallavamalla claim victories over the Pallavas and their city. The Kaḍaba plates[3] distinctly mention Vayiramēga as a surname of Dantidurga Rāshṭrakūṭa. Now, Vayiramēga is mentioned in Tirumangai Āḻvār's hymns on the deity of Ashṭabhuja in Kāñchīpuram along with the local ruler of Kāñchi.[4] The verse under consideration has reference to two rulers, the local Pallava ruler of Kāñchi and the foreign Rāshṭrakūṭa ruler Vayiramēga in occupation of Kāñchi just then. The

[1] *Sen-Tam.*, vol. xxii, pp. 10, 11.

[2] l. 56, Udayēndiram plates. P. T. Srinivasa Aiyangar's *Pallavas*. There are no independent references in the published records to prove that Pallavamalla performed an *Aśvamēdha* sacrifice. The reference to this sacrifice in the Udayēndiram plates does not specify that it was performed by this Pallava King.

[3] *Ep. Ind.*, vol. iv, p. 334.

[4] For a discussion on the identity of Vayiramēga see *Quart. Jour. Myth. Society*, vol. xiii, pp. 581-8 and pp. 698-700.

மன்னவன் தொண்டையர்கோன் வணங்கும் நீள்முடிமாலைவயிரமேகன்
தன்வலிதன்புகழ் சூழ்ந்தகச்சி அட்டபுயகரத்தாதிதன்னை
கன்னிநன் மாமதிள் மங்கை வேந்தன் காமருசீர்க்கலிகன்றி குன்றா
இன்னிசையாற்சொன்ன செஞ்சொல்மாலை ஏத்தவல்லார்க்கிடம் வைகுந்தமே.

P. T. ii. 9.

conquest of Kāñchi is also alluded to in the Ellora inscription as well as in the Bagumra plates [1] of Govinda III from which we learn that Dantidurga first reduced the lowermost (southern) country, then turned his enemies to Madhyadēśa and finally conquered the city of Kāñchi.[2] From the Vēlūrpāḷayam plates we learn that Nandivarman Pallavamalla's queen was called Rēva and that his son was called Dantivarman. From this it has been conjectured that there was soon after the invasions of Kāñchi by Dantidurga a marriage alliance [3] between the Pallava king and the daughter of Dantidurga, and the son born to the Rāshṭrakūṭa princess was called Dantivarman after the maternal grandfather. This Rāshṭrakūṭa-Pallava pact does not appear to have prevented Govinda III from leading another invasion on the Pallava capital and levying tribute from Dantiga of Kāñchi.[4]

Expedition against the Gangas.—The military exploits of Nandivarman II thus appear to have filled every part of his reign and almost all contemporary dynasties of the day seem to have come into hostile contact with him. To these powers, the Pāṇḍyas, the Rāshṭrakūtas, the eastern Chāḷukyas, the western Chāḷukyas, may be added the Gangas. What led to the conflict with the Gangas is not clearly stated, but *verse* 6 of the Taṇḍantōṭṭam plates make a specific reference to the fact that Nandivarman took away a neck ornament from which contained in it the gem called Ugrōdaya.[5] Although the name of the Ganga king is not mentioned, it may be presumed that he must have been either Śivamara or Śrīpurusha. As the earlier plates dated in the twenty-first and twenty-second years of his reign do not specify this detail this achievement probably took place in the later half of his reign.

Religious Leanings.—The religious leanings of Nandivarman Pallavamalla were towards Vaishṇavism. His celebrated

[1] *Ep. Ind.*, vol. ix, p. 24.
[2] *Verse* vi, *Ep. Ind.*, vol. ix, p. 24.
[3] Vēlūrpāḷayam plates, *verse* 18.
[4] *Ind. Ant.*, vol. x, p. 125.
[5] *S.I.I.*, vol. ii, part 5, p. 519.

contemporary seems to allude to his worshipful attitude in the present tense in his hymn on the God of Ashṭabhuja at Kāñchī. His copper-plates describe him as never accustomed to bowing 'excepting to the pair of worshipful feet of Mukunda' (Vishṇu)[1] as worshipping the feet of Hari.[2] The newly-found plates of Koṟṟanguḍi devote several invocatory verses to Vishṇu (*verses* 1 and 2). The unnamed Pallava king who is mentioned by Tirumaṅgai Āḷvār as having worshipped at Śrīrangam is presumably Nandivarman Pallavamalla[3] as also the king called Nandi in the Nandipuraviṇṇagarapatikam.

State of Learning during Nandivarman's Reign.—The copper-plates of this and following period give excellent glimpses into the nature of learning during this period as well as of government, etc. The donees enumerated in the Kaśākkuḍi plates and the Tanḍantōṭṭam plates numbering several

[1] *Verse* 12, Tanḍantōṭṭam plates. *Ibid.*

[2] *Verse* 30, Kāśākkuḍi plates. *Ibid.*

[3] Other details of the king in somewhat exaggerated terms are also available from this copper-plate grants. Some interesting personal accomplishments and qualities are furnished in the *praśasti* portion of the Kaśākkuḍi grant composed by Trivikrama. In *verse* 29 we read :—' This Śrīdhara (Pallavamalla) resembles Vijaya in battle, Karṇīsuta, in acquaintance with the arts, Rāma in archery, the king of Vatsa with reference to the science of elephants and to music, *Kāma* in the opinion of women, the first poet (Vālmīki) in the composition of poetry, the master of policy (Bṛhaspati) himself in suggesting expedients, and (*Dharma*) Yudhishtira in delighting the subjects.' *Verse* 2 of the Tanḍantōṭṭam plates say of him :—' From him (Hiraṇyavarman) was born the wise and the prosperous king called Nandivarman who was the home of prowess and conqueror of the hoards of his enemies, whose victorious elephant reached almost the shores of the four oceans, whose fame extended to the four quarters and who was praised in battle for his knowlede in the use of all weapons. Verse 3 of the same record says, ' The only one of name Raja that did not bow to him was the dead-rayed moon and the only country in this world that did not pay tribute to him was that where no men exist. And while this king comparable to Indra was ruling the earth, there was nothing unapproachable by the people except perhaps the way leading to hell.'

' He is the lord of the circle of good people as Hari is the possessor of the powerful weapon Chakra, him the wise cling to as Gods to Sakra (Indra).

' He wore on his breast, as it were the lord of serpents, the bed of Achyuta dwelling near his heart a necklace, which he had snatched away from the Ganga king and in which was the gem called Ugrōdaya like the Kaustuba (*verse* 6).'

hundreds are many of them, if we may judge from their titles, masters of three and four Vedas of the six angas, etc. Of the 244 and odd names that are mentioned in the Taṇḍantōṭṭam plates no less than a hundred were Chaturvēdis, 18 were Shaḍangavids, while there are several Kramavids, Bhaṭṭas and Trivēdis. The accomplishments of an average South Indian Brahman scholar in the field of Sanskrit learning during the eighth century may be gathered from the following description of the donee of the Kaśākkuḍi charter dated in the twenty-second year of Nandivarman II's reign the object of which was to register a gift of village to a Brahman scholar whose name was Jyēshṭapada Somayāji. The extract gives some idea of what the average Brahmanical educational curriculum consisted in those times :—

'While the twenty-second year of his reign was current, this Rājādhirāja-paramēśvara, the Mahārāja called Nandivarman, who is engaged in ruling the kingdom of Paramēśvarapōtarāja, . . . was himself pleased to give as a Brahmadēya, as requested by Brahmaśrīrāja . . . who just as Bṛhaspati is minister of Indra, the lord of heaven, is the chief minister of the handsome Nandin, the lord of the earth and the chief of the Pallavas, to Jyēshṭapada Somayājin, who has mastered the ocean-like Vedas, who chants the Sāman hymns which are pleasant on account of their melody (*rasa*) ; who has completed the rehearsal and the study of the six auxiliary works, namely, the ritual of the Veda, grammar, astronomy, etymology, phonetics and metrics ; who knows the properties of words, sentences and subjects ; who has drunk the elixir of the *śruti* and *smṛti* ; who is learned in the portion referring to rites (*Karmakāṇḍa*) and the portion referring to knowledge (*Jñānakāṇḍa*) ; who is skilled in the ways of the world and in the knowledge of the arts ; who is versed in the poems, dramas, stories, epics and legends ; in short who is skilled in all branches of (holy and profane) knowledge ; who is expert in the performance of all rites ; who is of good conduct ; (who illumines) the world as a lamp does a house ; who is courteous (in spite of) the honour paid to him and of noble birth; who is the only sun of the middle world, namely earth, because he has dispelled all ignorance or darkness; who is considered the best of fathers and grandfathers who ranks first among the twice born; who knows the Vedas; who conforms to the precepts of the Vedas; who follows the Chandōga-sūtra, who has performed Vājapēya and other sacrifices; who belongs to the Bhāradvāja-Gōtra; who resides at Puniya, an excellent settlement of Brāhmaṇas, in the Tuṇḍākarāshṭra; who is poor in sins, who is distinguished by his dress, who is a unique person; who cares for both worlds; who accomplishes the three objects of human life, who knows the four Vedas; whose chief objects are the five primary elements (*Panchamahābhūta*), who knows the six auxiliary works, who resembles the sun, who possesses good qualities and who is an excellent Brahman,—a whole village, the original name of which was Koḍukolli which on becoming a Brahmadēya received the new name of Ekadhīramangalam, in Uṇḍivanakōsṭhaka in the same rāshṭra. . . .'[1]

Some Celebrities of the Period.—It has already been pointed out that the king himself like other royal members of the family was a scholar of considerable reputation and is compared to Karṇīsuta for his acquaintance with arts and to Valmīki the first poet in the composition of poems (*v.* 28) while verse 4 of the Taṇḍantōṭṭam plates record the fact that the learned people cling to him as the gods to Śakra. Among the Sanskrit poets of this period mentioned in the royal charters may be mentioned Paramēśvara, Uttara Karanika, and Trivikrama the composers of the prasasti in the Udayēndiram. Taṇḍantōṭṭam and Kaśākkuḍi plates. The celebrated scholar and saint Tirumangai Āḷvār was his contemporary and is another product of the times reputed for his skill in dialectics and known as the master of four kinds of poetical compositions. (Chatushkavi, Nālukaviperumāḷ). His work in the *Nālāyiraprabhandam* exceeds those of any other Vaishṇava saint excepting that of Nammāḷvār and forms one

[1] ll. 71 to 103, Kaśākkudi plates, *S.I.I.*, vol. ii, part 2, pp. 358 ff.

of the most precious collections that have come down to us. His great regard for the Pallava family and individual Pallava kings and their services finds continuous mention in his hymns to an extent far greater than in the *Tēvāram* hymns, or other works by the Vaishṇava Āḻvārs themselves. He was for some time a petty chieftain of Ālināḍu in the Chōḷamaṇḍala before he became a devout Vaishṇava saint. His contributions° in the *Nālāyiraprabhandam* are *Periya-Tirumoḻi*, *Tirukuṟundāṇḍakam*, *Tiruneḍundaṇḍakam*, *Śiriya-Tirumaḍal*, *Periya-Tirumaḍal*, *Tiruveḻukkūṟṟirukkai*.

Among the temples attributable to Nandivarman II may be mentioned the Kēśavaperumaḷ temple at Kūram, the Muktēśvara temple at Kāñchīpuram, Vīraṭṭānēśvara at Tiruvadi and the Kunṟāṇḍarkōvil at Pudukotta. The Vaikuntaperumāḷ temple at Kāñchī, the Paramēśvaravinṇagaram of Tirumangai Āḻvār probably owes its origin to this king and named after his personal name which was Paramēśvaran. Extensive renovation works must have taken place in a large number of other temples, if we could judge from grants recorded to many of these.

The reign of Nandivarman Pallavamalla lasted for sixty-five years according to the inscription discovered recently at Mahabalipuram [1] and covered the greater part of the eighth century. He was succeeded on his death by his son called Dantivarman through the Rāshṭrakūṭa princess Rēva about A.D. 775. The notion that his reign was short having been distracted by continuous wars as a result of which his kingdom was much reduced now appears to be incorrect. The inscriptions so far discovered of his reign and that of his son have been found in regions as distant as Trichinopoly to Tirupati which probably comprised the extent of his dominions.

[1] Ep. Coll. 666 of 1922.

CHAPTER IX

SUCCESSORS OF PALLAVAMALLA

IT has already been pointed out that the newly discovered Inscription of Nandivarman at the Ādivarāha temple at Mahabalipuram dated in the sixty-fifth year probably represents the last year of Nandivarman Pallavamalla. If this is a genuine record the reign of this king must have come to a close about the year A.D. 775. For the succeeding period of a century and a quarter during which the Pallava power continued before the region comprised in their kingdom was annexed by the Chōḷas, we come across with the names of a number of kings who, to judge from their names, must have been members of the Pallava family. Of these it is a little difficult to separate the lineal descendants of Nandivarman Pallavamalla from the rest. We have for instance stone inscriptions or copper-plate records for Dantivarman, Nandivarman, Nripatungavarman, Kampavarman, Īśvaravarman, Narasimhavarman, Vayiramēgavarman and Chandrāditya, all of whom are ascribable to this period (circa A.D. 800–900). The task of distinguishing these kings and assigning them to particular periods on the evidence of inscriptions has been rendered not a little difficult by the use of certain prefixes and affixes to names which have bewildered some scholars and led them to postulate strange theories. The most important of these is what is known as the 'Ganga-Pallava theory' which was adopted by the official epigraphists[1] almost until recently. This may be illustrated by a specific

[1] *Ep. Ind.*, vol. iv, p. 182; *S.I.I.*, vol. ii, p. 344; *Ibid.*, p. 505.

The untenability of this theory is discussed by the late T. A. Gopinatha Rao in the *Madras Christian College Magazine*, vol. xxiv, pp. 530-9 and by Prof. Jouveau-Dubreuil in his *Pallavas*, pp. 47-58.

example. The Pallava king Dantivarman who is known to have ruled for over fifty years and succeeded Nandivarman Pallavamalla figures in inscriptions as Dantivarma-Mahārāja, Dantivikramavarman, Dantipōttaraśar, Dantivarman of the Pallavatilakakula, and Ko-Vijaya-Dantivikramavarma. Similarly in the case of Nandivarman it is equally difficult as this name occurs in the inscriptions and copper-plate records in the following varieties:—Nandipōttaraśar, Vijaya-Nandivikramavarman, Nandivarman of the Bhāradvāja Gotra, the victorious Nandipōttarayar of Teḷḷāṛu and Danti-Nandivarman. The difficulty is also intensified as the inscriptions of these kings have been found not indistinctly separate localities but indiscriminately throughout the region of the Pallava kingdom. As none of these records is dated in the Śaka or any known era their date has to be determined independently by means of palæography and other details noted in inscriptions.

The Probable Order of Succession.—It is well known that Toṇḍamaṇḍalam was conquered by Āditya before the twenty-first year of his reign. It is also clear that Parāntaka I ascended the Chōḷa throne in the year A.D. 907.[1] As the Brahmadēśam and Tirukaḻukkuṉṟam inscriptions are dated in the twenty-seventh year of Rājakēsarivarman, who is identical with Āditya I, it may be presumed that the first year of his reign was A.D. 880. One of his inscriptions in the North Arcot District in the twenty-first year of his reign which records a donation near Kāḷahasti shows that by A.D. 900 his empire had extended as far as Kāḷahasti thus covering the Pallava empire.[2] The reigns of Dantivarman, Nandivarman, Nripatungavarman, Aparājita, Kampavarman and the other miscellaneous kings of the Pallava family whose inscriptions have been discovered in these regions have to be assigned to the period between about A.D. 900 and the last quarter of the eighth century when Pallavamalla ceased to rule. Omitting the reigns of the miscellaneous rulers like Kampavarman, Vayiramēghavarman, Kāṭṭirai, etc., we find that the total

[1] Ins. 735 of 1905.

[2] Ep. Rep., 1907, p. 11.

reigns of the others so far known comprise a period of roughly 118 years.[1]

If the conquest of the Toṇḍamaṇḍalam and the victory over Aparājita recorded in the Tiruvālangāḍu plates,[2] may be assigned to the year A.D. 893, we may, by calculating backwards, assign the above-mentioned kings to the following periods which is in complete accordance with the evidence obtainable from contemporary Pallava inscriptions and copper-plates.[3] The reigns of the Pallava kings named Vijaya Kampavarman, Narasimhavarman, etc., most probably overlapped those of the last two members above mentioned. The probabilities seem to be that towards the last quarter of the ninth century several members of the family began to rule their own small territories styling themselves kings, and these chiefs largely figure in the inscriptions that have come down to us along with the others.

Dantivarman (circa 775 to 826).—We have ascertained the exact period of his accession to the throne of Kāñchīpuram by calculating back from the conquest of Toṇḍamaṇḍalam by Āditya. We possess inscriptions for Dantivarman dated from the second year of his reign (No. 256 of 1922) to fifty-first year (No. 262 of 1904). His records have been found from Trichinopoly District in the south to Tiruchchānūr in the north. According to the Vēlūrpāḷayam plates (*verse* 16) issued during the reign of his son Nandivarman III he was descended from Nandivarman Pallavamalla through Rēvā the Rāshṭrakūṭa princess.[4] Rēvā is here described as the chief queen who

[1]

Dantivarman	...	...	...	... 51 years.
Nandivarman (of Teḷḷāru)	...	...	...	... 23 ,,
Nripatunga	...	...		... 26 ,,
Aparājita	...	...	...	... 18 ,,
			Total	... 118 ,,

[2] *S.I.I.*, vol. iii, p. 396, verse 49.

[3]

Dantivarman	...	...	...	... 775-826
Nandivarman III	...	...	...	... 826-849
Nripatungavarman...		...	...	... 849-875
Aparājitavarman	...	...	...	... 875-893

[4] *S.I.I.*, vol. ii, part 5, p. 501.

"like the river Rēvā had her birth from a great king (from a high mountain).'[1] Dantivarman is stated to be 'a manifestation of the lotus-eyed Vishṇu himself, who was the delight of the earth whose object was the protection of the three worlds and in whom the group of pure qualities such as prowess, charity, and gratitude, attained eminence, as it were, after a long time enjoying the pleasures of each other's company.'[2] From verse 18 we learn that Dantivarman married a Kadamba princess called Aggaḷanimmaṭi described as the daughter of a Kadamba king—the crest-jewel of the Kadamba family. The name of this Kadamba king is not known. About the year A.D. 804 Govinda III, the Rāshṭrakūṭa king, appears to have invaded Kāñchi. A Rāshṭrakūṭa grant, dated Thursday the fifth *tithi* of the dark fortnight of the month of Vaiśāka of the year Subhānu, Śaka 726, expired, corresponding to Thursday, 4th April, A.D. 804, claims that Govinda III had conquered Dantiga, the ruler of Kāñchi and levied tribute from him.[3] The reasons prompting this Rāshṭrakūṭa attack on Kāñchi especially as Dantivarman the Pallava king was presumably a grandson of Dantidurga are not clear.

One of his Tamil inscriptions dated in the twelfth year of his reign has been discovered at the Pārthasārathi temple at Triplicane (Madras).[4] This inscription consists of nineteen lines of Tamil prose and is on a stone close to the entrance of the *garbhagṛha* of the temple. Dantivarman is here described as 'the ornament of the Pallava family' and as belonging to the Bhāradvāja Gotra. The object of the inscription is to record a gift of land. It is clear from this record that the Triplicane temple which is mentioned also in the hymns of the first Āḻvārs, continued to flourish during this period. Tirumangai Āḻvār, one of the Vaishṇava Āḻvārs, refers to this temple and the locality, and has recorded the important fact that a Pallava king constructed the temple.[5]

[1] *Ibid.*, p. 508, *vv.* 16, 17.
[2] *Ibid.*, p. 508, *vv.* 16, 17.
[3] *Ind. Ant.*, vol. xi, p. 127.
[4] *Ep. Ind.*, vol. viii, p. 291.
[5] This Pallava king referred to by Tirumangai Āḻvār was presumably an earlier king of Kāñchi who preceded Dantivarman.

Prof. Jouveau-Dubreuil argues,[1] from the fact that the inscription of Dantivarman ranging from the sixteenth year of his reign to the fifty-first year does not occur in any of the monuments found on the banks of the Kaveri while a dozen inscriptions of the Pāndyan king Māran Śaḍaiyan are found in the same region, that Dantivarman temporarily lost a part of his dominions in the south owing to the incursions of the Pāndyas. According to him Varaguṇa-Mahārāja led an invasion into the Pallava territory in the reign of Dantivarman. The Ambāsamudram inscription of the sixteenth year of this king is dated when this king was encamped in Araisūr on the banks of the Pennar. In the north, the Guḍimallam inscription shows that the Bāṇa king Vijayādityamāvalivāṇarāyar was a feudatory of Dantivarman. This record is dated in the forty-ninth year of Dantivarman.[2]

Nandivarman III (circa A. D. 826 to 849).—Dantivarman was succeeded on his death by his son Nandivarman III known in his inscriptions as Tellārrerinda Nandivarman, i.e. Nandivarman who defeated his enemies at Tellāru. According to the Vēlūrpāḷayam plates issued by this sovereign in his sixth year he is said to have, on the eve of his acquiring sovereignty, killed his enemies on the field of battle.[3] In the picturesque words of this record 'Nandivarman puffed up with the prowess of his arms acquired the prosperity of Pallava kingdom not easy for others to obtain by killing his enemies on the battle-field which was laughing as it were with the pearls dropping from the frontal globes of elephants slain by his unsheathed sword.' A contemporary Tamil work is *Nandikkalambakam*. A short account of this work appeared in the *Indian Antiquary* (vol. 37, pp. 170–173). The text of the poem which has long been out of print was published in

[1] *Pallavas*, p. 77.

[2] *Ep. Ind.*, vol. xi, p. 224.

[3] उत्खातखड्ग निहतद्विपकुम्भमुक्तमुक्ताफलप्रहसिते समरांगणे यः ।
शत्रून्निहत्य समवापदनन्यलभ्यां राज्यश्रियं स्वभुजविक्रमदर्पशाली ॥
v. 20.

1926 by Pandit V. Gopala Aiyar states that Nandivarman won a great victory against his enemies at the battle of Teḷḷāṟu. In the light of the information obtained from his other stone inscriptions it becomes clear that this must be the battle referred to in the Vēlūrpāḷayam plates quoted above. It has already been mentioned that towards the close of Dantivarman's reign the Pāṇḍyan forces under Varaguṇa made considerable inroads into the Pallava empire and had reached as far north[1] into Toṇḍamaṇḍalam as Araiśūr on the banks of the Pennar. By the time that Nandivarman III ascended the throne the forces of the opposing Pāṇḍyan king must have reached near Teḷḷāṟu not very distant from the Pallava capital when the forces of Nandivarman III inflicted a crushing defeat on them. Teḷḷāṟu the site of the battle may be correctly identified with the village of Teḷḷāṟu in the Wandiwash Taluk of North Arcot District.

Other Battles.—This victory against the Pāṇḍyans gave him the title by which his inscriptions thereafter mention him, namely, Teḷḷāṟṟerinda Nandipōtarayar. The Tamil panegyric in addition to the battle of Teḷḷāṟu [2] also refers to the other victories of Nandivarman such as those of Paḷayāṟu,[3] Veḷḷāṟu,[4] Nallāṟu,[5] and Kurugōḍu.[6] This series of further campaigns were evidently directed against the Pāṇḍyas themselves whom the Pallava king apparently pursued as they were retreating and inflicted defeats at Veḷḷāṟu, Paḷayāṟu, etc. One of the stanzas in the poem says that the Pallava army advanced as far as the banks of the Vaigai.[7] If this is correct we may presume that Nandivarman III marched as far as the Pāṇḍyan capital and defeated the Pāṇḍyas thoroughly.

Light thrown by 'Nandikkaḷambakam'.—This work makes it clear beyond doubt, that Nandivarman was a member of the

[1] Ep. Coll. No.105 of 1905.
[2] *Verses* 28, 33, 38, 49, 52, 53, 71, 75, 79, 80, 85, 86 and 96. The numbers refer to those of a MS. Edn., the work with the author.
[3] *Verse* 31. [4] *Verse* 23. [5] *Verse* 61.
[6] *Verses* 2, 35 and 84. [7] St. 4 and 81.

Pallava family as it calls him *Pallavarkōn* several times. The poem throws some light on the race of the Pallava family. Verse 39 refers to Nandivarman as '*Chandrakula-Prakāśan*' thus indicating that the Pallava family claimed their descent from the lunar race, a fact which is not however mentioned in any of the inscriptions. It is also clear from this work that Kāñchīpuram, Mallai (Mahābalipuram) and Mayilai (Mylāpur) were the chief Pallava cities during this period. The sway over these places is associated with the name of Nandivarman III by such references as '*Mallai-Vēndan*', '*Mayilai-Kāvalan*'. In this work his rule is also associated with the region of the Kavēri (*Kavirivaḷa-nāḍan*), the Kongu country, the Chēra land, the western regions as well as the northern. Inscriptions found in the northern regions of Pallava kingdom such as those of the Bāṇa king Vikramāditya clearly prove that his sway over the Bāṇas was not merely a poetic boast but real.[1] This king appears to have indulged his fancy in the assumption of a large number of surnames. This Tamil work enumerates the following surnames of this sovereign '*Avani-Nāraṇan*', '*Vidēlviḍugu*', '*Ugrakōpan*', '*Kuvalaya-Mārtānḍan*', '*Mānōdaya*', '*Vara-tungan*', etc. Nandivarman III appears to have patronized the Tamil poets very largely as is evident from allusion to this in *verses* 104 and 107 of the work. The author of the *Bhārata-Veṇbā, Perundevanar*, is taken to have flourished during his reign. The invocatory verses attached to the *Udyōgaparva* of this work, which alone has come down to us, mentions the defeat inflicted by Nandivarman III on his enemies at Teḷḷāṛu.[2]

Some interesting details may be gathered from the copper-plates of this period regarding the king and his rule. *Verse* 14 of the Bāhūr plates says that Nandivarman III had for his queen a Rāshṭrakūṭa princess called Śankā 'who was kind

[1] No. 229 of 1903 and *S.I.I.*, vol. viii, p. 93.

[2] Note by Editor.

to the people like a mother, was resplendent as Lakshmi incarnate.'

Verse 21 of the Vēlūrpāḷayam plates says of his rule: 'Never shone so (thoroughly a garden with the advent of) spring, nor men of high birth with (good) qualities, nor women with morality, nor a millionaire with charity, nor humility with knowledge, nor a lotus tank with the sun, nor the expanse of the sky with the moon at the end of the rainy season, as the people of this earth shone with the king.'

From the same record we learn that Nandivarman III was a devout worshipper of Śiva[1] and this is corroborated by *verse* 97 of *Nandikkaḷambakam*.

Nripatungavarman (circa 849 to 875).—Nripatungavarman known also as Nripatungavikramavarman and Nripatungapōtarayar succeeded his father Nandivarman about A.D. 850. The resemblance of his name to the Rāshṭrakūṭa Amogavarsha Nripatunga as well as the fact that his mother, the queen of Nandivarman III, is stated to be a Rāshṭrakūṭa princess in the Bāhūr plates[2] would indicate that this king was a grandson on the mother's side from Amogavarsha. Nripatunga appears to have continued the campaigns against the Pāṇḍyas who made inroads into the Pallava territory. The Bāhūr plates mention one of his victories on the banks of the Arichit (apparently a Sanskritized form of Ariśil) which has been identified with River Araśalār which flows near

[1] सुकृतमिदमजस्रम् रक्षतेति क्षितीशास्सकलनृपतिकेतुस्सोयमागामिनो वः ।
हरचरणसरोजोत्तंसचिह्नेन मूर्ध्ना मुकुळित करपद्मो वन्दते नन्दिवर्मा ॥ *S.I.I.*, vol. ii, part v, p. 509, ll. 64–5.

[2] *Ibid.*, vol. v, p. 515.

Kumbhakonam by the late Mr. T. A. Gopinatha Rao.[1] His adversary at this battle was probably Varaguṇa's son Śrī-Māra Parachakra-Kolāhala who according to the Tamil portion of the Śinnamanūr plates[2] is described as having repulsed the Gangas, the Pallavas, the Chōḷas, the Kalingas, and the Māgadhas who attacked him at *Kuḍamūkku*, the name by which the modern town of Kumbhakonam was known in the period before the tenth century.[3]

Extent of Empire.—The inscriptions of Nripatungavarman have been discovered all over the region from Pudukotta in the south to Guḍimallam in the north. From an inscription[4] of the Bāṇa king at the latter place—Vidyādhara—we learn that Nripatunga's sway was acknowledged by this Bāṇa chief. The Narthāmalai inscription of the Muṭṭaraiyan chief Śattan-Paḷiyili in the south who was one of Nripatunga's vassals shows that the authority of this king extended to the region of Pudukotta.[5] From the description contained in the Bāhūr plates that the glory of Nripatunga extended to other worlds as that of Rama, we may presume that here is an

[1] यत्प्रसादाज्जिता सेना पाण्ड्येन समरे पुरा ।
पारेरिच्चित्सराज्यश्चार्ददाह रिपुसंहतिम् ॥ v. 29.

v. 16. *S.I.I.*, vol. ii, part 5, p. 515.
The translation of the late T. A. Gopinatha Rao which Prof. Jouveau-Dubreuil follows requires to be reconsidered in view of an altered reading of the verse given in Dr. Hultzsch's of *verse* 16 (p. 50, *Pallavas*) text (*Ep. Ind.*, vol. xviii, p. 10) in which the sixteenth verse reads as follows :—

Yatprasādā(r)jjitāsēnā Paṇḍyēna Samarē purā |
Pārērichitsarājāgnirddadāha ripusaṃhatim ||

We have here no reference to the defeat sustained (by the Pallavas) at the hands of the Pāṇḍyas referred to in Gopinatha Rao's translation. Dr. Hultzsch translates the verse thus :—Resembling fire, this king (Nripatunga) by whose favour the Pāṇḍya had obtained an army formerly burnt a confederation of enemies on the further bank of the Arichit river. The supply of an army by Nripatunga to the Pāṇḍyan king, if the reading is correct, will necessitate a revision of our present views of the relationship of the Pallavas and Pāṇḍyas during this period.

[2] *M.E.R.*, 1907, pp. 63 ff.

[3] Inscription No. 13 of 1908 dated in the reign of Māran-Śaḍaiyan calls the place Tirukuḍamūkku. The *Tevaram* hymners also call the town Tirukuḍamūkku.

[4] No. 228 of 1903.

[5] No. 365 of 1904.

allusion perhaps to an unrecorded invasion of Ceylon during his reign.[1]

Educational Facilities.—A glimpse into the educational grants of the period is obtained from the Bāhūr plates[2] which were issued in the eighth year of this king. This record has for its object the registering of the gift of three villages—Chēṭṭupākkam, Iraipuṇaichēri and Viḷāngāṭṭangaḍuvanūr to the Vedic college at the village of Bāhūr[3] near Pondicheri in Aruvānāḍu. The grant was made by a member of the Pūśāli family and a descendant of the Kuru race (*verse* 18). This chief was the minister of Tungavarman, that is, Nripatunga who issued the necessary order for the grant of the villages (*verse* 21). The college at Bāhūr consisted of fourteen *gaṇas*, and was controlled by the learned men of the village, being organized and maintained by them. The fourteen *gaṇas* [4] are presumably the fourteen divisions of learning and consisted of—the Vedas (4), the Angas (6), Mīmāmsa (1), Nyāya (1), Purāṇa (1) and the Dharma-Śāstra (1).

Aparājitavarman (circa A.D. 875 to 883).—The order of succession after Nripatungavarman is not quite clear. According to the late Mr. Venkayya, Aparājita is the name of the son Nripatungavarman while T. A. Gopinatha Rao propounded the theory that the name Aparājita is merely another name for Nripatunga. In the inscriptions of this period we come across with several names such as Vijaya-Kampavarman, Vayiramēghavarman, Aparājitavarman and others. Of these we have inscriptions for Aparājitavarman ranging from the third to the eighteenth years of his reign in the region around Madras mostly from Tiruvoṟṟiyūr and Satyavēḍu. It is

[1] *Ibid.*, *verse* 17, *S.I.I.*, vol. ii, p. 515.

[2] This record which is now preserved in the *Bibliothèque Nationale*, Paris, has been recently re-edited with English translation and notes by the late Dr. E. Hultzsch who also furnishes two diagrams indicating the position of the villages granted in the charter which are reproduced elsewhere in this work. A palm-leaf MS. of this copper-plate containing different readings is now with Dr. S. Krishnaswami Aiyangar. *Ep. Ind.*, vol. xviii, p. 5.

[3] Vahūr and some of the village names mentioned in the detailed description of the boundaries in the grant survive to the present day.

[4] *See S.I.I.*, vol. ii, p. 514 footnote.

presumed that Kampavarman and Īśvaravarman as well as the other chiefs such as Vayiramēghan, whose inscriptions have been discovered at Kaveripākkam, Uttaramallūr, Olakkur and other parts of Chengleput District, enjoyed the rule of a part of the Pallava dominions along with Vayiramēghavarman.

Two important events are known regarding Aparājita. The first of these is the campaign against the Pāṇḍyas in which the Pallava king was allied with the Ganga king Prithivīpathi. According to the Udayēndiram plates[1] which enumerate the military exploits of the West Ganga Prithivīpathi I, he is described as 'having defeated by force the Pāṇḍya lord Varaguṇa at the head of a great battle of Śrīpurambiya and having thus made his friend's title Aparājita (the unconquered) significant, this hero entered heaven by sacrificing his own life.' We may identify Varaguṇa with the Pāṇḍya king of that name, Varaguṇa II, for whom we have a date for accession to the throne, namely, A.D. 862–863. The place of the battle Śrīpurambiyam has been identified by Dr. Hultzsch[2] with Tirupurambiyam near Kumbhakonam. 'How the Western Ganga king Prithivīpathi I whose dominions lay at least partly in the Mysore State and whose capital was Kolar, came to fight against the Pāṇḍya king Varaguṇa at Tirupurambiyam was hitherto inexplicable. From the two Ambur inscriptions[3] of the Ganga-Pallava king Nripatungavikramavarman we know that Prithivīpathi was his feudatory. It may, therefore, be presumed that Aparājita for whom the Western Ganga king fought was a Ganga-Pallava. If this be true Aparājita was perhaps the successor and presumably his son.'[4] The battle of Śrīpurambiyam may be dated with approximate accuracy about the year A.D. 880.

The Chōḷa Conquest of Toṇḍamaṇḍalam.—It has already been indicated that the Chōḷa king Āditya I who was making considerable inroads into the Pallava country brought about the defeat and ultimate conquest of the Toṇḍamaṇḍalam about

[1] *S.I.I.*, vol. ii, p. 384, *verse* 18.
[2] *Ibid.*, vol. ii, part 3, p. 381.
[3] *Ep. Ind.*, vol. iv, p. 182.
[4] *M.E.R. for 1906–7*, p. 47.

the close of the ninth century. This corresponded to the period before twenty-first year of Āditya. The latest of the Tirukaḷukkuṅṛaṃ inscriptions[1] is dated in the twenty-first year of Rājakēsarivarman. 'Taking this provisionally as the last year of Āditya's reign and deducting it from A.D. 907, the date of accession of his son Parāntaka I we get roughly to about A.D. 886 for the commencement of Āditya's reign.' It is presumable that the conquest of Toṇḍamaṇḍalam was effected considerably late in his reign and may be dated towards the end of the ninth century. The Tiruvālangāḍu plates say of the Chōḷa king Āditya I, son of Vijayālaya,[2] that 'having conquered in battle the Pallava with his brilliant army, though (he was) Aparājita (the unconquered) of his queen (viz.) and accomplished his object in this direction too.' In other words, the Chōḷa king Āditya I defeated the Pallava king Aparājitavarman and added the Toṇḍamaṇḍalam to his dominions. Thus the kingdom of Pallavas passed into the hands of the Chōḷas with the death of Aparājita.

The monuments belonging to this period are in the Aparājita style and, in the opinion of Jouveau-Dubreuil, very rare. The Vīraṭṭānēśvara temple at Tiruttaṇi, which contains inscriptions dated in the eighteenth year of Aparājitavarman is attributable to this king the Tamil verse[3] which is inscribed in this temple being supposed to have been composed by the king.

Other Miscellaneous Kings.—Some observations may be made on Kampavarman and Vayiramēghavarman before closing the survey. Over twenty inscriptions have been discovered dated in the regnal years ranging from the sixth to the twenty-fifth years[4] of Kampavarman who according to Hultzsch

[1] *Ep. Ind.*, vol. iii, p. 379. [2] v. 49. [3] Ins. No. 433 of 1905.

[4] His inscriptions have been found at the following :—

Sixth year	Uttaramallūr
Eighth year	do.
Tenth year	Ukkal.
Fifteenth year	Uttaramallūr
Seventeenth year	Kaveripākkam.
Twenty-third year	Uttaramallūr.

was a brother of Nripatungavarman. Whether this king succeeded Nandivarman III as king, or whether in the confusion that followed the death of Nripatunga he made himself an independent ruler in the North Arcot District and the region round about Kāñchi it is not clear from present evidence.

The inscriptions of this king are for the most part donative and do not furnish any historical details other than one record [1] which refers to the destruction of Olakkur and the death of a hero. This record is on a slab set up near the village-munsiff's *śāvaḍi* at Olakkur and is a *Vīragal* of the period of Kampaperumāḷ who may be identified with Kampavarman. It records the death of a hero on the occasion of the destruction of the place in the later part of the ninth century.

Vayiramēghavarman.—Two stone records have been discovered at the Agastyēśvara temple at Poyyanūr in the Arkonam Taluk which mentions the name of a new king apparently belonging to the Pallava family dated in the second year. According to the late V. Venkayya, the name Vayiramēgha was a *biruda* assumed by Dantivarman, and is the same name occurring in th eexpressions Vayiramēgataṭāka, Vayiramēghavāykkāl, etc., mentioned in the inscriptions. It has to be presumed that the name is more like Pallava than other dynastic names.

Chandrāditya (*No. 284 of 1916*).—This is a record written in the *Pallava-Grantha* on a pillar in the rock-cut temple at Mēlaichēri in the Gingee Taluk of the South Arcot District. It states that the Śiva temple called Śri-Śikhari-Pallavēśvaram was excavated by Chandrāditya at Śimhapura (Śingavaram). Prof. Jouveau-Dubreuil who discovered this inscription considers it probable that Chandrāditya was one of the names of Narasimhavarman I or Paramēsvaravarman I. This is, however, uncertain. There are in addition to these a few [2] inscriptions of this period belonging to Kāṭṭirai, Vijaya-Narasimhavarman

[1] No. 357 of 1909.

[2] Nos. 3 of 1899, 119 of 1897, also *Ep. Ind.*, vol. vii, p. 24, and vol. iv, p. 177.

and Vijaya-Īśvaravarman which need not be examined here as their position in the Pallava family is not clear.

With Nripatunga or Aparājita, the main line of the Pallava kings appears to have come to an end. But, however, a branch of them known as the Noḷambas claiming descent from Tṛnayana-Pallava continued to exercise sovereignty at Noḷaṃbavādi—thirty-two thousand. This region comprised the modern Bellary District and portions of Mysore. Here, as the records show, the Noḷamba chiefs continued in power as late as the thirteenth century A.D. The Hēmāvati Pillar inscription, which gives a genealogy of the Noḷambas, mentions that they belonged to the Īśvaravamsa and enumerates the names of several kings of this line. These include Mangala, Simhapota, Charuponnēra, Nanniga, Anniga, and Dilipa. Brief accounts of these are given in L. Rice's Mysore and Coorg from Inscriptions.[1]

[1] L. Rice, *Mysore and Coorg from Inscriptions*, pp. 55-59.

CHAPTER X

GENERAL CONSIDERATIONS OF PALLAVA RULE IN SOUTH INDIA

THE rule of the Pallava kings in the Tamil land for an unbroken period of nearly eight centuries resulted in stamping the administration of the country with a particular type of culture some of the aspects of which may now be briefly indicated. This is visible not only in the administration of government by the central and local authorities of the Pallava times (A.D. 200 to 900), but in practically every aspect of life, in religion, literature, art, etc. In studying the Pallava administration, literary history, art and religious movements, we are unfortunately not in the possession of all the materials that would help us to reconstruct the history of the culture and civilization of the times. We are dependent for the most part on the inscriptions and copper-plate grants of this period as well as the few monuments that have survived. It is, therefore, not strange that the picture obtained by us has many gaps that have to be filled up by future discoveries.

Administration.—In the numerous copper-plate charters that have been discovered from time to time by the officers of the Government Epigraphy Department and by the labours of private scholars we obtain excellent glimpses of certain aspects of Pallava polity. From the earliest of these, namely, the Hirahadagalli copper-plates issued from the capital Kāñchīpuram we learn that already in the middle of the third century there prevailed a system of administration with the king at the top and the provincial governors and several departmental ministers in charge of parks, public baths, forests, reminding us in several details of the Mauryan and in some respects the Gupta administration. From the grant of the king made at his palace office in the head-quarters in Kāñchīpura addressed to the provincial Viceroy at

Amarāvati [1] and several others which were issued in the following periods it is evident that during the early Pallava days the empire of the Pallavas was not unlike those of modern times divided into bigger and smaller divisions for the government of which officers of the state were appointed. The heads of departments were selected from among the members of the royal family such as the younger sons and distinguished members of the army. In Toṇḍamaṇḍalam the distinct division [2] into twenty-four kottams appears to have been introduced

[1] Lüders, *Ep. Ind.*, vol. x, App.

'From Kāñchīpura the righteous supreme king (*Dharmamahārāja*) of the great king of the Pallavas, Śivaskandavarman, a Bharadvāja and an officer of Agnishṭōma, Vājapēya and Aśvamēdha sacrifices issues the following orders :—

We send greetings to the princes (Rajkumara), rulers of districts (Raṭṭhika), chiefs of Madambas (customs officers), local prefects (Dēśādhikata) . . . the free-holders of the various villages (Gāma-gāmabhōjaka) . . . ministers (Amachcha), guards (Arakhadikata), captains (Gumikas), Dūtikas (Messengers ?), spies (Sanjarantakas) and warriors (Bhaḍamanuśas).

[2] These are enumerated in the Mackenzie MSS. as well as the Chingleput District Manual App. H. p. 438 and *in The Tamils 1800 years ago* and are as follows :

(1) Puḻal-Kōṭṭam, (2) Īkkūṭṭu-Kōṭṭam, (3) Maṇavīr-Kōṭṭam, (4) Śengāṭṭu-Kōṭṭam, (5) Paiyūr-Kōṭṭam, (6) Eyil-Kōṭṭam of which the principal town was Kāñchīpuram, (7) Dāmal-Kōṭṭam, (8) Uṟṟukāṭṭu-Kōṭṭam, (9) Kalattūr-Kōṭṭam, (10) Śembūr-Kōṭṭam, (11) Āmbur-Kōṭṭam, (12) Veṇkuṉṟakōṭṭam, (13) Palakuṉṟa-Kōṭṭam, (14) Ilangāṭṭu-Kōṭṭam, (15) Kaliyūr-Kōṭṭam, (16) Śengarai-Kōṭṭam, (17) Paḍuvūrkōṭṭam, (18) Kadikūr-Kōṭṭam, (19) Śendirukkai-Kōṭṭam, (20) Kuṉṟavaṭṭāna-Kōṭṭam, (21) Vēngaḍa-Kōṭṭam, (22) Velūr-Kōṭṭam, (23) Śettūr-Kōṭṭam and (24) Puliyūr-Kōṭṭam. This division of Toṇḍamaṇḍalam, the *Tundaka Rāshtra* of the copper-plates, seems to have come into existence prior to the period of the Pallava kings known to us from epigraphy, probably in the period of Chōḻa viceroyalty of Tondaman Iḷam-Tirayanat Kāñchi. Although these districts do not figure in the early copper-plates of the Pallavas they are rather frequent in the later stone inscriptions datable from the eighth and the ninth centuries. Puḻal-Kōṭṭam with its subdivision figures in the Velurpalayam plates of the sixth year of Nandivarman III (*S.I.I*, vol. ii, p. 509) while Kaḻaṭṭūr-Kōṭṭam, Īkkāṭṭu-Kōṭṭam, and Paḍuvūr-Kōṭṭam are mentioned in inscriptions dated in the fourteenth year of Nandivarman III, and the eleventh and the twenty-sixth years of Nripatungavarman, (Ep. Col. 349 of 1911, and 460 of 1905). Eyil-Kōṭṭam the division around Kāñchīpura also figures in the inscription dated in the fifteenth year of Nripatungavarman (Ep. Col. 461 of 1905). For the study of the ancient historical geography the references in the later Pallava inscriptions to these are very helpful. Some of the places such as Kaḻaṭṭūr, Dāmal, and Uṟṟukkāḍu which originally must have been important places after which the divisions were named have survived to the present day.

in an earlier period retained unaltered during the age of the Pallavas as we find them commonly figure in their inscriptions. The *Rāshṭras* which appear to be the equivalent of the *maṇḍala* were thus parcelled out into the hands of the viceroys called *Viṡhayikas* while the smaller divisions such as the Koshṭakas (*koṭṭam*) and Grāmas, were placed in charge of dēśatikadas and vapittas. The ministers and *rahasyādikadas* (privy councillors) were examined and consulted on state matters by the sovereign. Royal orders such as the one embodied in the Hirahadagalli plates were drawn by the king's private secretary. It is also learned from the early documents that there were officers in charge of the customs and the places or offices where they were collected were called *maṇḍapa* and the officers who were entrusted with the collection of the customs were known as *maṇḍapis*. There were also during this period special officers posted at bathing pools and tanks whose chief duties consisted in looking after the convenience of the bathers and their safety. They are called in this record as Tīrthikas (Superintendents of bathing places). The persons mentioned by the name of the Gumikas who are taken by some scholars as captains appear to have been officers in charge of forests, a fact which shows that there was something like a forest department. The term *neyka* which resembles the Sanskrit name Nāyaka probably stands for the military officer whose status was next to those of *Sēnāpatis* or Commanders of the army. All these clearly indicate an elaborate system of governmental organization which as already indicated above resemble the North Indian [1] rather than any southern system of administration that we know of.

The nature of village government at this period.—Whether or not the self-governing village corporation which, from the early Chōḷa times as we are familiar with, prevailed in the

[1] The administration of Government in North India was conducted in accordance with a series of books some of which were pre-christian and others post-christian. The chief works in this series were Kautilya's *Arthasastra*, Kamandakā's *Nītiśāstra* and *Śukranīti*.

early Pallava days we have not the material to judge from the ascertained facts at our disposal. But it appears that this later village organization with the characteristic features of committees, managing general village administration economic, financial, and judicial, existed in the later Pallava days for which we possess good evidence. That the system of government and administration was highly systematic, and even bureaucratic, we learn with the help of certain of the early Sanskrit charters mentioning the minute details of the boundaries of gifted lands and defining its situation—a fact which shows the efficiency of the land survey departments of the Pallavas. The Uruvapalli plates [1] give a typical example of such detailed-land survey. This is by no means the only instance of the elaborate arrangements and precautions taken in marking the village boundaries in the inscriptions. The Bāhūr plates belonging to the ninth century in recording a gift of the three villages near Pondicherry give similar details. 'According to the report submitted by the headman of the *nāḍu* the boundaries of the land granted (to the Bahur College) were as follows: Of the two villages of Viḷāṉgāṭṭangaduvanūr and Śēṭṭuppākkam, the eastern boundary is to the west of the boundary of a forest and of the boundary of Neṉmalippākkam; the southern boundary is to the north of the boundary of Neṉmalippākkam, of the boundary of Nelvāyippakkām, and of the boundary of Urattūr; the western boundary is to the east of the boundary of Māmbakkam and of sixty rice-fields which form a Brahmadēya

[1] *Ind. Ant.*, vol. v, 1876, p. 50.

' . . . In this village there are 200 entire *nivartanas*. The limit of these *nivartanas* are :—On the west the boundary of the Kēndūkūra village, are the limit; on the south River Suprayōga is the limit; on the east the same is the limit; to the north by the south there is a rock on the side of the great road proceeding thence to the north, there is a tamarind tree, proceeding thence to where there is a rock on the road to the village of Kurupura, and to the village of Kundukūra; proceeding thence to the north there is a heap of rocks; proceeding thence to the north there is rock on the limit of the cultivated field of the Brahman as in the village and proceeding to the west, the limit is the edge of the boundaries of the village of Kondamuruvīḍur.'

near Viḷāṇgaṭṭangaḍuvanūr; and the northern boundary is to the south of Vagūr.[1] . . .' It will be gathered from these records that the village and the central government of this period took the greatest pains in maintaining a detailed record of all the arable and waste lands, lakes, tanks, wells and rivers, rocks and even trees, for purposes of not only grants of land to temples and Brahmans, but also for revenue purposes.

Taxation and revenue.—From these we shall now proceed to the sources of taxation in the Pallava age that are mentioned in the records of the Pallava kings. We have no direct evidence of central or local finance during the early Chōḷa or Pallava times

[1] Dr. Hultzsch furnishes the following interesting plan indicating the relative position of the villages and boundaries referred to in the Tamil portion of the Bāhur plates. *Ep. Ind.*, vol. xviii. pp. 8-9.

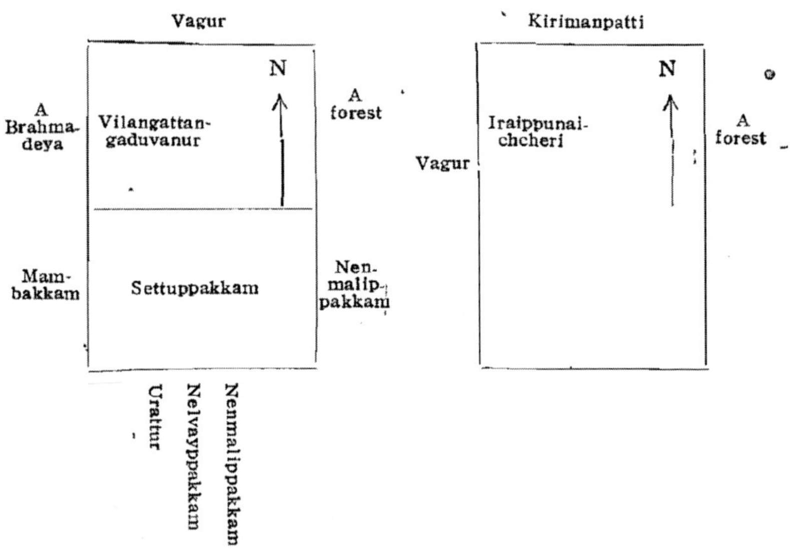

Of these villages, Vahūr survives as Bāhur, while Vilangaṭṭangaduvanūr and Kirmaṇpatti are identical with Kaduvanūr and Kiḻmāmbākkam situate to the west and north-east of Bahur, an important locality south of Pondicherry.

as none of the large number of records that have come down to us were intended to set forth exhaustively the financial machinery for the enlightenment of the modern scholar; we can however infer from the list of exemptions stated in the various records of lands and other grants at our disposal what taxes and dues a village was ordinarily subjected to if it was other than a land gifted to Brahmans or a temple in which case the exemptions were secured to the donee. First may be noted some of the seignorial rights mentioned in the earliest Pallava copper-plate charters. The Hirahadagalli plates already mentioned are very interesting in this respect. This record states that the garden Chillerakoḍuṁkā the object of the grant is to be free from the taking of sweet and sour milk and sugar . . . from taxes . . . forced labour free from the payment of the oxen in succession, free from the taking of grass and the wood . . . from the taking of vegetables and flowers. . . . It also mentions the important particular towards the close of the grant where it says that with these and other immunities of the eighteen kinds it must be exempted. It is thus clear from this early Pallava record that about the first quarter of the third century Pallava kings had laid claim to not less than eighteen[1] kinds of dues from the villagers (*Ashṭādaśaparihāras*) which they ordinarily could claim except in cases of gifted lands. The Mayidavolu plates of the Pallava king Śivaskandavarman [2] mentions among the immunities secured for the village of Viripara which was the object of the grant, freedom for the diggings of salt which shows that salt-manufacture was a royal monopoly, from the supply of bullocks in succession, the entrance of soldiers, the supply of boiled rice, etc. As we do not come across with some of

[1] It is important to note that these were not at all in the nature of taxes but more of free-will offerings of first fruits by gardeners to kings and of supplies of means of transport to royal officers while on tour. Mr. Longhurst is therefore wrong when he remarks on this that 'it is thus obvious that the people were liable to all these taxes and imposts on the ordinary necessaries of life,' and that it clearly shows that in the fourth century at any rate there was no 'Golden Age' in Southern India. (*An. Rep. of the Arch. Dep. of Southern Circle* 1918-1919, Part II, p. 21.)

[2] *Ep. Ind.*, vol. vi, pp. 88 ff.

these rights in the later records of the Pallavas it is probable that some of these rights fell out of use.

Passing on from the days of the early Pallavas to that of the later Pallavas, we notice in the Sanskrit charters of Paramēśvaravarman I, Nandivarman Pallavamalla and that of his grandson Nandivarman III more details regarding the rights of the Pallava kings of the period to other items of taxes and duties, are available. From a study of the Tamil portions of the Kaśākkuḍi, Kūram, the Tanḍantōṭṭam, Vēlūrpāḷayam and the Bāhūr plates we learn that during this period there were, what have been called profession-taxes but are really excise on local products, on oil mill-owners, potters, goldsmiths, toddy-drawers, as well as duties on areca-nuts exposed for sale and sold in the markets, duty on looms, presents on the occasion of new marriages and royalty on the manufacture of salt. Some of these such as the Īḻampūtchi[1] and Puthāḻi are inexplicable. Good specimens of this royal exemption order are contained in the Tamil portion of the Tanḍantōṭṭam plates dated in the fifty-eighth year of Nandivarman II, Pallavamalla: the immunities evidently indicate some of the taxes which were customary :—

'No tax of any kind such as duty on oil-press and looms, *Uḻaviyakūli*, the fee on marriages, *ūreṭṭu* fee on potters, *taṭṭukāyam*, duty on toddy-drawers and shepherds, fee on stalls, brokerage fee, *tirumugakkāṇam*, royalty paid for the manufacture of salt, the good cow, the good bull, *vaṭṭināḻi*, fee on basket of grain exposed for sale in the market, areca-nuts exposed for sale in the shops, *Budanāḻi*, and others which the king could take and enjoy. Damanagam may be planted; mansions and large edifices may be built of burnt bricks; reservoirs and wells may be sunk; cocoanut trees

[1] Of these terms some are obscure. Pūtchi seems to mean a kind of due and Īḻampūtchi might mean a duty on Iḻavar or toddy drawers. Tirumugakkaṇam apparently means a fee for the messenger bringing royal messages or orders. Ulaviyakkūli has been taken to mean the hire for well-diggers. The terms *putaḻi kannittukanam*, *arikoḻi*, *nedum parai* and *ūrettu* are not clear.

may be planted in groves; and large oil-presses may be used. . . .[1]

The emperor in these records is called Mahārāja and Dharmamahārāja. In the Gupta inscriptions of North India also, the emperor is called Mahārājādhirāja and Paramēśvara. In the Gupta Government the emperor is the centre of a group of subordinate kings. The territory of the empire was called a *Rājya* in the Gupta inscriptions as well as *Rāshṭra*, and *Dēśā* and *Maṇḍala* which occur also in the Pallava inscriptions. The territories in the Pallava Empire are divided in the records into Koṭṭāms and Nāḍus on the lines of the Gupta administration where they are similarly divided into *Bhukti*, *Vishaya*, and *Grāma*. There is a close resemblance between the sources of taxation and revenue between the early Pallava records and Gupta inscriptions. These may be gathered from the inscriptions recording various grants. These include several items such as Uparikara, Vāṭa Bhūta, Hiraṇya, Ädēya, etc. Several of the Gupta inscriptions as well as Pallava inscriptions indicate negatively the obligations imposed by the state. Several of the *Gupta Inscriptions*, may be compared with portions of the Pallava records dealing with exemption from taxes.[2]

About the beginning of the ninth century stone inscriptions of the Pallavas become abundant and in these we find interesting particulars of the activity of the village *Sabhās* all over the empire particularly in the Chingleput District. A perusal of the stone records of this period relating to these dated in the years of the later Pallava kings, Nandivarman II, Dantivarman, Nandivarman III and Aparājita shows that the following figure among the large numbers of places that enjoyed self-governing village *Sabhās*: Āḍambākkam,

[1] *S.?I. I.*, vol. ii, pp. 530–31.

[2] It (tho village rendered free) is not to pay taxes; it is not to be entered by the regular troops or by the umbrella.bearers; it does not carry with it the right to cows and bulls in succession of production, or to the abundance of flowers and milk, or to the pasturage, hides, and charcoal, or to the mines for the purchase of salt in a moist state . . . (*F. G. I.*, p. 242.)

Avaninārāyaṇachaturvēdimangalam (Kaveripakkam), Maṇali, Tiruvoṟṟiyūr, Kūram, Perumunaiyūr, Tiruviprambēḍu, Anbil Veṇkuṉṟam, Uttaramallūr, Perunguḷi, Tirukoilūr, and Ukkal. An account of the activities of these village assemblies in repairing tanks, accepting deposits for charitable purposes and other works has come down to us.

The Assemblies.—Though we know the existence of the village assemblies in the various parts of the Pallava empire we do not know the nature of the rules that regulated their constitution and working, their exact sphere of action and the relation of this to the central government. Inscriptions copied in the Chingleput District alone indicate that during the ninth century different types of village assemblies carried on their work. One of the most important of these was called the *Sabhā*. These were usually to be found in Brahmadēya villages granted to the Brahmaṇas and therefore were almost entirely run by the Brahmans. The rules laid down in the Uttaramallūr inscription[1] for the membership of the village assemblies applies in all probability to such *Sabhās*. A recently discovered inscription[2] dated in the thirty-first year of Māranśaḍaiyan throws some light on some of the rules of membership of the village *Sabhās* which differ from all those known till now. (i) It is stated in this record that of the children of the shareholders in the villages, only one who is well versed in the *Mantra-Brāhmaṇa* and one *Dharma*, and well-behaved, may be on the village assembly and only one of similar qualifications may be in the assembly for a share purchased, received as present, or acquired by him as *Strīdhana*; (ii) that shares purchased, presented, or acquired as *Strīdhana* could entitle one if at all, only to a full membership in the assembly, and in no case will quarter or half or three-quarter of the membership be recognized; (iii) that those who purchase shares should elect only such men to represent their share in the assembly as have critically studied a whole *Vēda* with their *pariśishṭas*; (iv) that those who do

[1] *A.S.R. for 1904-5*, pp. 13–145. [2] *M.E.R. for 1913*, para 23.

not possess full membership as laid down by Rule II cannot stand on any committee for the management of the village affairs; (v) that those who satisfy the prescribed conditions should in no case persistently oppose the proceedings of the assembly, by saying nay, nay, to every proposal brought up before the assembly; (vi) those who do this together with their supporters will pay a fine [1] of five *kāśu* on each item in which they have so behaved and still continue to submit to the same rules.[2]

The activities of the *Sabhās* were varied in character and they dealt with all important aspects of village life. From the Pallava inscriptions alone we gather that these *Sabhās* looked after the temple and its administration, and received the endowments made on behalf of temple services. In addition to this many of these *Sabhās* looked after the supervision and repairs to the village tanks which were brought into existence with considerable labour at the instance of the Pallava kings. Some of these immense irrigational tanks which must have engaged the skilled labour of a vast body of men have survived to our own times. These include, the Paramēśvara Taṭāka in Kūram near Kāñchīpuram, the Mahēndra Taṭāka in Mahēndravāḍi not far from Arkonam, Tirayanēri, Vayiramēga Taṭāka in Uttaramallūr, in the Madurantakam Taluk, Chitramēgha Taṭāka, Veḷḷēri and probably the large tank at Māmaṇḍûr which now irrigates a large area. The

[1] The last provision is rather ingenious in as much as it shows that as early as the ninth century the necessity to deal with the refractory and obstructionist tactics had been felt though the safeguard does not appeal to the modern mind.

[2] Fuller details are available in Chola inscriptions such as those of Parāntaka and his successors when the village assemblies not only managed all local affairs such as the collection of revenue, upkeep of tanks and irrigation canals, administration of temples but also looked after the local judicial administration, the education religious and secular of the young as well as the adult, and maintenance of hospitals for the diseased. The principle of election and the ballot box became very popular and local administration was conducted very efficiently. The annual change of office-bearers in the various committees extended to every villager the opportunity of getting acquainted with practical administration.

irrigation channels figuring in the Pallava inscriptions include the Perumbiḍugu Vāykkāl, the channel cut from the Pālār to Kūram and the Vayiramēga Vāykkāl, both of which probably owe their origin to the Pallava kings bearing these surnames. The supervision and upkeep of these tanks and channels must have entailed a great deal of labour and attention on the part of the village *Sabhās* many of which had a separate Tank Supervision Committee as is clear from one of the later inscriptions.[1] The great tank at Uttaramallūr owes its origin to one of the Pallava kings named Vayiramēgan and figures frequently in the inscriptions relating to the activities of the Uttaramallūr *Sabhā* during the reign of Dantivarman and Vijaya Kampavarman.[2]

The other important work of the village *Sabhās* of the Pallava age was the management of temple property and service. The temple appears to have played an important roie in the age of the Pallavas and must have attracted large numbers of people for various purposes. A close study of the inscriptions of this period shows that the Pallava kings took a great deal of interest in the building of these temples as well as their proper upkeep. These are scattered all over the Tamil districts, some of the most beautiful and important ones being found at the capital of the kingdom, Kāñchīpuram. The inscriptions at the Rājasimhēśvara and at the Vaikunṭaperumāḷ temples bear ample testimony to the great devotion of the Pallava kings but details of their management in those days are not available. It is quite probable that their management was entrusted to the temple committee of the city council in the days of Rājasimha and Paramēśvaravarman. In the actual management of the temple administration which involved the looking after of lands, appointment of contractors for the day-to-day supply of rice, ghee, flowers, etc., defalcations sometimes

[1] No. 84 of 1898, dated in the twenty-first year of Kampavarman mentions the name of this Committee as the Ēri-Vāriya-Perumakkaḷ.

[2] *Ep. Col.*, No. 74 of 1898, dated in the ninth year of Dantivarman; and *Ep. Col.*, No. 61 of 1898, dated in the twenty-first year of the same king and *Ep. Col.*, No. 84 of 1898, of Kampavarman.

occurred even leading to the reduction in the actual offering to the deity. One such instance is recorded in the Triplicane inscription of Dantivarman, dated in the twelfth year of his reign.[1] The temple management (*kulankiḻār*) having mortgaged one of the temple fields in Karumāracheri, the offering to the God fell short. This was restored however by the pious offices of one Pugaḻtuṇai-Vissiyarāyan who redeemed the mortgaged field.

Literature during the Pallava Age.—Another important benefit of the Pallava rule in South India was the impetus given to literature, particularly Sanskrit. The age of the Pallavas is also the period of the celebrated movements of the Āḻvars and the Aḍiyars which so much revolutionized the religious outlook of the people at that time. The Pallava kings on account partly of their having come from the north had distinct leanings from the beginning for Sanskrit literature and all their early charters with the exception of a few are written in Sanskrit. The *praśasti* portions in the later copper-plate charters such as the Kāśākkuḍi plates of Nandivarman Pallavamalla which furnish a historical account of the family of the donor appear to have been written by poets of considerable ability who adorned the contemporary Pallava court. It is only in the later Pallava period that a Tamil portion came to be added to the charters. The *praśasti* portions as well as the descriptive accounts (such as those of the battle of Peruvāḷanallūr)[2] of some of the plates compare very favourably with some of the best Sanskrit style of the classical *kavis*. We do not unfortunately possess any means whereby the names of the early Sanskrit poets of the Pallava kings before Simhavishṇu could be gathered. There is, however, no doubt whatever that Kāñchīpuram almost from the beginning of the Pallava rule was a centre of Sanskrit learning. The city appears to have been famous as a seat of Sanskrit learning as early as the second century B.C.; Patanjali discusses the derivation of the word

[1] Triplicane inscription of Dantivarman, *Ep. Ind.*, vol. viii, pp. 291 ff.
[2] Kūram plates; *S. I. I.*, vol. i, p. 153.

Kāñchīpuraka, possibly because it was famous for Sanskrit learning even then. Even in the Sangam age it will be remembered that Aṛavaṇa Aḍigaḷ taught Buddhistic philosophy at this place and at a subsequent period Dignāga the logician who is believed to have been the author of *Nyāyapravēśa* spent considerable time at Kāñchī and was perhaps a product of mediæval Pallava culture. Later, Mayūra Śarman, the progenitor of the Kadamba family, had to proceed to this place for the completion of the Vedic studies. It is not surprising therefore that Simhavishṇu about the close of the sixth century when he heard of Bhāravi staying with Durvinīta, the Western Ganga king, invited him to his court according to the *Avantisundarikathāsāra*.[1] It is by no means unlikely, that *Kirtārjunīya* the well-known work of this poet was composed about this period.

Of Mahēndravarman I, the illustrious son and successor of Simhavishṇu, more is known. His great command of Sanskrit is fully seen in his work *Mattavilāsà Prahasana* which has survived to our times. This has already been noticed while dealing with this king in an earlier chapter. The great musical inscription at Kuḍumiyāmalai about the same period, as well as the beautiful Sanskrit compositions at the Trichinopoly rock-cut temple and elsewhere are also indicative of the refined taste for Sanskrit composition at this period. It was during the reign of one of his successors that Daṇḍin, the celebrated savant, spent considerable time in the Pallava court, even paying a visit to the wonderful sculptures of Mahāmallapuram. It is not improbable that this was towards the close of the seventh century A.D. The *Avantisundarikathāsāra* contains interesting details of an earlier sojourn of Daṇḍin in the south, while quite young, when Kāñchīpuram was in the throes of foreign invasion and siege by the Chāḷukyas, when the citizens of the place had to desert the city temporarily. Daṇḍin returned to Kāñchī long after and in all probability flourished for long at the Pallava court. Mātṛidatta, a poet and scholar

[1] See App. *Avantisundarikathāsāra.*

and Rāma Śarman, also figure among the friends of Danḍin and wereperhaps associated with him at Kāñchīpuram. The names of Sanskrit poets at the Pallava court during this period other than these are not known. It is held by some scholars that the Sanskrit plays published recently in Trivandrum as Bhāsa's were abridgements made during this period of earlier works of Bhāsa and Śūdraka for being staged at the Pallava court. It has been suggested by Mr. L. D. Barnett that these are the works of an anonymous author in the court of the Pānḍyan King Rājasimha.[1] But as we have got evidence that the Pallava court was the great centre of Sanskrit learning during this period it seems to be more correct to regard that the dramas referred to above were intended to be staged at the Pallava court as is evident from the colophons of some of these plays.[2] It has been presumed also that the work was composed at Kāñchī from the occurrence of the name of Dantivarman in the manuscripts of *Mudrārākshasa* found in Malabar in the last benedictory verses.

The *Tēvāram* and the *Nālāyira Prabandham* hymns were also produced during the age of the Pallava monarchs. We have already seen that Appar, the first of the *Tēvāram* hymnists was the well-known contemporary of Mahēndravarman I who was converted to Śaivism by him. His hymns in the *Tēvāram* collection number over 3000 and are full of Sanskrit expressions and Brahmanical culture and tradition. Tiruñāna-Sambandar was his younger contemporary and flourished during the reign of Narasimhavarman I. During his period Śaivism was very much in the ascendant and Śiva temples were very numerous in South India. According to the *Periyapurāṇam* account he is said to have succeeded in converting Neḍumāṛan the contemporary Pandyan King to Śaivism after a successful disputation with the Śamaṇas who

[1] *J.R.A.S. for 1919*, p. 233.

[2] इमां सागरपर्यन्तां हिमवद्विन्ध्यकुण्डलाम् ।
पृथ्वीमेकातपत्राङ्कां राजसिंहः प्रशास्तु नः ॥

were very powerful at this period at Madura. His poems in the *Tēvāram* number nearly 4000. Sundarar the last of the sixty-three Śaiva saints appears to have lived in the ninth century and mentions Appar and Sambandar who preceded him. His *Tiruttoṇḍatokai* was the basis on which Nambiyāṇḍār Nambi composed his *Andādi* and these two formed the main sources of Śēkkiḷār for writing the *Periyapurāṇam.* Sundanar's hymns amount to eleven hundreds nearly in the *Tēvāram.*

About the age of Māṇikkavāśagar the well-known author of *Tiruvāśakam* and *Tirukkovai,* there exists some doubt. According to some Tamil scholars he preceded the three *Tēvāram* hymnists. But as he clearly refers to the Pandyan King Varaguṇa in his works there cannot be any doubt that he flourished in the earlier half of the ninth century. His *Tiruvāśakam* is a very popular work and celebrates Śiva's miracles in a simple and attractive style. His activities were confined to Chidambaram and its adjoining places and he does not appear to have come into active contact with the Pallavas.

Of the twelve Vaishṇava saints known as the Āḷvārs some of whom flourished during the Pallava age the first four—Pēyāḷvār, Budattāḷvār, Poygaiāḷvār and Tirumaḷiśaiāḷvār, appear to have been contemporaries and lived at a time before the advent of the Pallavas to Kāñchīpuram. Tradition however records that Tirumaḷiśai was a contemporary of one of the Pallava kings, perhaps Toṇḍamān-Iḷamtiraiyan. Of the others Tirumangaiāḷvār is the most important and has already been referred in a previous chapter. There is a credible Vaishṇava tradition that he held a successful disputation with the Śaiva saint Tiruñāna-Sambandar. If this can be relied on he should have lived an exceptionally long period of time. His work exceeds that of any other Āḷvar except Nammāḷvār and his peregrinations were spread all over South India. His great Pallava contemporary was Nandivarman Pallavamalla who reigned for an exceptionally long period of sixty-five years. This Āḷvār unlike the other Āḷvārs makes frequent mention of contemporary political occurrences including the martial exploits of the Pallava King referred to above. One of his verses contains an allusion to the repulse of the Chāḷukyan King which is corroborated by inscriptions. The war implements of the Pallavas as well as their other insignia also find mention in his hymns. The other Āḻvārs, such as Kulaśēkhara, Nammāḻvār, Periyāḻvār, Āṇḍāl, etc., did not flourish in Toṇḍamaṇḍalam and did not come into contact with the Pallava Kings.

The origin and evolution of Pallava art and architecture does not properly belong to this work and may be studied elsewhere.[1] It may be however noted here that it is a mistake to suppose that temples did not exist in South India before the Pallava age, for mention is made of them in early Śaṅgam works. They were then built only of wood and perishable material and consequently have not survived. The earliest inscriptional mention, in a Pallava record, of a temple occurs in the grant of Chārudēvi which evidences a donation of land to the temple of Nārāyaṇa at Dāḷūrā early in the fourth century. During the reign of Mahēndravarman I, a commencement was made[2] in the art of monolithic temple building. The first specimens were all of them excavations of hillsides into temples such as those at Trichinopoly, Vallam and Māmaṇḍūr, modelled after the caves at Uṇḍavalli. A later development was from the cave temples to the Rathas like those of Mahābalipuram. From these, in due course of evolution, came structural temples, among the earliest and best known of which are the Shore-temple at the Seven Pagodas, the Kailāsanātha temple at Kāñchi and at Panamalai. The evolution continued in the days of subsequent Pallava kings till the rise of what is a distinct Chola style.

[1] See the works of Prof. Jouveau-Dubreuil and Mr. Longhurst.
[2] According to Prof. Jouveau-Dubreuil.

APPENDIX A

A CHRONOLOGICAL INDEX OF PALLAVA INSCRIPTIONS

1. Nasik Buddhist Inscription of Śrī-Pulumāyi. *Ep. Ind.*, vol. viii, pp. 60ff.

   The inscription records in Prakrit, the gift of a cow to the community of monks, by Queen Gotami Bālaśrī, mother of Gotamiputrasātakarṇi, king of Aśmaka, Mulika, etc., who destroyed the Śakas, Yavanas, and the *Pahlavas*. A village was granted by the queen's grandson for the embellishment of the cave.

2. Junagaḍh Rock Inscription of Rudradāman. *Ep. Ind.*, vol. viii, pp. 36ff.

   Sanskrit fragment. Records the restoration of lake Śudarśana, situated at some distance from Girinagara (Girnar). The work was executed by Suviśāka, the son of Kulaipa, and a *Pahlava*, who had been appointed to rule the whole of Ānarta and Surāshṭra. He is described as having been able, patient, not wavering, not arrogant, upright, and by his good government and proper views and dealings in things temporal and spiritual, to have increased the attachment of the people and the spiritual fame and glory of his master.

3. The Myākadoni Inscription of Pulumāvi. *Ep. Ind.*, vol. xiv, p. 153. Also *Rep. for Epig., Madras, for 1915–16*, part ii, p. 112. Insc. No. 509, App. B.

   Prakrit record. This is dated in the eighth year of the Āndhra king Śrī-Pulumāvi, king of the Sātavāhana (family) and records the sinking of a reservoir by a resident of Vēpūraka, belonging to the Captain-Kumāradatta, in the country of Sātavāhani-Āhāra which belonged to the (great general) *Mahāsēnāpati-*

Khandanāga (Skandanāga). This inscription is important in so far as it establishes that the sway of the Sātavāhanas extended to the south of the Krishna.

4. Mayidavōlu plates of Śivaskandavarman. Hultzsch. *Ep. Ind.*, vol. vi, p. 84.

Eight copper-plates with a seal bearing in relief a bull and the legend *Śivaskandavarmaṇā*. The language is Prakrit, dialect different from literary Pāḷi, and the alphabet is considered an epigraphical curiosity.

The grant was issued by the heir-apparent (*Yuvamahārāja*) Śivaskandavarman of the Bhāradvāja-gōtra and of the Pallava family, and records the gift of a village (Viripara) to two Brahmans. The village is said to have belonged to Āndhrapathā and has not been identified. The record is dated in the fifth *tithi*, of the sixth fortnight of summer, in the tenth year of the reign of Śivaskandavarman's predecessor. The immunities secured by the village included, freedom from the diggings for salt, the supply of bullocks, in succession, the entrance of the soldiers, cots and dwellings.

5. Hirahadagalli plates of Śivaskandavarman. Bühler, *Ep. Ind.*, vol. i, p. 5. Final corrections by Hultzsch, *Ibid.*, vol. vi, p. 88.

Eight plates from Hirahadagalli, in the Bellari District. Prakrit. Records that the Pallava king Śivaskandavarman of Kāñchi, who belonged to the Bhāradvāja-gōtra and is said to have performed *Agnishṭôma*, *Vājapēya* and *Aśvamēdha* sacrifices, confirmed and enlarged in the eighth year of his reign a grant made formerly by the great king, the Lord-Bappa (his father), to certain Brahmans residing at Âpitti, and who are described as *bhojakas*, of the village of Chillarēkakoḍuṁka, in the Sātāhaniraṭṭha. The gift consisted of a garden in the above village, the income of which was to be divided in a specified manner.

The writer of the grant was the Privy-Councillor—(*Rahasadhikata*) Bhaṭṭi-Śarman. Among the other officials mentioned in this record are the Lords of Provinces, Royal Princes, Rulers of Districts, Custom-House Officers, Prefects of countries, Forest-officials, Sergeants, roaming spies, and others.

6. British Museum plates of Chārudēvi. Noticed by Fleet. *Ind. Ant.*, vol. ix, pp. 100ff. *Ep. Ind.*, vol. vi, p. 88, No. 10. Final correction by Hultzsch, *Ep. Ind.*, vol. viii, p. 143.

The original copper-plates secured by Sir Walter Elliot, are now in the British Museum. Language is mostly in Prakrit prose and partly in Sanskrit verse. The seal contains a standing animal, apparently a bull, the crest of the Pallavas.

The grant is dated in some year of Vijayaskandavarman (illegible). It records an order by the Queen Regent in behalf of the heir-apparent Vijaya-Buddhavarman who is described as a Pallava and affiliated to *Bhāradvāja-gōtra*. Dr. Hultzsch has read the name of the queen as Chārudēvi and that of the prince whose mother she claims to have been as Buddh (yan)kura. The grant supplies the genealogical order Mah. Vijayaskandavarman, his son Yuvamahārāja Vijaya Buddhavarman and his son Buddhyaṅkura.

The object of the grant is to register a gift of land made by Chārudēvi consisting of a field near the king's tank to Nārayaṇa of the Kuḷimahātāraka temple, at Dāḷūra. The village authorities were required to exempt the field from all immunities.

7. Allahabad Pillar Inscription of Samudragupta. Fleet, *Cor. Insc., Ind.*, vol. iii, pp. 1–17.

The inscription is written in an Asokan sandstone pillar. The characters belong to the Gupta alphabet, the language is partly Sanskrit prose and partly verse.

The record is undated. It gives abundant details as regards the conquests of Samudragupta, the divisions and kings of India in the fourth century A.D. Among the southern kings that Samudragupta conquered and released, the record mentions Mahēndra of Kosala, Vyāgrarāja of Mahākāntara, Mantarāja of Kaurāḷa, Mahēndra of Paishṭāpura, Svāmidatta of Koṭṭūra on the hill, Damana of Erāṇḍapalla, *Vishṇugōpa of Kāñchī*, Nīlarāja of Āvamukta, Hastivarman of Vēngi, Ugrasēna of Palakka, Kubhēra of Dēvarāshṭra, Danamjaya of Kausthalāpura, and all other kings of the region of the south. The inscription proves that Vishṇugōpa of Kāñchī, one of the several southern kings defeated by Samudragupta, flourished in the second quarter of the fourth century A.D.

8. Chendalūr plates of Kumāravishṇu II. *Ep. Ind.*, vol. viii, p. 233.

Five copper-plates from Chendalūr in the Ongole Taluk of the Nellore District.

Language is Sanskrit prose and the alphabets closely resemble those of Pikira, Uruvappalli, and Mangalūr plates. The inscription is an edict issued from Kāñchīpura in the second year of the reign of the Pallava-Mahārāja Kumāravishṇu (II) who is described as the son of Mah. Buddhavarman, the grandson of Mah. Kumāravishṇu (I), and the great-grandson of Mah. Skandavarman. The object of the grant is to register the gift of the king to a Brahman in the village of Chendalūra in *Kavichakārabhōga*, a subdivision of the district of Karmānkarāshṭra. Of the localities mentioned in the record Kanchīpuram is the well-known capital of the Pallavas and Chendalūr a village in the Nellore District.

9. Oṁgoḍu plates of Vijayaskandavarman (II). H. K. Sastri, *Ep. Ind.*, vol. xv, pp. 249ff.

Four copper-plates. Language, Sanskrit, characters belonging to the southern class. The grant is addressed from the Royal Camp the victorious Tāmbrāpasthāna. The record mentions in chronological order Mah. Kumāravishṇu, who is described as a Pallava king of the *Bhāradvāja gōtra* and a performer of the *Aśvamēdha* sacrifice, his son Mah. Skandavarman who acquired his kingdom by his own prowess, his son Vīravarman victorious in many battles and his son Vijayaskandavarman, the donor. The grant conveys an order to the officers of Oṁgoḍu and the residents that the village was given as a *Sātvika* gift with the eighteen kinds of exemptions to Gōlaśarman of the *Kaśyapa-gōtra*, a student of two Vēdas, and well versed in the six Angas. The grant was engraved in the victorious year 33, on the thirteenth day of the third fortnight of winter.

10. Darśi copper-plate fragment. Hultzsch, *Ep. Ind.*, vol. i, p. 397.

Language and script: Same as above. The grant consists of the beginning of a Sanskrit inscription engraved on one side of a copper-plate. The name of the donor of the plate is lost but the record gives the name of his great-grandfather —Śrī Vīrakōrchavarman—the laudatory verses attributed to him agreeing literally with those attributed to the Pallava kings Skandavarman I and Skandavarman II. The king's order was addressed from Vijaya-Daśanapura.

11. Pikīra Grant of Simhavarman. Hultzsch, *Ep. Ind.*, vol. viii, p. 159.

Five copper-plates with seal much worn but bearing in relief an animal perhaps the bull. Language is Sanskrit prose excepting the final imprecatory verses. The alphabet closely resembles the Uruvappalli plates.

The record opens with an invocation to Vishṇu (*Bhagavat*) and proceeds to record the grant of a village named Pikīra in the district of Muṇḍarāshṭra. It is dated in the fifth year of the reign of Mah. Simhavarman and issued from the camp at *Mēnmātūra*, in the Nellore District. Mah. Simhavarman, the donor is described as the son of Yuva Mah. Vishṇugōpa, the grandson of Mah. Skandavarman (II) and the great-grandson of Mah. Vīravarman. The term Yuva-mahārāja which is prefixed to Vishṇugōpa in the present grant as well as in the Uruvappalli grant suggests that he probably never ruled.

12. Mangalūr Grant of Simhavarman. Fleet, *Ind. Ant.*, vol. v, p. 154.

Six copper-plates. Language, Sanskrit in the southern characters. The grant which was issued from Daśanapura registers the gift of the village of Maṇgadūr, situated in the country of Vengorāshṭra to certain Brahmans. The record is dated in the eighth year of the reign of Simhavarman who is stated to have been the great-grandson of Mah. Śrī-Vīravarman, the grandson of Mah. Skandavarman. Dr. Fleet considered that Simhavarman was an elder brother of Yuva Mahārāja Vishṇugōpa one of whose grants is dated in the eleventh year of Simhavarman's reign.

13. Uruvappalli Grant of Yuva Mah. Vishṇugōpavarman. Fleet, *Ind. Ant.*, vol. v., p. 50. Also the *Bombay Gazetteer*, part ii, p. 320.

Language and characters same as above. The grant was issued from *Palakkada* and is dated in the eleventh year of Mah. Simhavarman. It mentions in genealogical order the names of four kings, Mah. Śrī Skandavarman, his son Mah. Śrīvīravarman, his son Mah. Skandavarman, and his son Yuva Mah. Vishṇugōpavarman the donor who is described as the most divine worshipper of the divine one (*Paramabhāgavata*). The object of the grant is to register a gift of 200 *nivartanas* of land in the village of Uruvappalli in the Muṇḍarāshṭra country to the temple of God *Vishṇuhāra* established by Senāpati Vishṇuvarman at the village of Kūndukura. A minute description of the boundaries of the land is furnished.

14. Ōṁgōḍu Plates of Simhavarman II. H. K. Sastri, *Ep. Ind.*, vol. xiv, p. 252; also *Mad. Ep. Rep. for 1916*, Pt. ii, p. 113.

Five copper-plates on a ring with no seal. Sanskrit language: characters same. The object of the grant is to register a gift of the village of Ōṁgōḍu in Karmarāshṭra to a certain Dēvaśarman, who was a resident of Kēndūr and belonged to *Kasyapagōtra*. The grant was made in the fourth year of the reign, in the month of *Vaiśākha Śuklapaksha Panchami*. It is taken as having been given on the occasion of an eclipse. The donor Simhavarman (II) is stated to have been the son of Yuva Mahārāja Vishṇugōpa, grandson of Mah. Skandavarman, and the great-grandson of Mah. Vīravarman.

15. Udayēndiram plates (spurious) of Nandivarman. Kielhorn, *Ep. Ind.*, vol. iii, p. 142; also *Ind. Ant.*, vol. iii, p. 167.

Three copper-plates with a circular seal containing in bas-relief a standing bull. Language, Sanskrit in the southern script.

The donor of the inscription is said to have been a devout worshipper of Vishṇu and the law-abiding Mahārāja Nandivarman of the *Bhāradvājagōtra*. He is said to have been the son of Mah. Skandavarman, the grandson of Mah. Simhavarman, and the great-grandson of Mah. Skandavarman. It registers the order of the King conveyed from Vijaya-Kānchīpura recording a gift of the village of Kānchivāyil, and four pieces of forest land situated in the district of Aḍayāra to a Brahman inhabitant of Kānchivāyil named Kuḷaśarman. The grant was issued in the fifth lunar day of *Vaiśākhā* in the first year of the reign. The Tamil endorsement on the first plate which is dated in the twenty-sixth year of *Madiraikoṇḍa-Ko-Parakēśari* records the amalgamation of two villages.

16. Chura Plates of Vijaya-Vishṇugōpavarman. *Mad. Ep. Rep. for 1914*, part ii, p. 82.

Sanskrit and Telugu. This record which is not dated, was issued from Vijayapālōṭkaṭa and registers a grant of land by the donor Vijaya-Vishṇugōpavarman, to a certain Chasmiśarman of the *Kaśyapagōtra* and a resident of Kundūr. According to this record Vijaya-Vishṇugōpavarman was the son of Simhavarman, grandson of Mah. Vishṇugōpavarman and the great-grandson of Skandavarman.

17. Tāḷgunḍa Pillar Inscription of Kakutsthavarman. Bühler, *Ind. Ant.*, vol. xxv, p. 27; Fleet, *Dynasties*, pp. 286 ff; Rice, *Ep. Carn.*, vol. vii, p. 200; Kielhorn, *Ep. Ind.*, vol. viii, pp. 24 ff.

The inscription which was discovered by L. Rice is written in Sanskrit in the box-headed variety of the Southern characters. It relates to the excavation of a tank near an ancient Śiva temple at Sthāṇukunḍūr, commenced by the Kadamba king Kakutsthavarman and completed by his son Śāntivarman. The author of the record which is written in high *Kāvya* style was Kubja. The greater portion of this inscription is devoted to an account of the early kings of Kadamba dynasty which is interesting for the information it gives of the relation of the Kadambas with the Pallava kings, the Bāṇas, etc. According to the inscription the Kadāmbas were a Brahman family belonging to the *Māṇavyasagōtra* and descended from *Hārītiputra*. In this family was born Mayūraśarman who went to Kāñchī in order to study and there was involved in a quarrel with the Pallava rulers. He took up arms against them and after a prolonged struggle, the kings of Kānchī, conferred upon him the territory between *Amarārṇava* and *Prēmāra*. He was succeeded by his son Kangavarman, his son Bhagīratha, and his two sons Raghu and Kakutsthavarman. His successor was

Śāntivarman during whose reign this record was composed.

18. The Penugoṇḍa Plates of Mādhava II. Rice, *Ep. Ind.*, vol. xiv, pp. 331 ff. also *Mad. Ep. Rep. for 1914*, p. 83, para 3.

Old type of Kannaḍa Characters. (Telugu-Canarese). The plates mention in order Konkaṇivarma Dharma-Mahādhirāja of the *Kāṇvāyanagōtra*, his son Mādhava Mahādhirāja I, who was an able exponent of the science of polity, his son Āryavarman who is described to have been 'duly installed on the throne by Simhavarma-Mahārāja, the lord of the prosperous Pallava family' and his son Mādhava Mahādhirāja II who was duly installed on the throne by the illustrious Pallava king Skandavarman. The object of the grant is to register sixty-five paddy-fields in *Paruvivishaya* to Kumāra-Śarman of the *Vatsagōtra*.

Exception has been taken by Dr. Fleet to this copper-plate grant. He considers them genuine as against others and the mention of the contemporaneous Pallava kings Simhavarma-Mahārāja and Skanda-varma-Mahārāja is important. It is probable that they were related as father and son.

19. Śīyamangalam Cave Inscription of Mahēndravarman. Madras. *Ep. Coll.*, No. 67 of 1900; Hultzsch, *Ep. Ind.*, vol. vi, No. 32, p. 319.

This inscription is engraved on the rock-cut pillars in the Śiva temple called *Sthambēśvara*, in the village of Śīyamangalam, Wandiwash Taluk, North Arcot District. It consists of a single Sanskrit verse written in an archaic alphabet resembling the cave inscriptions at Trichinopoly and Mahēndravāḍi, and records the fact that the temple called *Avani-bhājana-Pallavēśvara* was caused to be excavated by a king called *Lalitānkura* who has been identified with Mahēndravarman I of the Pallava kings.

20. Vallam Cave Inscription of Mahēndrapōtarāja. Hultzsch, *S.I.I.*, vol. ii, part iii, pp. 34ff.

This inscription, written in archaic Tamil, is engraved on the upper portions of the doorpillars of the Vasantēśvara temple at Vallam, near Chingleput. It records that one Vasantapriyarāja, the servant of *Pahāppiḍugu* alias *Lalitāṅkuran*, *Śatrumallan*, *Guṇabharan*, *Mahēndrapōla-Raja* caused the temple to be executed. The surnames belong to Mahēndravarman I.

21. Mahēndravāḍi Inscription of Guṇabhara. Hultzsch, *Ep. Ind.*, vol. iv, pp. 152ff.

This inscription is written in the same archaic Pallava alphabet as the Trichinopoly rock inscription and consists of a single Sanskrit verse in the *kōkilaka* metre, inscribed on the pilaster on the left end of the *facade* in the rock-cut temple here. It records the fact that Guṇabhara caused the temple to be cut out of the rock and that it was dedicated to Vishṇu and bore the name *Mahēndra Vishṇugṛiha*, i.e. the Vishṇu temple of Mahēndra, that it stood on the bank of the *Mahēndrataṭāka*, i.e. the tank of Mahēndra and that it was situated in *Mahēndrapura*, the City of Mahēndra. Mahēndrapura is probably identical with Mahēndravāḍi and Guṇabhara with Mahēndravarman I.

22. Trichinopoly Cave Inscriptions of Mahēndra. Hultzsch, *S.I.I.*, vol. i, pp. 28–30.

Two inscriptions in Sanskrit in archaic Pallava-Grantha characters on two pillars in the upper cave of the Rock at Trichinopoly record that a king called Guṇabhara, who bore the *birudas*, *Purushōttama*, *Satyasaṁdha* and *Śatrumalla*, constructed a temple on the top of the mountain and placed in it a *linga* and a statue of himself. As the Kāvēri is here called 'the beloved of the Pallavas' and as the inscription is found in the Chōḷa territory it is clear that the Pallavas had extended their dominions during this period to the region of the Kāvēri.

23. Maṇḍagappaṭṭu Inscription of Vichitrachitta. Jouveau-Dubreuil, *Conjeevaram Insc. of Mahēndravarman*, p. 2. *Ep. Ind.*, vol. xvii, p. 14.

The record is written in the Pallava-Grantha characters of the seventh century A.D., and is a Sanskrit verse in the *Giti* metre. It is somewhat damaged and can be read only with difficulty. It states that King Vichitrachitta caused to be constructed a temple for *Brahma*, *Īśvara* and *Vishṇu*, without the use of bricks, timber, metals and mortar. Vichitrachitta is a surname of Mahēndravarman I.

24. Daḷavānūr Cave Inscription of Narēndra. Hultzsch, *Ep. Ind*. vol. xii, p. 225 ; *Ep. Col.*, Nos. 50 and 51 of 1905.

Sanskrit and Tamil. The inscriptions are written on a pillar in a rock-cut cave at Daḷavānūr in the Tindivanam Taluk of the South Arcot District. The first inscription consists of a single Sanskrit *slōka* which states that the cave-temple containing the inscription was executed at the order of Śatrumalla and named Śatrumallēśvarālaya. The second is divided into two sections of which one is Tamil verse and the other prose, and records the same fact. The name of the locality is stated to be Veṇpaṭṭu. Narēndra is only a surname of Pallava Mahēndravarman I and the reference to the donor as *Toṇḍaiyaṁtārvēndan* confirms this surmise.

25. Pallavaram Inscription of Mahēndravikrama. *Mad. Ep. Rep. for 1909*, p. 75.

This inscription written on the beams of the upper and lower verandahs of the cave temple at Pallavaram in archaic Pallava-grantha-characters. Fragment. It gives a list of *birudas* of which some are Sanskrit, others Telugu. Of these *Śrī-Mahēndravikrama*, *Mattavilāsa*, *Chēṭhakāri*, *Vichitrachitta*, *Aluptakāma*, *Kalahapriya*, and *Sankīrṇajāti* are in

Sanskrit and *Nilvilonayambu*, *Ventulavittu*, etc., are in Telugu. Some of these *birudas* are those of Mahēndravarman.

26. Conjeevaram Inscription of Mahēndravarman. *Ep. Col.*, No. 82 of 1921. Also see Jouveau-Dubreuil, *Conjeevaram Inscription of Mahēndravarman.* Pallava-Grantha.

This is engraved on the pillar of the *Paurṇami Maṇḍapa* to the south of the central sanctuary of the Ekāmbaranāthasvāmi temple, and consists of a series of *birudas* of the king who got them engraved such as *Abhimukha*, *Chitrakārap-puli*, *Vambara*, *Dṛḍabhakti*, etc. As some of these surnames occur in his other cave inscriptions it is probable that they belong to Mahēndravarman I.

27. Kuḍimiyāmalai Inscription of music. P. R. Bhandarkar, *Ep. Ind.*, vol. xii, p. 226; *Mad. Ep. Rep. for 1905*, p. 47 ; *Ep. Col.*, No. 354 of 1904.

The inscription is written in Sanskrit in the Pallava-grantha characters of the seventh century, on a rock behind the Sikhānāthasvāmi temple in Kuḍumiyāmalai (Pudukotta State). The inscription is divided into seven sections, corresponding to the seven classical *rāgas* and was engraved at the instance of an unnamed king who was a disciple of Rudrāchārya for the benefit of his pupils.

28. Aihoḷe inscription of Puḷakēsin II. Kielhorn, *Ep. Ind.*, vol. vi, p. 4.

Sanskrit in characters of the southern class. The inscription is a poem by a certain Ravikīrti who during the reign of Pulakēśin II founded the temple of Jinēndra on which it is engraved. It bears the date Śaka Samvat 556 corresponding to A.D. 634–35. It gives an eulogistic account of the history of Chāḷukya family especially, of the exploits of Pulakēśin II who is described to have besieged Banavāsi, subdued the Gangas, the Ālūpas, and the

Mauryas in the Konkaṇas, besieged Puri, subdued the Lāṭas, Māḷavas, and the Gūrjaras, defeated Harsha of Kanauj, fought with the Kalingas and the Kosalas, captured Pishṭapura, fought at the Kaunāḷa, defeated the Pallavas of Kāñchīpuram (' causing the splendour of the lord of the Pallavas who had opposed the rise of his power to be obscured by the dust of his army, and to vanish behind the walls of Kāñchīpuram '), crossed the River Kāvērī and caused prosperity to the Chōḷas, Kēraḷas and the Pāṇḍyas. The fame of the composer of this poem is said to have exceeded that of Kālidāsa and Bhāravi, thus showing that already in the seventh century the fame of Kālidāsa had spread so as to be quoted in contemporary inscriptions.

29. Tirukkaḷukkuṅṛam Inscription of Rājakēsarivarman. Tamil. Venkayya. *Ep. Ind.*, vol. iii, p. 276.

This inscription is dated in the twenty-seventh year of the reign of Rājakēsarivarman and records that at the request of a certain Puttan a grant which had been made by Skandaśishya and confirmed by Vātāpi-konda-Narasingapōtarayar was renewed. The gift was originally made to the Mūlasthānattu-Perumān, which has not been identified. Both the kings are spoken of as former kings. On paleographical grounds the grant may be dated in the ninth century A.D. Tirukkaḷukkuṅṛam is spoken of as being in the Kaḷattūrkoṭṭam. Skandaśishya may be Skandavarman and Vātāpikonda-Narasingapōtarayar is Narasimhavarman I.

30. Bādāmi Stone Inscription (fragment). Fleet, *Ind. Ant.*, vol. ix, p. 99.

This fragmentary inscription engraved on the north side of a shapeless rock lying to the north-west of the temple of Jeggina Īrappa in the Badami Taluq in the Biyapur District. The characters are of the same type as those of the Pallava grants of

Vishṇugōpavarman. The fragment is of great interest as mentioning Badami under the ancient name of Vātāpi and speaking (l. 4) of 'the Pallava, the foremost of kings'. It refers also to Narasimhavishṇu and contains a reference to the occupation of the city by Māmalla.

31. Dharmarājaratha Stone Inscription at Mahābalipuram—Hultzsch, *Ep. Ind.*, vol. x, pp. 5ff., also *S.I.I.*, vol. i, p. 1.

These inscriptions consist of a number of words in the nominative case. The characters resemble the Mahēndravādi and Śīyamangalam inscriptions of Mahēndravarman I. The language is Sanskrit. They do not contain any date and their approximate time has to be fixed on palæographical grounds. They appear from a comparative study to belong to Narasimhavarman I. Narasimha is twice mentioned. From the archaic nature of the alphabets Dr. Hultzsch thinks that the Narasimha of the Dharmarājaratha may be identified with the Narasimha I of the Pallavas. The identification is made almost certain by a reference to the published facsimile of the Badami stone inscription of Narasimhavarman I the alphabets of which are nearly identical with those of the Dharmarājaratha Inscriptions. Dharmarājaratha was probably sculptured in the first half of the seventh century A.D.

32. Gaṇēśa temple Inscription of Paramēśvaravarman I. Hultzsch, *Ep. Ind.*, vol. x, pp. 8ff. Eleven *verses* in Sanskrit.

This inscription records that the monolith on which it is engraved was a Śiva temple and was called the Īśvara temple of Atyantakāma-Pallava. From *slōka* 2 of this inscription Dr. Hultzsch has concluded that Atyantakāma must be either Paramēśvaravarman I, father of Rājasimha, or Paramēśvaravarman II, his son, preferably the former. The alphabets of Atyantakāma's inscription of the Seven Pagodas bear so close a resemblance to Kailāsanātha temple epigraphs of Rājasimha that both of them may be assigned to about the same period (viz.) the third quarter of the seventh century A.D. Among Atyantakāma's surnames the following are given—*Śrīnidhi*, *Śrībhara*, *Raṇajaya*, *Taruṇāṅkura*, *Kāmarāga*.

33. Dharmarāja Maṇḍapa Inscriptions. Hultzsch, *Ep. Ind.*, vol. x, No. 22, pp. 10 and 11.

This is a duplicate of Gaṇēśa temple inscription and proves that the cave-temple now called Dharmarāja Maṇḍapa was in reality a Śiva temple and that it was erected at the orders of the Pallava king Paramēśvara, who named it Atyantakāma-Pallavēśvara after one of his own surnames Atyantakāma.

34. Inscription of Paramēśvaravarman at the Rāmānuja Maṇḍapa. *Ibid.*, p. 11.

This inscription consists of the last *śloka* of the preceding inscription and the cave-temple on which it is inscribed accordingly was a Śiva temple having been excavated during the reign of the Pallava king Paramēśvaravarman.

35. Sāḷuvankuppam Inscriptions of Atiraṇachaṇḍa. Hultzsch, *Ep. Ind.*, vol. x, p. 12.

This inscription on the left of the cave-temple at Sāḷuvankuppam records that the excavation was a temple of Śiva and that it was made by King Atiraṇachaṇḍa who named it after himself Atiraṇachaṇḍēśvara. *Verses* 1, 2 and 4 are identical with Paramēśvaravarman's Mahābalipuram inscription. It contains the *birudas*, *Atyantakāma*, *Śrīnidhi*, *Kāmarāga*, *Śrībhara*, *Raṇajaya*, *Anugraśila*, *Kālakāla*, *Samaradanaṁjaya* and *Sangrāmadhīra*. Most of these are applied to Rājasimha in his inscriptions at Kāñchī. The alphabet resembles those of Kaśākkuḍi plates of Nandivarman II. The name Atiraṇachaṇḍa is unknown from other sources.

Nos. 24, 25 and 26 are Nāgari copies of the above.

36. Kūram plates of Paramēśvaravarman I. Hultzsch, *S.I.I.*, vol. i, pp. 144ff.

Seven copper-plates from Kūṛam near Conjeevaram. The seal bears the usual Pallava symbol the seated bull facing the left. The language is partly in Sanskrit verse and prose and the rest Tamil and the script *Pallava-Grantha.* The Sanskrit portion opens with benedictory verses of which the first two are addressed to Śiva. Then follows a mythical genealogy from Brahma to Pallava after whom are mentioned Mahēndravarman, his son Narasimhavarman, who is stated to have repeatedly defeated the Cholas, the Kēraḷas, the Kaḷabhras and the Pāṇḍyas, and who vanquished Pulakēsin in the battles of Pariyaḷa, Maṇimangala, and Śūramāra and destroyed his capital Vātāpi. Of Paramēśvaravarman himself is given a long description of military exploits which mentions that he made Vikramāditya whose army consisted of several *lakshas* take to flight covered only by a rag. The object of the Kūṛam grant is a gift of the village of Paramēśvaramangalam made to the temple of Śiva which had been built at Kūṛam by Vidyāvinīta-Pallava. The village was evidently named after the king himself and divided into twenty-five parts of which three were to be enjōyed by two Brahmans Anantaśivāchārya and Pullaśarman who looked after the divine service of the temple. The fourth part was set aside for the cost of providing water and fire for the temple *maṇḍapa*, the fifth for the reading of the *Bhārata* at this place while the remaining twenty parts were given to twenty *Chaturvēdins.* Kūram is mentioned as belonging to Manyavāntararāshṭra of Nirvēḷūr, a division of Uṛṛukāṭṭukkōṭṭam. The village of Paramēśvaramangalam belonged to Panmā-Nāḍu Patmamānyāvāntararāshṭra, a sub-division of Manavīrkoṭṭam.

37. Gadvāl Plates of Vikramāditya, A.D. 674. Hultzsch, *Ep. Ind.*, vol. x, No. 22, p. 101.

Three copper-plates. Language is Sanskrit prose and verse; alphabet like other Chāḷukyan grants. The inscription records the grant of land by the Western-Chāḷukya king Vikramāditya I, the son of Satyāśraya, (Pulakēśin II) grandson of Kīrtivarman (I) and great grandson of Pulakēśin (I). Several surnames of the king are mentioned such as *Śrīvallabha*, *Raṇarasika*, *Rājamalla*. *Ślōka* 3 states that he defeated Narasimha, Mahēndra and Īśvara, the three successive Pallava kings, Narasimhavarman I, Mahēndravarman II and Paramēśvaravarman I. *Ślōkā* 4 alludes to the conquest of Kāñchī the capital of the Pallavas. *Ślōka* 5 states that Vikramāditya first destroyed the Mahāmalla family. At the time of the grant Vikramāditya's army having invaded the Chōḷa province was encamped in Uragapura on the southern bank of the Kāvēri (ii. 25ff). The date of the grant was the full-moon *tithi* of *Vaiśākha* in the twentieth year of the reign which was current after 596 Śāka, equivalent to Tuesday, 25th April, A.D. 674. (Dr. Hultzsch identified Uragapuram with Negapatam in the Tanjore District and Venkayya with Uraiyūr near Trichinopoly Town, the ancient Chola capital.)

38. Panamalai Inscription of Rājasimha. *Mad. Ep. Rep. for 1916*, p. 114; *Ep. Col.*, No. 616 of 1915; also, *Pallava Ant.*, vol. i, p. 1.

The beginning and end of this inscription found in the Talapurīśvara temple at Panamalai are covered by a paved floor. The record which consists of six verses is in the floried Grantha-Pallava characters and is written right round the temple as in the Kailāsanātha temple inscription of Rājasimha at

Kāñchīpura. The existing portion mentions Aśvattāma, his son Pallava, who was the progenetor of the great Pallava family the members of which, washed their sins away by *Aśvamēdha* sacrifices and belonged to the Bhāradvājavaṁśa. Rājasimha is described as a famous king of the line who was born from Paramēśvara as 'Guha from Śiva'. Under his care the tree of Dharma is said to have thriven even though oppressed by the hot sun, the Kali age.

39. Rājasimhēśvara Shrine Inscriptions of Rājasimha. Hultzsch, *S.I.I.*, vol. i, No. 24, p. 13.

Twelve Sanskrit verses in the Grantha-Pallava running round the outside of the central shrine. The record opens with a benediction addressed to Ganga, and then gives a mythical pedigree of Pallava from (Brahman). It further says that in the race of the Pallavas was born Ugradaṇḍa, the destroyer of the city of Raṇarasika whose son was Rājasimha who bore the *surnames Atyantakāma*, *Raṇajaya*, *Śrībhara*; he is said to have built the Śiva temple round which the inscription is written and called it after his own name Rājasimha-Pallavēśvara or Rājasimhēśvara.

40. Inscription of Rangapatāka. Hultzsch, *S.I.I.*, vol. i, No. 29, pp. 23–24.

The record consisting of three Sanskrit verses in characters similar to Rājasimha's records that the small Śiva shrine was founded by Rangapatāka the wife of Narasimhavishṇu or Kālakāla whose sign was the Bull.

41. Panamalai Cave Inscription of Rājasimha. Hultzsch, *S.I.I.*, vol. i, No. 31, p. 24.

This record consists of a single Sanskrit *sloka* in Grantha-Pallava characters and is identical with the last verse of Rājasimha's Kāñchī inscription (*S.I.I.*, vol. i, No. 24). It mentions the *birudas* of Rājasimha, *Srībhara*, *Chitrakārmuka*, *Ēkavīra*, and *Śivachuḍāmaṇi*. Dr. Hultzsch from a study of this inscription concludes that the Panamalai cave was founded by Rājasimha and that the Pallava rule extended as far south as Panamaḷai at this period.

42. Shore Temple Inscription of Rājasimha. *Ep. Col.*, 566 of 1912. *Mad. Ep. Rep. for 1913*, paras 8 and 9.

This record consisting of about six Sanskrit verses is inscribed round the plinths of the two *bali-pīṭhas* recently excavated in the shore-temple. The record is not complete but contains an eulogy of a Pallava king whose attributes were *Atyantakāma*, *Aparājita*, *Śivachūḍāmaṇi*, etc. Another verse refers to him as Rājasimha, Raṇajaya, Śrībhara and Chitrakārmuka and is identical with the twelfth verse of the Kāñchīpuram inscription of Rājasimha. The mention in the record of the king as the ruling sovereign makes it probable that he was Rājasimha son of Paramēśvaravarman I, who bore the surnames Kshatriyasimha and Rājasimha. The two Śiva temples of the Shore Temple Kshatriyasimha and Rājasimhapallavēśvaram were evidently contemporary with Rājasimhapallavēśvaram of Kāñchīpuram and named after Rājasimha.

43. Vāyalūr stone pillar Inscription of Rājasimha. *Mad. Ep. Rep. for 1909*, part ii, para 16, p. 17. Joveau-Dubreuil, *Pallavas*, ch. ii, pp. 19–21; *Ep. Col.*, No. 368 of 1908; H. K. Sāstri, *Ep. Ind.*, vol. xviii, p. 145.

This record is engraved on a cubical pillar in the Vyāghrapurīśvara temple at Vāyalūr. It is written in the usual Grantha-Pallava characters of the florid type used in the Ramānuja *maṇḍapa* and the Ganeśa temple inscriptions at Mahābalipuram, and the Kailasanātha inscription at Kāñchīpura. It gives a list of the Pallava kings in genealogical order. Beginning with the names of Brahma, Angirasa, etc., it proceeds to mention the names of Aśoka, Harigupta, Āryavarman, Bhūtadatta, etc. and a long list of further names obviously in the order of descent. These include Sūryavarman, Rūpamalla, Dhṛitaka Vimala Konkaṇika, Kālabhartṛ, Chūta-Pallava, Vīrakūrcha, Vishṇugōpa, Skandavarman, Kumāravishṇu, among the early Pallava kings of the copper-plates. Then are mentioned the names of Simhavarman, Nandivarman, Simhavishṇu, Mahēndravarman, Narasimhavarman and Paramēśvaravarman and Rājasimha. The value of the record consists in the connection which it establishes between the Pallavas of the Prakrit charters and those of the Sanskrit charters and the connection of these again with those of the Simhavishṇu line.

44. Inscription in the Kailāsanātha temple of Mahēndravarman II. Hultzsch, *S.I.I.*, vol. i, No. 27, p. 22.

The record consists of four Sanskrit verses in Grantha-Pallava characters of Rājasimha's period and registers the fact that Mahēndra, the son of Rājasimha and grandson of Lokāditya built a temple of Śiva and called it Mahēndrēśvara after his own name. The record is engraved round the smaller shrine which stands in front of Rājasimha's Kailāsanātha shrine. It speaks of Lokāditya that 'his valour dried up the army of Raṇarasika, just as the heat of the sun does the mud.'

45. Vīraṭṭānēśvara temple Inscription of Paramēśvaravarman II. *Ep. Col.*, No. 56 of 1903. Tamil.

This inscription engraved on a slab lying in front of the Vīraṭṭānēśvara temple at Tiruvādi records in Tamil a gift of gold and is dated in the third year of Paramēśvarapotarayar.

46. Vaikunṭhaperumāḷ Inscription. *Mad. Ep. Rep. for 1906*, part. ii, pp. 62–63; *Ep. Col.*, No. 37 of 1888. Text, *S.I.I.*, vol. iv, pp. 10ff. Also see *Ep. Ind.*, vol. xviii, p. 117.

This is not a single record but a series of inscriptions each explaining the group of sculptures below which it is put up. They are in the nature of explanatory notes denoting particular events in Pallava history. The portion relating to the events leading to the accession of Pallavamalla is very important and contains a full account of the circumstances under which Nandivarman (II) succeeded to the Pallava throne which is depicted in twelve sculptured scenes on the south wall of the *veranda* running round the central shrine. It is stated therein that after the death of Paramēśvaravarman II a deputation of the officials and citizens waited on Hiraṇyavarma-Mahāraja for the selection of a sovereign to the Pallava throne. Hīraṇyavarman, thereupon, held an important consultation with the chief potentates and his sons. Ultimately Pallavamalla the twelve-year-old son of Hiraṇyavarman was selected by common consent and was crowned king under the name Nandivarman, and with the Pallava insignia and war instruments—*Samudraghōsha*, *Khaṭvāngadhvaja* and *Vrishabha-lāñchana*. The members of the Merchants'-guild, the City-Council, and the Ubhaiya-gaṇa of Kāñchī are also mentioned as having taken an important part in the above events.

47. Sthambēśvara Temple Inscription of Vijaya-Nandi-vikramavarman. *Ep. Col.*, No. 68 of 1900.

Tamil record, dated in the third year of Vijaya-Nandi-vikramavarman records the building of a temple *maṇḍapa* at Sthambēśvara temple at Śīyamangalam (South Arcot District).

48. Vīraṭṭānēśvara Temple Inscription of Nandivikrama-varman. *Ep. Col.*, No. 300 of 1902.

Tamil record inscribed on a rock in the *prākāra* of the Vīraṭṭānēśvara temple, Kiḻūr, near Tirukkoilūr, dated in the fourth year of Nandivikramavarman registering gift of gold for lamp.

49. In the same place. *Ep. Col.*, No. 295 of 1902. Tamil inscription dated in the eleventh year of Vijaya-Nandivikramavarman records a gift of gold,

50. *Ep. Col.*, No. 49 of 1905.
This is a Tamil inscription found on the south wall of the rock-cut cave at Daḷavānūr (South Arcot District,) is dated in the fifteenth year of Vijaya-Nandivikramavarman. Much damaged.

51. *Ep. Col.*, No. 296 of 1902.
Tamil inscription, dated in the sixteenth year of Vijaya-Nandivikramavarman recording gift of gold for a lamp found in the *prākāra* of the Vīraṭṭānēśvara temple at Kīḻūr near Tirukkoilūr.

52. *Ep. Col.*, No. 220 of 1902.
Tamil inscription dated in the ninteenth year of Vijaya-Nandivikramavarman found on the west wall of the Rishabhanātha temple records gift of paddy. Incomplete.

53. Udayēndiram Plates of Nandivarman Pallavamalla. Hultzsch, *S.I.I.*, vol. ii, p. 365. Sanskrit and Tamil. The grant consists of two parts, the first a grant of the Pallava king Nandivarman Pallavamalla in the Sanskrit, and the other an inscription of the time of the Chōḷa king *Madiraikoṇḍa-Kō-Parakēsari-varman* in Tamil.
The object of the Sanskrit portion is to register a grant made at the request of one of his military officers Udayachandra by Nandivarman Pallavamalla in the twenty-first year of the reign. Udayachandra is described as belonging to the Pūchan family and as residing in the city of Villivala on the River Vēgavati. The record gives the mythical genealogy, and the race of Simhavishṇu and his successors. It describes Nandivarman-Pallavamalla as the son of Paramēśvara-varman II. The most interesting part of the grant is that relating to the services rendered by Udaya-chandra to Pallavamalla which included the release of his sovereign from Nandipura where he was besieged by the Tamil kings, the killing of Chitramāya, defeat of the Śabara king Udayaṇa, the Nishāda chief

Prithivī-Vyāghra, and the subjection of the district of Vishṇurāja to the Pallava, etc. The donees were hundred and eight Brāhmans, while the grant consisted of Kumāramangala-Veḷḷātur and two water-levers. The Tamil endorsement dated in the twenty-sixth year of Ko-Parakēśarivarman relates to the agreement of two villages Udayachandramangalam and the neighbouring village of Kânchivāyil to form one village of the two.

54. Kaśākkuḍi plates of Nandivarman Pallavamalla. Eleven copper-plates with a seal containing the figure of a bull facing left. Hultzsch, *S.I.I.*, vol. ii, p. 346.

Sanskrit and Tamil. The characters of the plates belong to the Pallava-grantha, and bear a close resemblance to the Kūram plates. The grant part of the record is preceded by an account of the ancestors of the donor Nandivarman Pallavamalla which was composed by Trivikrama. After the mythical genealogy from Brahma to Aśokavarman, the record mentions the Pallava kings Skandavarman, Kalindavarman, Kāṇagōpa, Vīrakūrcha, Vīrasimha, Simhavarman and Vishṇusimha. Then are mentioned Simhavishṇu called Avanisimha, Mahēndravarman (I), his son Narasimhavarman (I), his son Mahēndravarman II, his son Paramēśvaravarman (I), his son Narasimhavarman II, his son Paramēśvaravarman (II). The donor Nandivarman Pallavamalla in whose twenty-second year the record is dated is described as being descended from Simhavishṇu's younger brother Bhīmavarman, between whom and Nandivarman (II) there intervened the kings Bhīmavarman, Ādityavarman, Govindavarman and Hiraṇya, the father of Nandivarman. The object of the grant which was made at the request of Brahmaśrīrāja was Koḍukoḷḷi which received the name of Ēkadhīramangalam. The donee was Jyēshṭhapāda-Sōmayājin who belonged to the Bhāradvājagōtra a Vedic scholar, and a student of *Kalpa*, *Vyākaraṇa*, *Jyōtisha*, *Nirukta*, etc., and who lived in Pūniya in Tuṇḍāka-Rāshṭra. There is an interesting list of immunities secured by the donee. Mention is also made of local officials and His Majesty's Treasurer *Śrī-Paramēśvara-Mahākōshṭhāgārin*.

55. *Ep. Col.*, No. 14 of 1893. Tamil.

This inscription found in the west and east walls of the Muktēśvara temple of Conjeevaram is dated in the twenty-eighth year of Nandivarman and gives the ancient name of the temple as Dharmamahādēvīśvara evidently after Dharmamahādēvi, a Pallava Queen.

56. Panchapāṇḍavamalai Inscription of Nandipōttaraśar. *Ep. Col.*, No. 10 of 1895.

This inscription written in very archaic Tamil characters consists of a single sentence in Tamil, records in the fiftieth year of Nandipōttaraśar an inhabitant of Pugaḻalaimangalam caused to be engraved an image of Ponniyakkiyār attended by the preceptor Nāganandin.

57. *Ep. Col.*, No. 27 of 1887.

Tamil fragmentary inscription on a stone in the Grāma-dēvata temple at Saduppēri is dated in the fifty-second year of Kō-Vijaya-Nandivikramavarman.

58. *Ep. Col.*, No. 154 of 1921.

Tamil inscription, dated in the fifty-second year of Vijaya-Nandīśvaravarman found in Kuludikkai, North Arcot District, records the death of Kannāḍu-Perungangar, chief of Karkāṭṭūr who at the instance of the great Bāṇa king fought and fell on the day of the great Pallava invasion against Permānaḍigal and the destruction of Perunguḻikoṭṭai.

59. Taṇḍantōṭṭam plates of Kōvijaya-Nandivikramavarman H. K. Sastri. *S.I.I.*, vol. ii, part v, p. 517. Also *Mad. Ep. Rep. for 1912*, paras 4 and 5.

Fourteen copper-plates from Taṇḍanōṭṭam with seal bearing in relief a couchant Bull facing right.

Sanskrit and Tamil in the *Grantha-Pallava* characters. Some of the introductory plates containing the genealogy of the Pallava kings are missing. The existing plates commence with the information that a particular king conquered the south, after which the birth of Hiraṇyavarman is recorded. From him was born Nandivarman who bore the *biruda* Ēkadhīra. Of him it is recorded that he took away from an unnamed Ganga-king a neck ornament which contained in it the gem called *Ugrōdaya*. The inscription also gives the name of Nandivarman's elephant as *Paṭṭavardhana* (v. 7.). The object of the grant was to register the gift of a village called Dayāmukha-mangalam to 308 Brahmans learned in the *Vēdas*, and *Smṛtis* who were *Chaturvēdis*, *Trivēdis*, *Sōmayājins*, *Bhaṭṭas*, *Shaḍangavids*, *Kramavids*, etc. Provision was made for the conduct of worship to the local Vishṇu and the Śiva temples, and also for the recitation of the *Mahābhārata* in the temple-hall. The Sanskrit part of the record ends with the portion which mentions that the *āgñapti* of the charter was Kumāra, the Chief of the Treasury, and the composer of the Praśasti, the poet Paramēśvara-Uttarakāraṇika, the Tamil portion is dated in the fifty-eighth year of Kōviśaiya-Nandivikramavarman and records an order which was issued to the residents of Tenkarainādu, a district of Śoḻanāḍu. The donees whose enumeration occupies more than eleven plates, number 244. To judge from their titles it may be presumed that most of them were learned. The concluding portion enumerates the obligations and the immunities of taxation secured by the donees.

60. Tiruvallam Rock Inscription of Vijaya-Nandivikrama-varman. *Ep. Col.*, No. 76 of 1899 and *S.I.I.*, vol. iii, p. 90.

Tamil record. This inscription is engraved on the surface of a large boulder in the bed of the Nīva river, near Tiruvallam, and is written in archaic *Grantha-Tamil* characters. It is dated in the sixty-second year of Vijaya-Nandivikramavarman while Māvali-Vāṇarāya was ruling, the Vaḍuga-vaḷi-Twelve-thousand ; it registers a gift of land for the renewal of a temple Vaḍaśikharakovil, at Vāṇapuram by a goldsmith called Aridhīran, a resident of Aḷiṅgaṇappākkam in the district of Ūṟṟukāṭṭukōṭṭam.

61. Koṟṟanguḍi Plates No. 5 of App. A, 1922–3. *Q.J M.S.*, vol. xiv, pp. 125–139. Also *Ep. Ind.*, vol. xviii, pp. 115 ff.

Five copper-plates written on eight sides unearthed from a hamlet of Kottamangalam in Tanjore District. The engraving is partly in Grantha and partly Tamil. The record consists of eleven Sanskrit verses and a prose passage in Tamil. It opens with invocatory verses to Vishṇu. Then is given the usual mythical genealogy of Pallava through Brahma, Angīras, Bṛahaspati, etc. Verses 4 and 5 give a panegyric account of the Pallava family. The historical account which begins with (v. 6.) states that after Virākūrcha and others had gone to heaven, Hiraṇyavarma became king. Then came Nandivarma while yet he was very young and his conquests over Vallabha, Kaḷabhra, Kēraḷa Pandya and Chola, are detailed. The Tamil portion is dated in the sixty-first year of the reign of Ko. Vij. Nandivikramavarman and registers a gift of land which was received by *the Brahmans* of Nalgūr. The names of the donees are then enumerated.

62. *Ādivarāha temple* inscription of *Mahābalipuram*, No. 666, 1922. *Ep. Col.* No. 666 of 1922.

This Grantha-Tamil inscription is written on two sides of a slab lying in the court-yard of the Ādivarāha temple at Mahābalipuram. It is dated in the 65th year of Nandipotavarman and registers a gift of land by purchase from the citizens of Mahāmallapuram.

63. Kāñchi inscription of Vikramāditya II. Dr. Hultzsch, *Ep. Ind.*, vol. iii, p. 359. The inscription is in

Kanarese prose and is engraved on the back of the pillar of the *maṇḍapa* in front of the Rājasimhēśvara shrine. It records that Vikramāditya Satyāśraya after his conquest of Kāñchī, did not confiscate the property of Rājasimhēśvara temple but granted large sums of money to the temple. The inscription ends with the imprecation that those who destroy the letters of the record and the stability of the king's charity, shall incur the sin of those who killed the men of the assembly of the city (Ghaṭikaiyār).

64. Vakkalēri plates of Kīrtivarman. Rice, *Ind. Ant.*, vol. viii, p. 23, also Kielhorn, *Ep. Ind.*, vol. v, p. 200.

Five copper-plates first brought to notice by L. Rice. The language of the record is Sanskrit and mostly prose. The record belongs to the Western Chāḷukya king Kīrtivarman II whose ancestors are mentioned between lines 2–59. The object of the inscription is to record in the eleventh year of his reign, 679 *Śāka*, the gift of Śuḷḷiyūr and two other villages to Mādhava-Śarman. The gift was made while the king was encamped on the northern bank of Bhīmarathi.

The historical portion of the grant mentions the origin and exploits of the early Chāḷukyan Kings, Pulakēśin, Satyāśraya-Vikramāditya of whom it is said that he forced the king of Kāñchī 'who had never bowed to any man to lay his crown at his feet'. Of his son Vinayāditya it is said that he captured the whole army of Trairājya-Pallava and also levied tribute from the rulers of Kavēra, Pārasika, Simhaḷa, and other islands. Then Vijayāditya's exploits are mentioned and is followed by an account of Vikramāditya who immediately after his coronation, being resolved to root out the Pallavas (who are described as the obscurers of the splendours of the former kings of his line and their natural enemies) entered the Tuṇḍākarāshṭra, slew the Pallava king Nandipōtavarman, captured his trophies, elephants and rubies, etc., triumphantly entered Kāñchī and without plundering it caused the statues in the Rājasimhēśvara to be overlaid with gold. Of Kīrtivarman the donor of the grant, the inscription records that, while yet a *Yuvarāja*, he marched into the city of Kāñchī scattered the forces of the Pallava king who had to take refuge in a hill-fort, and returned with a large booty which he delivered to his father and in due course became a *Sārvabhauma*.

65. Kēndūr plates of Kīrtivarman II. Pathak, *Ep. Ind.*, vol. ix, p. 200, *Śaka* 672.

The record belongs to the Western Chāḷukya king Kīrtivarman II. The language of the inscription is in Sanskrit and in prose while the characters belong to the southern class of alphabets.

After recounting the exploits of Kīrtivarman I and Pulakēśin II it says of Vikramāditya I, that he recovered part of the Chāḷukyan dominions by means of his horse Chitrakāṇtha which had been previously overrun by the Pallavas and had obeisance done to him by them. Vijayāditya though he was taken prisoner, contrived to effect a skilful escape. Of Vikramāditya II the record says that he led an excursion to the Tuṇḍākavishaya, defeated his natural foe, entered the Pallava capital Kāñchī and restored to Rājasimhēśvara and the other temples, heaps of gold and rubies which had been taken away from them. He was succeeded by Kīrtivarman II, the donor of the grant. The object of the grant is to register the gift of the village of Bēpatti made at the request of his queen in the sixth year of his reign in *Śāka* 672 on the occasion of a lunar eclipse.

66. Vēlvikkuḍi Plates of Neḍunjaḍaiyan. *Mad. Ep. Rep. for 1908*, p. 62; *Ep. Ind.*, vol. xvii, pp. 291 ff.

The record consists of Sanskrit and Tamil, the Sanskrit portion being written in *Grantha* characters while the

Tamil portion is written in Vaṭṭeḻuttu characters. The Sanskrit portion after giving a mythical origin of the Pāṇḍya kings mentions Māravarman who is said to have performed the *tulābhāra* ceremony; his son was Raṇadhīra; his son was Māravarman Rājaśimha who is stated to have defeated Pallavamalla in battle, and performed the *tulābhara* and *hemagarbha* ceremonies. Jaṭila was his son born through a Maḷava princess whom he had married. His son was Rājasimha the donor of the present record. The *praśasti* was composed by Varōdayabhaṭṭa.

The Tamil portion refers to the grant of Vēḷvikkuḍi by Palyāgaśālai-mudukuḍumi-peruvaḷudi to Korkaikiḻān-Narkoṟṟan and mentions the Kaḷabhṟa-occupation of the country. Then it proceeds to record the re-establishment of the Pāṇḍya power under Kaḍungōn whose son was Adhirāja-Māravarman-Avani-Śūḷāmaṇi. His son was Śeḻiyan-Śēndan famous for his heroism, his son Arikēśarin Asamasaman-Māravarman of whom it is recorded that he overcame the ocean-like army of the Vilvēli in the battle of Nelvēli, conquered the king of Kēraḷa and performed several times the ceremonies of *Hēmagarba* and the *Tulābhāra.* His son Kō-Śaḍaiyan is said to have destroyed at Marudūr the army, and at Mangaḷapura the Mahāratha who was overcome and destroyed. Tēr-Māran, his son, fought the battles of Neḍuvayal, Kuṟumaḍai, Maṇṇi-kurichchi, Tirumangai, Pūvāḷūr, Koḍumbāḷūr, and Kuḷumbūr against the Pallava. He is further credited with having subdued Maḷakongam, entered into relations with the Gangarāja, renewed the walls of Kūḍal, Vañji and Koḻi. His son was Tennan-vānavan-Neḍuñjaḍayan, who is stated to have conquered at Peṇṇāgaḍam, the Āyavēḷ and the Kuṟumbas at the battle of Nāṭṭukuṟumbu. In the third year of his reign he renewed a land grant made by Palyāgaśālai-mudukuḍumi-Peruvaḷudi to the palace singer. The *āgnapti* of the grant was Māran-Kāri and the poet who composed the Tamil portion of the grant was Ēnādi *alias* Śāttan.

67. Bigger Sinnamanur Plates of Rājasimha. *Mad. Ep. Rep. for 1907*, pp. 63 ff.

Sanskrit and Tamil in *Grantha* and *Vatteluttu* characters. The Sanskrit portion occupies four plates. After enumeration of the names of a number of mythical kings are mentioned Arikēśarin, Jaṭila, Rājaśimha, Varaguṇa, and Māravarman who held the *birudas* Ēkadhīra and Śrīvallabha. He is said to have conquered Māyapāṇḍya, Kēraḷa, Simhaḷa and Pallava, and Vallabha; Varaguṇavarman, Parāntaka and Rājaśimha are then mentioned in order, the last being the donor of the grant, the object of which was to record the gift of Narcheigai-puttūr in Aḷanādu to one Parāntaka of *Kausika-gōtra*.

The Tamil portion which is written in Vatteḷuttu characters after mentioning the mythical and semi-mythical exploits of early Pāṇḍyan kings makes mention of the Tamil translation of the *Mahābārata*, and the establishment of the Madura College (*Śangam*). Then are mentioned Parānkuśa who is said to have conquered the Pallavas at Śankaramangai, his grandson Rājasimha Varaguṇamahārāja, his son Parachakrakōlāhala, who gained victories at Kunnūr, Śingaḷam, and Viḷiñam, and defeated at Kuḍamūkku, the Gangas, the Pallavas, the Cholas, the Kalingas and the Māgadhas: then came Varaguṇavarman, his younger brother Parāntakan Śaḍaiyan who fought at Kharagiri and destroyed Peṇṇāgaḍam; then came Rājasimha the donor.

68. Madras Museum Plates of Jaṭilavarman. Venkayya, *Ind. Ant.*, 1893, pp. 57ff. The Sanskrit portion is in Grantha characters and the Tamil in Vaṭṭeḷuttu characters. After invocatory verses to Brahma, Vishṇu and Śiva, Māravarman is mentioned as having

been born in the Pāṇḍya race and is credited with having destroyed the Pallavas. In the Tamil portion his son Jāṭila is described as having destroyed his enemies at Viḻiñam, Śeḻiyakkuḍi and Veḷḷūr and as having advanced against an enemy who was joined by the Pallava and the Kēraḷa. He is also stated to have captured the Western-Kongu king, entered the village of Kānchivāyil and there built a temple to Vishṇu. He also destroyed the town of Viḻiñam and the king of Vēn. (Vēṇadu or Travancore.) The object of the record is to register the gift of a village Vēlanguḍi to Sujjalabhaṭṭa, a learned Brahman.

69. *Ep. Col.*, No. 256 of 1922. Tamil.

This record written on a slab built into the floor of the *manḍapa* in front of the Vāṇādhīśvara temple, Vayalakāvur (Conjeevaram Taluk) is dated in the second year of the reign of Vijaya-Danṭivikrama-varman and registers a gift of paddy by five private individuals for offerings and lamp for the Bhaṭāra of the village.

70. Tiruveḷḷarai Inscription of Dantivarman. Fifth year. *Ep. Col.*, No. 541 of 1905. K. V. S. Ayyar, *Ep. Ind.*, vol. xi, p. 156.

Tamil prose and verse. This inscription is engraved in one of the stones of the well, south of the Punḍarīkāksha Perumāḷ temple at Tiruveḷḷarai near Trichinopoly. The object of the inscription is to record the construction of a well called Mārpiḍugu-perunginaṟu by one Kamban-Araiyan, the younger brother of a certain Viśaiya-Nallulān of Ālambākkam. The work was commenced according to the record, in the fourth year of Dantivarman of the *Pallava-tilaka* family and sprung from *Bhāradvāja-Gōtra*, and completed in the fifth year. The village and the tank may be identified with the modern village and tank of Ālambākkam situated at a distance of twelve miles from Lalguḍi in the Trichinopoly District.

71. Toṇḍūr Inscription of Dantivikramavarman. Tamil. *Ep. Col.*, No. 283 of 1916.

This is a Tamil inscription on a boulder in a field near the Viṇṇambārai rock near Toṇḍūr. The object of the inscription is to register in the sixth year of Vijaya-Dantivikramavarman a gift of gold by Viṇṇakōvaraiyar to the temple of Kunrānār-Bhaṭṭāri for the merit of Udāradhī and Nambi who fell in a cattle raid. The gold was received by the residents of Kīlvaḷi-Aruvāgūr in Singapuranāḍu.

72. Tamil Record at Uttaramallūr. *Ep. Col.*, No. 80 of 1898. Fragmentary-Tamil inscription is dated in the seventh year of Dantivarman recording sale of land.

73. Uttaramallūr Inscription of Dantipōttaraśar. *Ep. Col.*, No. 74 of 1898.

This is a Tamil inscription engraved in the south wall of the Vaikunṭhaperumāḷ temple at Uttaramallūr dated in the ninth year of Dantipōttaraśar. The object of the inscription is to register a gift of gold for digging a tank.

74. Uttaramallūr Tamil Inscription. *Ep. Col.*, No. 51 of 1898. This Tamil fragmentary inscription found in the Sundaravaradaperumāḷ temple at Uttaramallūr is dated in the tenth year of Vijaya-Dantivikramavarman.

75. Triplicane Inscription of Dantivarman. Venkayya, *Ep. Ind.*, vol. viii, No. 29, p. 291.

This inscription consists of nineteen lines of Tamil prose and is found in the *garbhagṛha* of the Pārthasārathi temple at Triplicane. It is dated in the twelfth year of Dantivarma-Mahāraja who is described as the ornament of the Pallava family, and as belonging to the *Bhāradvāja-gōtra*. The object of the inscription is to record that the priests of the temple had mortgaged a field belonging to the temple and in consequence the interest of forty-five *kādis* of paddy fell short in the rice-offerings presented to the God. This was restored by a certain Pugaḻtuṇai-Viśaiyarāyan who redeemed the gold by a gift of thirty *kādis* of paddy and five *kaḻañjus* of gold.

76. Uttaramallūr Tamil Inscription. *Ep. Col.*, No. 61 of 1898.

This inscription engraved on the south wall of the Vaikunṭhaperumāḷ temple at Uttaramallūr is dated in the twenty-first year of Dantivikramavarman and records a certain resolution of the Village Assembly.

77. *Ep. Col.*, No. 262 of 1904.

This inscription is written on a detached stone lying outside the temple at Tiruchānūr dated in the fifty-first year of Vijaya-Dantivikrama records a gift of lamp by Ulagaperumānār to the shrine of Tiruviḷangovil-Perumānaḍigaḷ in *Tiruchokinūr* in Kaḍavūr-Nāḍu, a subdivision of Tiruvēngaḍakōṭṭam.

78. *Ep. Col.*, No. 226 of 1903. Venkayya, *Ep. Ind.*, vol. xi, p. 224.

Tamil. This record written on a stone in the Paramēśvara temple at Guḍimallam. It is dated in the forty-ninth year of Vijaya-Dantivikramavarman, while Vijayāditya-Māvalivāṇarāyar was ruling the earth, and registers the gift of land called Nandikundil to the tank *Veḷḷēri*. Out of the produce of this land was to be met the charges for digging pits in the tank and depositing it in the bund.

79. *Ep. Col.*, No. 89 of 1921. Tamil.

This inscription dated in Dantivikramavarman's reign is engraved on a slab in the shrine of Tirumēṟṟali in Pillaipāḷayam. It mentions a certain Muttaraiyan who had petitioned for certain charities to the temple of Tirumēṟṟaḷi and a certain *maṭha* attached. The portion recording the regnal year in which the record was inscribed is damaged.

80. Govinda's Copper-plate Inscription. A.D. 804. *Ind. Ant.*, vol. xi, p. 125.

This copper-plate grant records the grant made by Govinda III while encamped on the bank of the River Tungabhadra to Gôrava a Śaiva priest. The record is dated Thursday, the fifth *tithi* of the dark fortnight of the month of Vaiśāka, of the year Subhānu, *Śāka* 726 expired, corresponding to Thursday, 4th April, A.D. 804. The record mentions that Govinda had conquered Dantiga the ruler of Kāñchī and as having levied tribute from him.

81. *Ep. Col.*, No. 347 of 1914.

This is a Tamil inscription written in the rock-cut cave of Parvatagirīśvara temple at Kunnāṇdār koil (Pudukotta) in the third year of Nandipōttaraśar and registers a gift of rice for feeding 100 persons on the day of *Tiruvādirai* by a resident of Vaḷuvūr.

82. The Vēlūrpāḷayam Plates. H. K. Sastri, *S.I.I.*, vol. ii, No. 98, pp. 507 ff.

Five copper-plates in Sanskrit and Tamil, the seal bearing a Pallava bull in a recumbent posture facing the proper right. After invocatory verses to the supreme being, the legendary origin of the Pallavas is given from Vishṇu to Pallava through Brahma, Angirasa, Bṛhaspati, Śamyu, Bhāradvāja, Drōṇa and Aśvattāma. Then occur the names of Aśōkavarman, Kāḷabhartṛ, his son Chūta-Pallava, Vīrakūrcha, of whom it is stated that he acquired the emblems of sovereignty on marrying the daughter of the Lord of the Serpants. Their son Skandaśishya is said to have seized the *Ghaṭika* of the Brahmans from Satyasēna. After him was born Kumāravishṇu who is stated to have captured Kāñchī. His son Buddhavarman is described to have been a submarine fire to the ocean of the Chōḷa army. After Vishṇugōpa and several other kings had passed away Nandivarman I was born who is credited with having subjected a powerful snake called Drishṭivisha. Simhavarman is introduced in verse 10 as the father of Simhavishṇu the latter being described as the conqueror of the Chōḷa country. The subsequent verses repeat the names and exploits of the members of the Simhavishṇu line supplied by Kaśākkuḍi and other plates. Two successions after Nandivarman Pallavamalla are supplied by these plates. Dantivarman was the son of Nandivarman II through Rēva (*Śloka* 18). His son through Aggaḷanimmati the Kadamba princess was King Nandivarman III, the donor. The object of the grant which was made in the sixth year of the reign was the gift of the village of Śrīkāṭṭupaḷḷi to the Śiva temple built by a certain Yagñabhaṭṭa on the request of a Chōḷa Mahārāja, Kumārānkuśa. A long list of exemptions stating sources of royal revenue is given. The village has been identified with Kāṭṭupaḷḷi in Ponnēri Tāluk.

83. *Ep. Col.*, No. 52 of 1895.

This is a Tamil inscription dated in the tenth year of *Tellāṟṟerinda-Nandipōttarayar*, (i.e.) Nandipōttarayar the victor at Teḷḷār, engraved in the entrance of Grithasthānēśvara temple at Tillasthānam. The object of the inscription is to register a gift of gold for a perpetual lamp.

84. *Ep. Col.*, No. 11 of 1899. Twelfth year. Tamil.

This inscription which is written in the first pillar in the *manḍapa* of Sundarēśvara temple at Śendalai, records in the twelfth year of Nandipōttarayar who defeated his enemies at Teḷḷāṟu, a gift of land to the temple.

85. Tiruvallam Inscription of Vijaya Nandivikramavarman. Hultzsch, *S.I.I.*, vol. iii, p. 93.

Tamil. This inscription which is found in the Śiva temple of Bilvanāthēśvara at Tiruvallam belongs to the seventeenth year of the reign of Vijaya Nandivikramavarman three villages which were clubbed together and called Viḍēlviḍugu-Vikramāditya-Chaturvēdimangalam, were given away to Śiva at

Tīkkālivallam in Mīyāṟunāḍu, a subdivision of the Paḍuvūrkōṭṭam. It stipulates that the Assembly should pay 2000 *kādi* of paddy and twenty *Kaḻanju* of gold to the temple for the feeding of Śiva Brahmans, the drum-beaters and other temple servants including the singers of *Tirupadiyam* as well as for perpetual lamps, anointment of idols, temple repairs, etc. The mention of *Tirupadiyam* at this early period is significant.

86. *Ep. Col.*, No. 12 of 1895. Venkayya. *M.C.C. Mag.*, vol. viii, p. 102.

This is a Tamil inscription engraved on a stone built into the veranda round the *garbagṛha* of the Ulagaḷanda-Perumāḷ temple at Kāñchīpuram, dated in the eighteenth year of the Nandipōttarāyar who was victorious at Teḷḷāṟu. It registers a license to the villagers of Viḍēlviḍugu-Kudiraichēriyār to carry on trade in all goods from camphor on one side and shoes on the other side. This was done at the request of Anuttara-Pallavarāyan. The *Āgñapti* was Kāḍupaṭṭi Tamiḻappērarayan.

87. *Ep. Col.*, 283 of 1901.

This inscription is engraved into the entrance to the Śaḍāiyar temple at Tiruchannambūṇḍi near Koviladi, Tanjore District and registers, in the eighteenth year of Nandipōttarāyar who was victorious at Teḷḷāṟu, a gift of two lamps to the temple.

88. *Ep. Col.*, No. 180 of 1907.

This inscription engraved in the twenty-second year of Nandipōttarāyar, the victor at Teḷḷāṟu, in a stone in the north wall of the Ādimūlēśvara temple at Tirupaḷātturai registers a gift of gold for two lamps in the temple of Mahādevabhaṭara at Tiruparāyturai.

89. Guḍimallam Bāṇa Inscription of the twenty-third year of Nandipōttarāśar. Veṇkayya. Five Baṇa inscriptions of Guḍimallam. *Ep. Ind.*, vol. xi, pp. 224 ff.

This is a Bāṇa inscription in Tamil found in the Paramēś-vara temple at Guḍimallam. It records, in the twenty-third year of the glorious Nandipōttaraśar, while Vikramāditya-Māvalivāṇarāya was ruling the *Vaḍugavaḷimērku*, one of the members of the committee administering the Tiruviprambēḍu, purchased by a deed of sale a field from one Agniśarman and made a gift of it to the God Mahādēva of the temple of Paraśurāmēśvara for ghee and sacred lamps. The Assembly accordingly ordered that all the oil-mills in the village should be set up and the oil secured.

90. *Ep. Col.*, No. 68 of 1908.

This Tamil inscription, dated in the sixth year of Nripatungapōtarāyar is written on a slab set up near the sluice of a tank at Vaḷuvūr and registers the construction of a sluice by a private individual.

91. *Ep. Col.*, No. 365 of 1904.

Tamil, dated in the seventh year of Vijaya-Nṛpatunga-varman and engraved in the north base of a ruined *manḍapa* in a rock-cut Śiva shrine at Narttāmalai refers to the excavation of the temple by Śāttan Paḷiyili, son of Viḍēlviḍugu Muttaraiyan.

92. Bāhūr plates of Nripatungavarman. Hultzsch. *Ep. Ind.*, vol. iv, pp. 180 ff. Text of the record in H. K. Sastri, *S.I.I.*, vol. ii, part v, p. 515. Translation of Sanskrit portion in Jouveau-Dubreuil's *Pallavas*, pp. 49 ff. Freshly edited with text and translation in *Ep. Ind.*, vol. xviii, pp. 5 ff. by E. Hultzsch.

Original plates missing. The record which is in Sanskrit and Tamil consists of about thirty verses in Sanskrit. The first contains an invocation to Vishṇu while the next five furnish the mythical pedigree from Brahma to Pallava, through Āngirasa and Śamyu, Bhāradvāja, Drōṇa and Aśvattāman. In the lineage of the Pallava was born Vimala, Konkaṇika, etc., after whose demise came Dantivarman a devotee of Vishṇu who was equal to Indra and who had obeisance done to him by other Kings. From Dantivarman was born the powerful Nandivarman, who is described as having taken the earth unaided in battle, and who had married Śankā born in the Rāshṭrakūta family. Their son was Nṛpatungadēva who was the donor famous in other worlds, as Rama was and who is said to have been victorious in the battle of Kālava (?) and who defeated the Pāṇḍyan armies on the banks of the Arichit. The object of the record is to register the gift of three villages, Chēṭṭupākkam, Viḷāngāṭṭukaḍuvanur, and Iraippuṇaichēri to the College of Vedic studies at Bāhūr (*Vidyāsthāna*). The villages were freed from all taxes. The Tamil portion dated in the eighth year of Vijaya-Nṛpatungavarman records the announcement of the gift to the residents of the Bāhūr village and refers to Viḍēlviḍugu-Kāḍupaṭṭi-Tamiḷapēraraiyan as the Āgñapti, and that the villages as being situated in the subdivision of Aruvānāḍu.

93. *Ep. Col.*, No. 460 of 1905.

This is a Tamil inscription found in the first *prākara* wall of the Naṭarājasvāmi shrine, in the Vaṭāraṇyeśvara temple at Tiruvālangāḍu records in the eleventh year of Nṛpatunga's reign that the Queen Kāḍavan Mahādēviyar made a gift of 108 *kaḷanju* of gold to the temple of Tiruvālangāḍu in the Paḷayanūrnāḍu.

94. *Ep. Col.*, No. 457 of 1912.

This is a Tamil stone inscription written in a slab lying in a big irrigation tank in the village of Marudāḍu which records that in the twelfth year of Kō-Vijaya Nṛpatungavarman a certain Kongarayarninṛa-Perumān constructed a bank of stones to the tank at Marudāḍu and also renovated the head of the irrigation channel.

95. *Ep. Col.*, No. 257 of 1912. Tamil. Sixteenth year of Nṛpatunga.

This is a Tamil inscription found near a Gaṇēśa image outside Kailāsanātha temple at Paramēśvaramangalam and registers a gift of eleven *kaḷanjus* of gold in the sixteenth year of Nṛpatunga for offerings to the God Mahādēva in the temple of Śailēśvara at Paramēśvaramangalam. The amount of the gift was deposited on interest with the *Gaṇaperumakkaḷ* of Śailēśvara by Nandiniraimati.

96. *Ep. Col.*, No. 33 of 1900. Tamil record on the north wall of the Kēśavaperumāḷ temple at Kūram registers a sale of land.

97. *Ep. Col.*, No. 277 of 1902. Venkayya, *Ep. Ind.*, vol. vii, p. 139.

This inscription records in Tamil that in the twenty-first year of Vijaya-Nṛpatungavarman—one Nannan Koṛṛan made a gift of twelve *Kaḷanju* of gold for a perpetual lamp to the God Mahādēva of Tiruvīraṭṭanam temple at Tirukōvilūr situated in Kurukkaikūṛṛam, a sub-division of Milāḍu. The citizens of Tirukōvilūr accepted the gift and promised to carry out the donor's wish.

98. *Ep. Col.*, No. 303 of 1902.

99. *Ep. Col.*, No. 300 of 1901.

This is a Tamil inscription dated in the twenty-second year of Vijaya Nṛpatungavikramavarman and is found on a pillar in the Śaḍaiyar temple at Tiruchennambūnḍi near Kōviladi. The object of the inscription is to record the gift of gold by a Pallava Queen to the temple of Tirukaḍaimuḍi-Mahādēva.

100. *Ep. Col.*, No. 301 of 1901. Same year, gift by another individual to the same temple.

101. *Ep. Col.*, No. 17 of 1895.

This inscription is found at the Vīraṭṭanēśvara temple at Kanḍiyūr and is dated in the twenty-first year of Vijaya-Nṛpatungavikramavarman.

102. *Ep. Col.*, No. 37 of 1900.

This is a much damaged Tamil inscription engraved on

a pillar on a Śiva temple and dated in the twenty-first year of Nṛpatungavarman's reign. It records a resolution of the Assembly at Kūram.

103. *Ep. Col.*, No. 84 of 1892.

This Tamil inscription found in a niche of the north wall of the *prākāra* of the Saptarshīśvara temple at Lālguḍi is dated in the twenty-second year of Kōvijaya Nṛpatungavikramavarman and registers a gift of lamp and offerings to God.

104. *Ep. Col.*, No. 179 of 1915.

This is a Tamil inscription inscribed on a beam in the Venketēśaperumāl temple at Tirumukkūḍal in the Madurāntakam Taluk dated in the twenty-fourth year of Vijaya Nṛpatungavarman. Its object is to register a gift of gold to the temple of Vishṇubhaṭāra by Arigandaperumānār, son of Kāḍupaṭṭi-Muttaraiyar. The Assembly of Śiyyapuram in the Ūṛrukāṭṭukoṭṭam took charge of the gift.

105. Five Bāna inscriptions. *Ind. Ant.*, 1911, April, p. 113; T. A. G. Row, *Ep. Col.*, No. 228 of 1902.

This inscription found in the Paramēśvara temple at Guḍimallam in Kāḷahasti zamindari is dated in the twenty-fourth year of Vijaya Nṛpatungavarman while Māvali-Vāṇarāya was ruling the west of the Vaḍugavaḷimērku. It makes mention of the members of the Assembly of Tiruviprambēḍu, which is mentioned as being situated in Śilaināḍu a sub-division of Tiruvēngaḍakōṭṭam.

106. *Ep. Col.*, No. 397 of 1905.

This Tamil inscriptional fragment found on the ceiling of the *maṇḍapa* in front of the Varadarājā temple at Kāveripākkam records the gift of gold in the twenty-fifth year of Vijaya Nṛpatungavikrama.

107. *Ep. Col.*, No. 394 of 1905. Undated.

This inscription found in the north wall of the *maṇḍapa* in front of the Varadarājā temple at Kāveripākkam mentions Māngāḍunaḍu, a sub-division of Paḍuvūrkoṭṭam and Kāvidipākkam, *alias* Avaninārāyaṇa-chaturvēdimangalam in the same *kōṭṭam*.

108. Two Āmbur Inscriptions. Hultzsch, *Ep. Ind.*, vol. iv, pp. 182, 183 and plate.

The two slabs bear on their top a Tamil inscription and below on a counter-sunk surface a bas relief representing a warrior holding a bow and sword. These are dated in the twenty-sixth year of Kō-Vijaya Nṛpatungavarman and record the death of the servant of Pirudi Gangarāyar when the army of the Noḷamba attacked Amayūr, in Mēl-Aḍayāṛunāḍu, a sub-division of Paḍuvūrkōṭṭam for lifting cattle. (Dr. Hultzsch held the view that Pirudi-Gangarâyar of these inscriptions is perhaps identical with the Western-Ganga King Prthivīpati I.)

109. Copper-Plate Inscription of the sixth year of Nṛpatunga-varman. Sewell's *List of Antiquities*, vol. ii, No. 209, p. 30.

A set of seven copper-plates having a seal with several emblems the principal figure being a bull. The language of the first three plates is Sanskrit in the old Grantha characters, the remaining plates in Tamil. The object of the record is to record the grant of Śrī-Nṛpatunga, in the sixth year of his reign, a gift of the village of Pratimadēvi-Chaturvēdi-mangalam to certain Brahmans. The genealogy of the donor is traced from Vishṇu to Pallava through Āngirasa, Bharadvāja, Drōṇa and Drōni, and from Pallava througn Harigupta, Aśokavarman, Kalarvya-varma, Narasimha, Mahēndra, Nṛpati, Rājasimha, to Śrī-Dantivarman the father of the donor.

INSCRIPTIONS OF MISCELLANEOUS PALLAVA CHIEFS OF THE SECOND HALF OF THE NINTH CENTURY

110. Kampavarman. *Ep. Col.*, No. 64 of 1898.

Tamil insciiption dated in the sixth year of Vijaya-

Kampavarman recording gift of gold to the Vishṇu temple at Gōvardhana at Uttaramallūr.

111. Another Tamil Record, *Ep. Col.*, No. 398 of 1905, dated in the sixth year of the same king's rule but fragmentary, is found in the Varadarāja-perumāḷ temple at Kavēripākkam.

112. *Ep. Col.*, No. 3 of 1898.
Tamil inscription written in the west wall of the Vaikunṭha-perumāḷ temple at Uttaramallūr records the gift of gold to the Mahādēva in the neighbouring village in the eighth year of the reign.

113. *Ep. Col.*, No. 85 of 1898. Records a sale of land, in the eighth year.

114. *Ep. Col.*, No. 6 of 1898, found in the Vaikunṭha-perumāḷ temple wall records a gift to Mahāvishṇu, and is dated in the eighth year of the same reign.

115. *Ep. Col.*, No. 7 of 1898.
Tamil inscription in the walls of the Vaikunṭhaperumāḷ temple at Uttaramallūr. Incomplete. Records a sale of land in the ninth year of Vijayakampavarman's reign.

116. *Ep. Col.*, No. 429 of 1902 ; *Ep. Ind.*, vol. vii, pp. 192–3.
Tamil inscription, dated in the eighth year of Vijayakampavarman's reign written in a long stone in a *tope* opposite to the ruined Īśvara temple at Śoḷapuram near Vellore. The record consists of two Sanskrit verses and a half in the *Grantha* characters and a passage in Tamil prose. The Tamil portion which is dated in the eighth year states that a chief named Rājāditya built a Śiva temple and a tomb in memory of his deceased father Prithivī-Gangarāyar. The mutilated Sanskrit portions give a genealogical account of Rājāditya and mentions Mādhavā as the earliest ancestor of his son Atvivarman, and another whose name is illegible. Rājādityā is described as the son of Prthivī-Gangarāyar and the contemporary of Vijayakampa.

117. *Ep. Col.*, No. 11 of 1898.
Damaged Tamil inscription at Uttaramallūr Vaikunṭhaperumāḷ temple, dated in the tenth year of the same king.

118. *S.I.I.*, vol. iii, No. 8, p. 13. Hultzsch.
This Tamil inscription on the south wall of the Vishṇu temple at Ukkal records in Tamil that one Saḍaiyan gave 400 *kādis* of paddy to the villagers of Ukkal in the tenth year of Kampavarman to feed the Brahmans.

119. *Ep. Col.*, No. 207 of 1901.
Tamil inscription on the south wall of the Lakshmi-Nārāyaṇa temple of Kāvāntanḍlam records in the fourteenth year of Kampavarman that one Mānasarpa an inhabitant of Kuḷanur in Vēngai Nādu made a gift of land to the Vishṇu temple at Kāvāntanḍlam. (Chenglepat District).

120. *Ep. Col.*, No. 42 of 1898.
Tamil record in the Vaikunṭhaperumāḷ temple at Uttaramallūr registers a gift of gold to the temple in the fifteenth year of Vijayakampavarman.

121. *Ep. Col.*, same place. Another damaged. Tamil inscription in the fifteenth year of the same king.

122. *S.I.I.*, vol. iii, No. 5, p. 8. Hultzsch.
Tamil inscription engraved on the south wall of the Vishṇu temple of Ukkal, dated in the fifteenth year of the reign of Kampavarman. The inscription records that a certain Śaḍaiyan gave over 1000 *kādi* of paddy to the Assembly of Ukkal, who pledged themselves to supply in return 500 *kādi* of paddy per year for some unspecified purpose.

123. *Ep. Col.*, No. 391 of 1905.
This is a Tamil inscription engraved on a stone built into a floor close to the south wall of the Varadarāja-perumāḷ temple at Kāvēripākkam. It is dated in the seventeenth year of Vijayakampavarman and records a gift of gold and mentions Avani-Nārāyaṇachaturvēdimangalam, an alternative name of Kāvēripākkam.

124. *Ep. Col.*, No. 208 of 1901.

This Tamil inscription put up in the south wall of the Lakshmī-Nārāyaṇa temple at Kāvāntanḍlam records in the eighteenth year of Kampavarman the celebration of certain festivals at Mānasarpa-Vishṇugṛha.

125. *Ep. Col.*, No. 84 of 1898.

This is a Tamil inscription at the Vaikunṭha-perumāḷ temple at Uttaramallūr and records the gift of gold in the twenty-first year of Vijayakampavarman for the repair of a local tank.

126. *Ep. Col.*, No. 86 of 1898.

Tamil inscription on one of the walls of the Vaikunṭha-perumāḷ temple of Uttaramallūr records, in the twenty-thiid year of Kampa-Perumān, an allotment of gold and paddy.

127. *Ep. Ind.*, vol. vii, p. 93. Śoḷapuram Tamil inscription.

This inscription in the north wall of the Perumāḷ temple at Śoḷapuram near Vellore records the building of a temple of Nārayāṇa at Kāṭṭutumbūr, that is, Śoḷavaram called Kanakavalli-Vishṇugṛha identical with the temple in which the inscription is engraved. Kāṭṭutumbūr is described as being in Pangaḷa-Nāḍu, a subdivision of Paḍuvūr-kōṭṭam.

128. *Ep. Col.*, No. 174 of 1912.

This is a Tamil inscription engraved in one of the slabs built into the floor of the Ādhipurēśvara temple at Tiruvoṟṟiyūr. The object of the inscription is to record a gift of twenty-seven *kaḷanjus* of gold for offerings by Pūdi-Arindigai wife of Viḍēlviḍugu Iḷangōvēḷār of Koḍumbāḷūr in Konāḍu. The amount was placed in the hands of the residents of Vaikāṭṭūr, a suburb of Tiruvoṟṟiyūr on interest at three *manjāḍi* per *kaḷanju* per annum.

129. *Ep. Col.*, No. 357 of 1909.

This inscription is written on a slab set up near the Village Munsiff's śavadi at Olakkūr and is a Vīragal of the period of Kampaperumāḷ. It records the death of a hero on the occasion when the town was destroyed. The characters in which the inscription is recorded are old enough to be ascribed to the time of the later Pallava kings of the ninth century. The hero who met with his death is represented by a standing figure with a drawn sword in the right hand.

130. *Ep. Col.*, No. 351 of 1908.

This inscription found in the slabs at Vallēśvara temple at Māngāḍu records in the third year of Kō-Vijaya-Aparājitavarman a gift of gold for lamp and offerings to the temple of Tiruveiḷikiḷ-Mahādēva at Māngāḍu in Kachchipēḍu.

131. *Ep. Col.*, No. 158 of 1912.

This is a Tamil inscription engraved on a slab in the floor of the verandah of the Ādhipurēśvara shrine at Tiruvoṛṛiyūr belonging to the fourth year of Kō-Vijaya-Aparājitavarman. The object of this record is to register the gift of thirty *kaḷanjus of ūrkārchemmai* gold for a lamp to the god of Tiruvoṛṛiyūr (Mahādēva) by Amatti *alias* Kurumbakoḷari a concubine of Vayiramēghan *alias* Vāṇakōvaraiyar son of Perunangai. The amount was deposited with the Assembly of Āḍambākkam a hamlet of Tiruvoṛṛiyūr and the *Amiṛtagaṇa* (committee) on interest of three *manjāḍi* per *kaḷanju*, every year.

132. *Ep. Col.*, No. 31 of 1912.

This Tamil inscription written on a stone lying in the Matangēśvara temple at Satyavēḍu is dated in the fourth year of Aparājitavarman records the village of Turaiyūr with its income consisting of *pon* and *puravu* for worship in the Mahādēva temple at Matangapaḷḷi in Tekkūrnāḍu a sub-division of Paiyūr-Iḷangōṭṭam by Kumarāṇḍai-Kurumbarādittan *alias* Kāḍupaṭṭi Pērariyan of Śēranāḍu.

133. *Ep. Col.*, No. 161 of 1912.

This is a stone inscription in Tamil dated in the fourth year of Kō-Vijaya-Aparājitavarman, and records the gift of thirty *kaḷañju* of gold for a lamp to the temple of Tiruvoṛṛiyūr Mahādēva by Ṣappakkan *alias* Patradāni who was a concubine of Vairamēghan *alias* Vāṇakovaraiyan son of Śāmi-Akkan. It mentions the assembly of Āḍambākkam a suburb of Tiruvoṛṛiyūr and Amṛtagaṇattār, the village committee who took charge of the money-gift.

134. *Ep. Col.*, No. 32 of 1912.

This is a Tamil inscription engraved in the *Ardhamaṇḍapa* of the same temple records in the fifth year of Aparājitā gift of 100 sheep for a lamp by Poṛṛinangai wife of Kāḍupaṭṭipērariyan, a chief mentioned in a previous inscription. It also mentions the measure called the *Viḍēlviḍugu.*

135. *Ep. Col.*, No. 190 of 1912.

This Tamil inscription records that in the sixth year of Kō-Vijaya-Aparājitavarman a gift of gold for two lamps by the community of the Mahēśvaras which was accepted by the assembly of Maṇali a village near Tiruvoṛṛiyūr.

136. *Ep. Col.*, No. 162 of 1912.

This Tamil inscription on a slab inside the Ādhipurēśvara temple records in the seventh year of Kō-Vijaya-Aparājitavarman a gift of gold for a lamp to the temple by the Queen Mahādevi Adigal. The Assembly of Adambakkam received it on interest.

137. *Ep. Col.*, No. 159 of 1912.

This is a Grantha-Tamil inscription of the eighth year of Kō-Vijaya-Aparājitavarman engraved on a slab built into the verānda of the Ādhipurēśvara temple in Tiruvoṛṛiyūr. The object of the inscription is to record the gift of fifty *kaḷañju* of ūrkarchemmai gold for offerings and a lamp by Paittāngikaṇḍan, chief of Kāṭṭūr in Vaḍagarai-Innambarnāḍu in Cholanāḍu. The provisions made were elaborate and included rice, ghee, plantain, sugar, vegetables, arecanuts, betel-leaves, tender cocoanuts, *pancha-gavya*, sandal-paste and camphor.

138. *Ep. Col.*, No. 180 of 1912.

This inscription which is found in the temple of Oṟṟimūdūr records a gift of land by purchase from the residents of Iganaimūdūr for offering to a shrine called Cholamallēśvara by a donor whose name is lost.

139. *Ep. Col.*, No. 435 of 1905.

This inscription in Tamil verse on the south wall of the Vīrāṭṭānēśvara shrine at Tiruttaṇi records in the eighteenth year of Vijaya-Aparājitavarman a gift of 1000 *kuḻi* of land by Nambi-Appi to the temple.

140. *Ep. Col.*, No. 433 of 1905.

This is another inscription in Tamil verse in the same place and records that a certain Nambi-Appi built a temple of Tiruttaṇiyal of granite. The verse is said to have been composed by the king whose name is not however given.

141. Udayēndiram Plates of Prithivīpati II. *S.I.I.*, vol. ii, part iii, p. 380.

Sanskrit and Tamil copper-plates. The Sanskrit portion gives a genealogy of the Ganga-Bāṇa king Prithivīpati II, surnamed Hastimalla (*verses* 12-23) and the information that, with the permission of his sovereign Parakēsari-Parāntaka I he granted the village of Kaḍaikōṭṭūr to the village of Udaiyēndra-Chaturvēdimangalam. The Tamil portion gives the boundaries of the granted land and is dated in the fifteenth year of Parāntaka I. The genealogical portion records the military exploits of Prithivīpati I in several verses one of which (*verse* 18) says that, 'having defeated by force the Pāṇḍya's lord Varaguṇa at the head of the great battle of Śrīpurambiya and having thus made his friend's title Aparājita significant, the hero entered heaven by sacrificing his own life.' (It has been surmised from this that the battle of Śrīpurambiya was fought by the Pallava king Aparājita against Varaguṇa and that the former had for his ally the Western Ganga king Prithivīpati and that the battle ended in favour of Aparājita though his ally lost his life in it.)

142. Tiruvālangāḍu plates of Rajēndrachoḷa. H. K. Sastri, *S.I.I.*, vol. ii, part iii, No. 205.

The Tiruvālangāḍu plates of Rajēndrachoḷa belonging to the sixth year of Rajēndra, while describing the achievements of the ancestors of Rajēndra, record (*verse* 49) that the Choḷa king Āditya 'having conquered in battle the Pallava with his brilliant army though he was Aparājita, he took possession of his queen, the earth and accomplished his object in this direction too'. This Aparājita is evidently identical with the Aparājita-Vikramavarman whose inscription at Tiruttaṇi is dated in the eighteenth year and who, along with Western Ganga king Prithivīpati for his ally, fought against the Pānḍya king Varaguṇa at the battle of Śrīpurambiya.

143. *Ep. Col.*, No. 119 of 1897.

This is a Tamil inscription of the third year of Vijaya-Narasimhavarman and records that Atimāttūr-marugan, an inhabitant of Pākkam and a servant of Valimadura having recovered the cattle, in a cattle raid fell in the same cause.

144. Hultzsch, *Ep. Ind.*, vol. iv, p. 177. Kīḷ-Muttugūr inscription of Narasimhavarman.

This inscription consists of nine lines on a rough stone slab in Kīḷ-Muttugūr, a village in Guḍiyāttam Taluk of the North Arcot District. The alphabet is in Tamil and resembles the Vaṭṭeḻuttu inscriptions. 'The inscription records in Tamil the gift of land and houses at Mukkudūr to a Brahman in the eighteenth year of Kō-Vijaya Narasimhavarman. Below the inscription is a bas-relief with two central figures of elephant and goose from which Dr. Hultzsch has drawn the inference that Narasimhavarman belonged to the Western-Ganga dynasty.

145. This is an archaic Tamil inscription of the twenty-fourth year of Kō-Vijaya Narasimhavikramavarman and records the death of a hero in the service of Skanda, the Ādhirāja of the Bāṇās and who fell in the recovery of cattle lifted by three persons.

146. Vijaya-Īśvaravarman. *Ep. Ind.*, vol. vii, p. 24.

This Tamil inscription in Vaṭṭeḻuttu characters records in the twelfth year of Vijaya-Īśvaravarman the death of a hero who was killed by a Bāṇā chief called Kārōniṛi at Śiṛaiyūr.

147. *Ep. Ind.*, vol. vii, p. 23.

Two inscriptions in a field at Hanumantapuram in Ḍharmapuri Taluk, Salem District, record that in the seventeenth year of king Vijaya-Īśvaravarman, Śāttan of Pudūr and Kaḍadi Kārākkan fell.

148. *Ep. Col.*, No. 150 of 1916.

This is a Tamil inscription engraved on a slab built into the north wall of the Agastyēśvara temple at Poyyanūr, Arkonam Taluk, records in Tamil the gift for offerings in the second year of Vayiramēgha-varman for the temple of Tiruvagattīśvarmuḍaya-Mahādēva at Poygainallūr in Dāmalkōṭṭam.

149. *Ep. Col.*, No. 152 of 1916.

This is a similar record dated in the second year of Vayiramēghavarman and registers a gift for conducting Śrībali in the temple of Tirukulicharattu Āḻvār at Pālakalam.

150. Kāṭṭirai, *Ep. Ind.*, vol. vii, p. 25.

This is a Tamil inscription put up on a rock near Taṇdlam, Arkonam Taluk, dated in the tenth year of Śatti, the king of Kāḍavas. It consists of two Tamil verses each of which states that a Pallava-mahārāja built a sluice for the tank at Tandlam.

151. *Ep. Col.*, No. 284 of 1916. Jouveau-Dubreuil, *Pall. Ant.*, vol. ii, pp. 65–6.
This inscription engraved in *Pallava-Grantha* on a pillar in a rock-cut cave at Mēlachēri, Gingee Taluk, states that the Śiva temple called Śrī-Śikhari-Pallavēśvaraṁ was excavated by King Chandrāditya at Simhapura.

SOME INSCRIPTIONS IN ORIGINAL

Mayidavolu Plates

Diṭha[ṁ] || Kāṁchīpurato Yuvamahārājo Bhāradāyasagotto Pallavānaṁ Śivakha[ṁ]da vammo Daṁñakaḍevapataṁ ānapayati [|]amhehi ḍāni amha-vejayike ya [dhaṁ]m-āyu-bala-vadhanike bamhanānaṁ Agivesa sagottasa Puvakoṭujasa Agī(gi)vesa-sagottasa Goṇaṁdijasa Aṃdhāpatī (thī) ya-gāmo (Virīpa)ram amhehi udak-ādiṁ saṁpadato [|] etasa gāmasa Virīparasa sava-bamhadeyapa (r)i(ha)ro(re) vitaraṁ a [|] alona [kh]ādakaṁ araṭhasaṁ (vi) nāyikaṁ aparaṁ parābaliva[daṁ] abhaḍapapesasaṁ akūracholakavināsikhaṭ [a] saṁvāsam [|] etehi anēhicha savabamhadēya-majādāya sava-pariharehi pariharito [|] pariharatha parihārāpetha cha[|] jo amha-sāsanaṁ atichhitūna pīlā badh[a]karejjā [vāta] kārāpejjā vā tasa amho Sārīra [ṁ] sāsanaṁ karejāmo [|] sa[ṁ]vachhara [ṃ] dasamaṁ[1] 10 gimhā pakho chhaṭho 6 divasaṁ paṁchami 5 [|] ānatī sayattī dattā paṭṭikā [||].

Ep. Ind., vol. vi, pp. 86–8.

British Museum Plates of Chārudēvi

Siddha || Siri-Vijaya-Khandavam[m]a-Mahārājassa Samvachchar[ā] . . . [|] yuvamahārājassa Bhāraddāyassa Pallavānam si(r)i-Vijaya-Buddhavammassadevī [Bu]ddhi. kurajānavī (janani) Chārudevi ka [ḍake] vīya . . (vīyāpataṁ) Rājatalākaheṭ [ṭh]e pāṇiya (paniya-kupād) päd pāse Ātukassa kasita. (Kasitavvaṁ) chhettaṁ Dālūre Kūḷi-Mahātaraka

(Mahātaraka) devakula [ssa] bhagavan-Narāyaṇassa amhaṁ āyu-baḷavaddhāniyaṁ kātūṇa bhūmī-nivattaṇā chattāri 4 amhehiṁ sampadattā [|] taṁ nātūṇa gāmeyi(ya)kā āyuttā savva-pariharēhi pariharatha pariharāpe [tha] [|] . . . . . Ānatti Rohan(i)gu[tt]ātti.

Ep. Ind., vol. viii, p. 145.

TRICHINOPOLY INSCRIPTION OF MAHENDRAVARMAN I

कावेरीन्नयनाभिराममलिलामाराममालाधरां
देवो वीक्ष्य नदोप्रियः प्रियगुणामप्येष रज्येदिति ।
साशङ्का गिरिकन्यका पितृकुलं हित्वेह मन्येगिरौ
नित्यन्तिष्ठति पल्लवस्यदयितामेतां ब्रुवाणा नदीम् ॥ 1 ॥
गुणभरनामनि राजन्यनेन लिङ्गेन लिङ्गिनि ज्ञानम् ।
प्रथताश्चिराय लोके विपक्षवृत्तेः परावृत्तम् ॥ 2 ॥
चोलविषयस्य शैलोमौलिरिवायं महामणिरिवास्य ।
हरगृहमेतज्ज्योतिस्तदीयमिव शांकरं ज्योतिः ॥ 3 ॥
शिलाकारेण जनिता सत्यसन्धस्य भौतिकी ।
मूर्तिः कीर्तिमयीचास्य कृता तेनैव शाश्वती ॥ 4 ॥
निष्कृष्य चला समधायि गुणभरे भक्तिः—

S. I. I., vol. i, p. 28.

MAHENDRAVADI INSCRIPTION OF GUNABHARA

महिततमं सतामुपमहेन्द्रतटाकमिदं
स्थिरमुह कारितं गुणभरेण विदार्य शिलाम् ।
जनंनयनाभिरामगुरुधाम महेन्द्रपुरे
महति महेन्द्रविष्णु गृहनाम मुरारिगृहम् ॥

Ep. Ind., vol. iv, p. 153.

ŚĪYAMANGALAM INSCRIPTION

ललिताङ्कुरेण राज्ञावनिभाजनपल्लवेश्वरन्नाम ।
कारितमेतत् स्वेभ्राच्काच्ककरण्डमिव पुण्यरत्नानाम् ॥

Ep. Ind., vol. vi, p. 320.

DALAVĀNUR INSCRIPTION OF NARENDRA

दण्डानतनरेन्द्रेण नरेन्द्रेणैषकारितः ।
शत्रुमल्लेन शैलेस्मिन् शत्रुमल्लेश्वरालयः ॥

Ep. Ind., vol. xii, p. 225.

APPENDIX B

THE *MAHAVAMSA*, Ch. XLVII

AND when that King Hattha-daṭha II was dead Māṇavamma became king. (Who is this Māṇavamma?), what family came he from, and whose son was he, and how did he take possession of the kingdom? He was sprung from the race of Mahasammata, and inherited the great virtues of that line of princes. He was the son of Kassapa, who destroyed the Thuparama. And his queen was Sangha, the daughter of the Raja of Malaya. After he had obtained the hand of this princess in marriage he lived secretly with her in the northern country until it came to the ears of Hattha-daṭha, whereupon he went over to India and having made himself known to King Narasiha, he entered his service and with much labour found favour in the sight of that king. And when he saw that the king's friendship was unfeigned, he brought his wife also to India and lived there with her, ministering to the king by day and night and another king, Kaṇḍuveṭhi, with whom also he had found favour gave him such great possessions that it seemed as if the whole of that king's dominions had been granted to him; and while he was living in this way his wife Sangha bore him four sons and four daughters.

And it happened one day as the king, Narasiha, was out on his elephant on pleasure attended by Māṇavamma, he became thirsty and drank of the water of a tender cocoanut sitting on his elephant and gave the nut (of which he had drunk with the water that was left therein) to Māṇavamma thinking him to be some other attendant. And Māṇavamma took the nut that was offered to him and communed thus with himself: 'This king is a friend to me and, considered in its true light, what is there mean or degrading in eating the remnants of that which another had partaken? It can in no wise harm me, therefore, to drink this.' Then he drank off the nut. Yes, so great are the efforts of exceeding prudent men who are resolved to overcome difficulties! And the king (happening at that moment to turn round) perceived the error he had made, and fearing (lest what he had done should grieve his friend, and desiring also to repair the wrong he had unwittingly done to him) seized the nut and himself drank off what had been left in it by his friend. In such manner do honourable men always conduct themselves.

Thenceforth the king Narasiha placed Māṇavamma on an equal footing with himself, regarding food, and lodging, and honour and equipage.

And while they were living there together, a king, Vallabha, came to make war against Narasiha. And the king Narasiha reflected within himself in this wise: 'This man (Māṇavamma) has served me diligently by day and night, so that with my help he might obtain the kingdom which is his birthright. Wherefore if he should now follow me to the place of battle and lose his life in the field, his purpose, and my desire also to help him, would be of no avail.' Therefore the king left Māṇavamma in the city, and went alone to the place of battle, and began to prepare for war against Vallabha. And (after his departure) Māṇavamma thought to himself: 'It would advantage me no wise to survive the king if he should be slain in battle (as I would then be left without a friend and with none to help me). If such an event should happen, my friendship should have been formed in vain. For what purpose, besides, has the king treated me as an equal (unless he expected that I might be of service to him in difficulties)? Wherefore it is meet that I should follow the king to the place of battle, and join him in the field, and share either of defeat or victory, of life or of death, with my friend the king.' And for this end he raised a large army, and having equipped it fully, he mounted on a noble elephant and set out for the place of battle, and showed himself before Narasiha. And king Narasiha was greatly delighted at the sight, and exclaimed with great emotion, 'Surely, now know I the trust I had placed on him has been rightly placed.'

And afterwards the forces of Māṇa as well as those of the king joined together, and crushed the army of Vallabha.

And Māṇavamma displayed great valour in the field of battle, beating down the enemy on all sides like unto Narayana in the battle of the gods. And Narasiha was greatly pleased with the valour of Māṇavamma, and embraced him fondly, and exclaimed, 'Of a truth thou hast been to me the giver of victory!' And he returned thence to his own city and held a feast in honour of his victory, and rewarded the army of Māṇavamma with all the honours that were due. And in course of time the king thought thus within himself: 'This my friend has left naught undone to prove his love for me; he is no longer my debtor. My debt to him must I now repay by what it is my duty to do, even though grateful men are hardly found who know the value of services done for them.' He then assembled his officers together and spake to them in this wise: 'You yourselves are witnesses of the deeds of valour done by my friend here. And now it is my duty to do for him that which will be a benefit unto him, remembering that to give help unto one who had given help in the past, is the duty of the righteous man.' And when these words were said, all the ministers replied, 'Whatsoever your majesty desireth, even that is our desire also.'

And the king then granted unto Māṇavamma an army with all the equipage and material and all kinds of artificers, and gave him leave to proceed (to his country and gain for himself the sovereignty thereof). And when Māṇavamma was leaving the country together with his army, the king wept sore as if he had been separated from his own son.

Māṇavamma then took ship and crossed the sea (with his army), and having made a fast voyage, landed at Lanka with his forces, and began to subdue the country (around).

And when Dathopatissa heard of this invasion, he fled (from the capital); and Māṇavamma entered the city and took it, and tarried not to be crowned, but straightway closely pursued the fugitive king (taking with him only a small force). (But he was soon compelled to give up the pursuit, for) that portion of his Tamil army that he had left in the city deserted from him when false tidings were brought that he had been stricken with a serious illness. And Dathopatissa also, when he heard of this defection, raised a large army and prepared for war against Māṇavamma, who, when he saw that (save a few followers) his whole army had deserted from him, and that (if he should carry on the war with so small a force) his enemy might get a chance to triumph over his defeat and his death, resolved to return to India and pursuade his friend to help him yet another time, by giving him an army to conquer the kingdom. Accordingly he returned to India, and showed himself again to his friend, Narasiha, and entered his service a second time, and having regained his favour, dwelt at his court until four kings had reigned in this island.

And Narasiha thus thought within himself: 'This my friend, who seeketh most resolutely after fame, hath now spent many years of his life in my service that so he might get back his kingdom. And lo! he will soon have grown old. How then can I now reign (in comfort) and see him (thus miserable). Assuredly I shall this time restore to him his kingdom by sending my army thither. Else what advantageth my life to me?' Thereupon the king gathered his army together, and having equipped it well, gave Māṇavamma all things that he desired to have, and himself accompanied the army to the sea-coast where a mighty array of ships of burden, gaily ornamented, had been prepared for them. And when the king reached the harbour he gave orders to all his officers that they should embark and accompany Māṇavamma; but they all showed unwillingness to do so (without their king).

And Narasiha, having pondered well over the matter, resolved on this stratagem. Keeping himself so that his army might not see him, he gave over to Māṇavamma all his retinue and insignia of royalty together with the ornaments with which he adorned his person, and sent him (secretly) on board the ship, bidding him take the royal drum, the *koṭṭha* with him, and sound it from the deck of the vessel. And Māṇavamma did as he was directed; and the soldiers thinking that it was the king (who was sounding the call), embarked, leaving him alone on land. Then Māṇa began his voyage with the army and all the material of war, which, with the ships in which they were borne, was like unto a city floating down the sea. And in due time reached the port and disembarked with the army. And after the men had been made to rest there for a few days, he began to fight, and took the northern country and subdued the inhabitants thereof, and then put himself at the head of his invincible army and marched against the city. And Pottha-kuṭṭha, having heard thereof, went forth with a large army to meet the enemy. And the two armies encountered each other like unto two seas that had burst their bounds. And, Māṇavamma clad himself in his armour, and led his men, mounted on his elephant; and he broke through the forces of Pottha-kuṭṭha and the king (Hattha-daṭṭha), and scattered them on all sides. And Hattha-daṭṭha, the king, as he was fieeing from the field of battle, was seized by some country people. And they cut off his head and brought it to Māṇavamma.

And Pottha-kuṭṭha, who escaped from the field of battle, took refuge in Merukandara. And the lord of that country (from whom he sought protection), when he saw him (under his roof), communed thus within himself, 'Yea, now for a long time has this man been my friend: how can I reject him, nor yet how can I keep clear of offence to my lord the king and to this my friend?' And so (as he could not escape from this portion by reason of its hardship, he resolved to kill himself, and) ate of some poisoned cakes, so that he died. And when Pottha-kuṭṭha heard what had befallen his friend, he ate also of one of the cakes and died. Thus did the island fall into the hands of Māṇavamma, freed from dangerous foes that are like unto thorns.

And Māṇavamma then lifted his parasol of sovereignty over the island, as if he thereby sheltered the inhabitants thereof from the afflictions which had rained on them. And the good deeds that he did were many in number and of great value. Who can enumerate them all one by one? And this great and renowned man built these buildings: the terraced house called Kappagama, Sepaṇṇi, Siriat Paḍhanarakha Vihāra, and the beautiful terraced house at Siri Sanghabodhi Vihāra. He covered also the roof of the house at Thuparama. And he built a terraced house at the Thuparama and gave it to the Pansukulika monks. He repaired also the old canopy on the top of the Cetiya and many buildings there that had gone to decay.

APPENDIX C

THE 'AVANTISUNDARIKATHĀSARA'

THE *Avantisundarikathā* and the *Avantisundarikathāsara* are two old Sanskrit manuscripts discovered by the search party of the Madras Oriental Manuscript Library some years ago.[1] Of these the former is a prose work with a poetic introduction while the other is a summary of this work in verse. While the MSS. are interesting to the students of Sanskrit literature the poetical introduction prefixed to the prose work is of particular interest to the students of Pallava history inasmuch as it shows the literary patronage of some of the Pallava kings of the Simhavishṇu line and the connection of some of the well-known Sanskrit poets with Kanchipuram. It is agreed that this prose work was written by Daṇḍin and the introductory chapter gives some valuable data for fixing the date and place of Daṇḍin and his connection with Bhāravi as well as the Pallava kings and their interest in architecture and literature. The literary and historical importance of the work have been discussed in full by Mr. Ramakrishnakavi in his paper on '*Avantisundarikathā of Daṇḍin*'[2] which may be referred to. Mr. Harihara Sastri of Trivandrum has questioned the tenability of the identity of Damodara and Bhāravi and the relationship of Bhāravi and Daṇḍin suggested by Mr. Kavi in the light of his discovery of the corresponding prose passage from Trivandrum Manuscript Library. The following are extracts from Mr. Ramakrishnakavi's edition which has the advantage of supplying a number of correct readings not found in the Manuscript acquired by the Government Oriental Manuscript Library.

[1] See para 108, of the Report on the working of Perip. party of Goverment Oriental Manuscript Library, Madras, for 1916-17 to 1918-19.

[2] Proc. and Trans. of the Second Oriental Conference, Calcutta, pp. 192-200. See his paper in the Fourth Session of the Oriental Conference entitled 'Bhāravi and Daṇḍin'.

। श्रीः ।

॥ अवन्तिसुन्दरीकथासारः ॥

सत्कथाकथनप्रोत्या तथापि कथयाम्यहम् ।
कान्तामवन्तिसुन्दर्याः कथामनतिविस्तराम् ॥ ॥ १० ॥

अस्तिप्रासादविस्तारग्रस्तव्योमान्तरा पुरी ।
काञ्चीपुराख्या कल्याणी ककु (भः) कुम्भजन्मनः ॥ ॥ ११ ॥

या मृग्यविगलद्भोगै रसंख्यवसुभिर्जनैः ।
भोगवत्यमरावत्यौ न्यक्कुर्वाणेव गर्विता ॥ ॥ १२ ॥

तस्यां जज्ञे बुधव्रातध्वस्ताखिलविपल्लवः ।
पल्लवेषु महीपालः सिंहविष्णुरिति श्रुतः ॥ ॥ १३ ॥

गरिम्णा स्थावरान् सर्वानोजसा जङ्गमानपि ।
यो विजिग्ये भुजश्लाघी भूभर्तॄनुभयानपि ॥ ॥ १४ ॥

अदृष्टपूर्वो गन्धर्वस्तं सभासदमेकदा ।
उदञ्जलिर्महीपालमुपावीणयदार्यया ॥ ॥ १५ ॥

दनुजपतिहृदयभूधर-
विभेदविज्ञातशक्तिनखकुलिशम् ।
जगदुदयहेतु विष्णो-
रवतु वपुर्नरसिंहं वः ॥ ॥ १६ ॥

श्रुत्वैनामत्युदारार्थां कुतूहलखला (लो) कृतः ।
अब्रवीद्भद्र केनेयं निर्मिता वर्णपद्धतिः ॥ ॥ १७ ॥

इत्यूचिवांसं प्रत्यूचे गन्धर्वस्तं धने (रे) श्वरम् ।
देव त्वनुगृहीतोऽस्मि श्रूयतामवधानतः ॥ ॥ १८ ॥

अस्त्यानन्दपुरं नाम प्रदेशे पश्चिमोत्तरे ।
आर्यदेशशिखारत्नं तत्रासन् बहवो द्विजाः ॥ ॥ १९ ॥

ततोऽभिनिःसृता काचित् कौशिकब्रह्मसन्ततिः ।
ब्रह्मलोकादिवायन्ती पुण्यतीर्था सरस्वती ॥ ॥ २० ॥

नासिक्यभूमावौत्सुक्यान्मूलदेवनिवेशिताम् ।
प्राप्याचलपु (रं नाम पु) रोमधिवसत्यसौ ॥ ॥ २१ ॥

तस्यां नारायणस्वामिनाम्नो नारायणोदरात् ।
दामोदर इति श्रीमानादिदेव इवाभवत् ॥ ॥ २२ ।

स मेधावी कविर्विद्वान् भारविः प्रभ (वं) वो गिराम् ।
अनुरुध्याकरोन्मैत्रीं नरेन्द्रे विष्णुवर्धनो (ने) ॥ ॥ २३ ।

क्षुधाविष्टेन तद्विद्रमामिषं मृगयान्तरे ।
अनिष्टशिष्टं हा! कष्टं तेनाभोज्यमभुज्यत ॥ ॥ २४ ॥

अगच्छन्नन्तिकं पित्रोः सतपस्तोर्थयात्रया ।
चरन् भेवर (?). मापेदे कस्यापि शुभजन्मनः ॥ ॥ २५ ॥

स दुर्विनीतनामासीदनन्वर्थाभिधानवान् ।
तस्यान्तिके वसत्येष तेनार्येयमुदीरिता ॥ । २६ ॥

इति श्रुत्वा महीपालस्तदालोकनलोलुपः ।
अनेकश्रीमुखाकृष्टमकरोदमुमात्मसात् ॥ । २७ ॥

स्वर्विशेषैरविगतैस्तमाचारैरतोषयत् ।
अभूषयच्च भूपालमग्राम्यैः स सुभाषितैः ॥ ॥ २८ ॥

नृपनिर्बन्धनिर्दिष्टे प्रकृष्टविभवे गृहे ।
वहतः पैतृकीं वृत्तिं तस्यासीत् तनयत्रयम् ॥ ॥ २९ ॥

मनोरथाङ्कयस्तेषां मध्यमो वंशवर्धनः ।
ततस्तनूजाश्चत्वारः स्रष्टुर्वेदा इवाभवन् ॥ ॥ ३० ॥

श्रीवीरदत्त इत्येषामुत्तमस्तत्त्ववेदिनाम् ।
यवीयानस्य च श्लाघ्या गौरीनामाभवत् प्रिया ॥ ॥ ३१ ॥

ततः कथंचित् सा गौरी द्विजाधिपशिखामणेः ।
कुमारं दण्डिनामानं व्यक्तशक्तिमजीजनत् ॥ ॥ ३२ ॥

स बाल एव मात्रा च पित्रा चापि व्ययुज्यत ।
अयुज्यत गरीयस्या सरस्वत्या श्रुतेन च ॥ ॥ ३३ ॥

सविक्रये पुरे तस्मिन् परचक्रोपरोधतः ।
स चचार शुभाचारः सर्वामुर्वीमुदारधीः ॥ ॥ ३४ ॥

अथाश्रमेष्वधीयानः शास्त्रेषु च कृतश्रमः ।
पश्यन् पुण्यान्यरण्यानि न्यवसद्दिवसान् बहून् ॥ ॥ ३५ ॥

अथाहूतः क्षितीशेन प्रशान्तोपद्रवे पुरे ।
स्वसुहृद्बन्धुमध्यस्थः स भेजे निजमास्पदम् ॥ ॥ ३६ ॥

एकदा वास्तुशास्त्रज्ञस्तक्षमर्मविचक्षणः ।
स्थपतिः कश्चिदभ्येत्य प्रणिपत्योपतस्थिवान् ॥ ॥ ३७ ॥

अनल्पकल्पिताश्चित्रा विकल्पाः शिल्पकर्मिणाम् ।
अत्र त्वष्टामुनैवेत्थं तत्रस्थास्तमशंसिषुः ॥ ॥ ३८ ॥

स तु शिल्पिवरस्तेषामाक्षिप्य स्तुतिमात्मनः ।
मूर्धन्यञ्जलिमाबध्नन्नथ दण्डिनमभ्यधात ॥ ॥ ३९ ॥

अस्ति विज्ञाप्यमस्माकमन्तग्राह्योऽस्मि यद्यहम् ।
प्रार्थनां वितथीकर्तुं प्रभवो न भवादृशाः ॥ ॥ ४० ॥

महामल्लपुरे देवः स्वैरं वारिधिसन्निधौ ।
आस्ते मुकुन्दः सानन्दं फणीन्द्र इव मन्दिरे ॥ ॥ ४१ ॥

भग्नः केनापि तस्यासीत् कारणेनासुरद्विषः ।
मणिबन्धे महाबाहुः स मया सन्धितोऽधुना ॥ ॥ ४२ ॥

तदालोकितुमर्हन्ति भवन्तः साधु वा न वा ।
एतावता प्रयासेन प्रसादातिशयोऽस्तु नः ॥ ॥ ४३ ॥

श्रुत्वा सेनापतेः पुत्रः कलाकौशलपेशलः ।
पार्श्ववर्ती परां मैत्रीं बिभ्रद्दण्डिनमभ्यधात् ॥ ॥ ४४ ॥

आर्य संभाव्यतामस्य स्थपतेः प्रणयस्त्वया ।
अपि च स्पृहणीयं ते सुहृदामपि दर्शनम् । ॥ ४५ ॥

मित्राणि मातृदत्ताद्याः केरळेभ्यो द्विजोत्तमाः ।
त्वद्दर्शनार्थमायातास्तस्मिन् सन्निदधत्यमी ॥ ॥ ४६ ॥

इति श्रुत्वा ततः प्रीतस्तं विसृज्यपरेऽहनि ।
सुहृद्भिः सह तं देशं ययौ तेन च शिल्पिना ॥ ॥ ४७ ॥

अथोत्तरङ्गभङ्गालीविलसद्बाहुलील्या ।
नृत्यन्तमिव गम्भीरमम्भोराशिं ददर्श सः ॥ ॥ ४८ ॥

ततः सागरकल्लोलक्षिप्तक्षोदाम्बुबिन्दुना ।
सेव्यमानं सुखामोदक्षारिणा वनवायुना ॥ ॥ ४९ ॥

तत्रोदारं मुदा पश्यन्नदूरे राजमन्दिरम् ।
गच्छन् वेलापथेनाथ प्रपेदे मन्दिरं हरेः ॥ ॥ ५० ॥

तरङ्गबाहुसंबाह्यचरणाम्बुरुहद्वयम् ।
उदन्वता मुदाविष्टो ददर्श मुरशासनम् ॥ ॥ ५१ ॥
प्रविश्य प्रतिमाभ्यर्णं गत्वा निर्वर्णयन्नयम् ।
नाध्यगच्छत् सुसंहत्या सन्धानं मणिबन्धके ॥ ॥ ५२ ॥
तस्यापहसितत्वष्टुस्तक्षकर्मणि शिक्षया ।
विस्मितोऽयं स्मितं कुर्वन्नर्घ्यैरर्चयति स्मतम् ॥ ॥ ५३ ॥
तस्मिन् काले जलोद्देशे ददर्शे मुक्तवारिजम् ।
उदयारुणमार्तण्डमण्डलाकारि वारिधौ ॥ ॥ ५४ ॥
तत्तु प्रत्यक्षमेवैषां तरङ्गप्रेषितं हरेः ।
चरणाम्बुरुहस्पर्शात् सद्यो विद्याधरोऽभवत् ॥ ॥ ५५ ॥
ततः किरीटी केयूरी कृपाणी कवची च सः ।
भूत्वा तपस्वी भूतेशं प्रणम्योदपतद्दिवम् ॥ ॥ ५६ ॥
दृष्ट्वा दण्डिनमाचष्ट स्नेहादिष्टतमः सुहृत् ।
गोरीपुत्रोऽपि नन्वेतद्विस्पष्टं दृष्टवानिति ॥ ॥ ५७ ॥
पश्यन्नाचार्यरूपं तं चिन्तयित्वा किमित्यसौ ।
कौतुकाकृष्टदृष्टिभ्यस्तेभ्यः संभाव्यमभ्यधात् ॥ ॥ ५८ ॥
पद्मसंबन्धिनो नूनममुना मुनिशापतः ।
पद्मीभूय प्रमुक्तेन भाव्यं दिव्येन केन चित् ॥ ॥ ५९ ॥
अथ वा देवमाराध्य प्रसादान्मुरशासनम् ।
अत्याहितमिदं वेत्तुमत्यर्थमहमुत्सहे ॥ ॥ ६० ॥
ततः स्वभवनं गत्वा दर्भशय्यामुपेयुषे ।
कथयामास तत्सर्वं भूतार्थं भूतभावनः ॥ ॥ ६१ ॥

पृथुकान्तिमवन्तिसुन्दरीति
प्रथितां विक्रमरत्नराजहंसाम् ।
सरसां रहसि प्रियामिवार्द्रा-
मुपलेभे पुरुषोत्तमप्रसादात् ॥ ॥ ६२ ॥

मुक्त्वा शय्यां मिलितपुलकव्रातमुत्थाय भूयः
प्राप्तानन्दो विरतिसमये प्राक्तनीनां क्रियाणाम् ।
स प्रारेभे सपदि सकलां स्वप्नलब्धां सुहृद्भ्यः
शुश्रूषुभ्यः पृथुमथ कथां विस्तरेणाभिधातुम् ॥ ६३ ॥

इत्यवन्तिसुन्दरीकथासारे
प्रथमः परिच्छेदः ॥

ADDITIONAL NOTES BY THE EDITOR

Page 10, note 2.

This work traces the descent of Daṇḍin in its introductory chapter. In doing so it brings his great grandfather Gopala as a fellow-pupil of Bhāravi whom it brings into contact with three kings of South India, namely, Vishṇuvardhana, the father of Jayasimha I of the Chāḷukyas of Bādāmi; of Durvinīta, among the Gangas who was his own pupil and commented up on the 15th Sarga of the *Kirātarjunīya* and wrote a Sanskrit version of the *Bṛhatkathā* and Simhavishṇu of Kanchi. These details come out clearly from the MS. copy of the prose work *Avantisundarikathā*, not the versified *sāra* or abridgement, as shown by Pandit Harihara Sastri, Curator of Sanskrit MSS., Trivandram, in a paper presented to the fourth Oriental Conference in Allahabad.

Page 11, note 2.

The discovery of these panels raises the question as to the religion of the kings and the existence of the place. Simhavishṇu was a Vaishṇava as he is described as Simhavishṇu who worshipped Vishṇu in devotion; *Bhaktyārādhita Vishṇuḥ Simhavishṇuḥ*. His son and successor Mahendra is said to have been a Jain originally and then become a convert to Śaivism through Appar. It seems likely that he was Jain as in the *Mattavilāsa* he brings into ridicule the Śaiva Kāpālika and the Śākyas or Buddhists. He has no reference to the Jains. His father's devotion to Vaishṇavism may explain its omission. His portrait in the Varāha cave may be due to the fact that he was there a prince with his father and like him, he may then have been a Vaishṇava. This raises the question of the origin of the place. There is little doubt that the place existed before whatever Mahamalla may have done to enlarge and beautify it.

Page 101, note 1.

The style of pillar described does mark a distinct class of pillars. If Mahamalla originated it, as probably he did, his successors continued it, and we find this kind of pillar in buildings of later times of different ages. To mark it distinctly as having been originated by Mahāmalla we want a few undoubted examples of these ascribable to his age. We cannot say we get that in Mahābalipuram.

Page 102, note 1.

There is no evidence in support of the assertion that Narasimhavarman Mahāmalla founded the town. The town had the vernacular name *Mallai* and in that name was known earlier, as Bhūtattāḻvār, a native of the place refers to the place by that name. Tirumangai Āḻvar a contemporary of Nandivarman Pallavamalla refers to the place as *kaḍal mallai-Talaśayanam*, meaning Mallai close to the sea which is otherwise known *Talaśayanam*, lying on land. This last is in reference to Vishṇu who is abed on the earth, as though on the sea usually, to let a devotee have a view of him in that posture. It was called kaḍal-Mallai to distinguish it from other Mallais clearly indicating that it is an ordinary native name. This is distinct from the Māmallapuram given to it by Mahāmalla, as is very commonly the case in South India. The village Mallai became the city Māmallapuram by this rechristening. Pandit M. Raghavaiyangar has suggested, from a reference in the Śangam classic *Perumbāṇāṟṟuppaḍai*, the identification of this place with *Nīrpeyarttu* in the poem in the *Journal of Oriental Research*. This term means that which has the name of water and the Pandit finds justification for it in the name *Jalaśayanam* given to the Shore-temple in one of the later inscriptions. Tirumangai Āḻvar's reference is *Talaśayanam* and not *Jalaśayanam*. It would be difficult to find a reason for the alteration. It must also be noted that *Jalasayanam* is given to the *Śiva shrine* in the inscription. While the Pandit deserves credit for the suggestion, *Nīr-peyarttu* is more likely to refer to another place *Tiru-Nīr-Malai* near Pallāvaram and the poem has to be examined closely to see whether this is the place actually meant. (See *Indian Antiquary*, 1917; *The Antiquities of Mahābalipuram*, pp. 49 ff.)

Page 120, note 2.

The views of the late Mr. H. K. Sastri seem to have been due entirely to a misconstruction of the *śloka* in the Taṇḍantoṭṭam plates and a misunderstanding of the word *punaḥ* (again). The previous verse refers to the conquest of the south and refers obviously to the exploits of Simhavishṇu of the main line. From these the genealogy passes on to the descendants of his younger brother Bhīmavarman. The first important character in this line is Hiraṇyavarma whose son Nandivarman Pallavamalla became a great Pallava ruler. The poet apparently spoke of Simhavishṇu as an *avatar* of Vishṇu and refers to Hiraṇya similarly as a second *avatar* of the same Vishṇu (Bhuraṇyutējaḥ). The use of the *punaḥ* (again) is then quite justified. There is no need to identify this Nandivarman with Nandi of Teḷḷāru and create difficulties to surmount. The first is given his peculiar title Ēkadhīra and he is described as a *Paramavaishṇava*. The other is described as an equally devout Śaiva. Each of them gives himself credit for such allegiance in religion in the concluding verses. There is no room for a second Hiraṇyavarma nor is there any need.

Page 138, note 2.

The name of this author Perundēvanār and his work *Bhārata-veṇbā* have been too readily identified with the author Bhāratam-pāḍiya Peruṁdēvanār and his *Bhāratam*. The first refers himself and his work to the reign of Nandivarman of Teḷḷāru and therefore to the ninth century beyond a doubt. In regard to the other however we have neither the work nor any extracts. He is regarded as the author of the invocatory poems to the eight Śangam collections of which the *Ahanānūru* collection was made for Ugra-Pāṇḍya by Rudra Śarman. An ancient Pāṇḍya, anterior to the genealogical lists, is given credit for having got the *Bhāratam* done into Tamil in the larger Ṣinnamanūr plates. This achievement is put on a footing of equality with the victory at Talaiālangānam and the establishment of the Śangam in Madura. In the face of these distinctive features the identifications of the two Perundēvans would be impossible and the *Bhāraṭam* of the earlier Perundēvan cannot be the *veṇbā* that has come down to us in part.

ERRATA

Page	Line	
39	25	*for* Kūlimaharaṭha, *read* Kulimahātāraka.
42	12	*for* Simhavarman and Skandavarman, *read* Mādhavavarman.
,,	15	*for* Simhavarman, *read* Mādhavavarman.
71	25	*for* fifth, *read* fourth.
,,	29	*for* sixth, *read* fifth.
104	12	for *circa* 600, read *circa* 655.
108	f.n. 2 line 1	*for* क्षण *read* रक्षण.
	,, 2	*for* अवारप्य *read* अवाप्य.
113	Gen. Table	*for* Simhavarman *read* Simhavishnu.
116	f.n. 1 line 8	for *Malaprakritis*, read *Mūlaprakritis*.
137	f.n. 2 line 2	*for* the work, *read* of the work.
160	7	*for* Sundanar, *read* Sundarar.
169	2	*for* vol. xiv, *read* vol. xv.

N.B.—A few other errors mostly in diacritical marks have not been noticed here as being too obvious.

INDEX

(References are to pages)

G

H

I

J

K

L

M

Published by

Facsimile Publisher
Ashok Vihar, Delhi-110052 (India)
Website: www.facsimilepublishers.com

Distributed by

Gyan Books Pvt. Ltd.
5, Ansari Road, Daryaganj, New Delhi-110002 (India)
E-mail: books@gyanbooks.com, Website: www.gyanbooks.com

9 789333 401197